A DELICIOUS COUNTRY

ALSO BY SCOTT HULER

A Little Bit Sideways:
One Week inside a NASCAR
Winston Cup Race Team

On Being Brown:
What It Means to Be a Cleveland Browns Fan

Defining the Wind:
The Beaufort Scale, and How a 19th-Century
Admiral Turned Science into Poetry

No-Man's Lands:
One Man's Odyssey Through "The Odyssey"

On the Grid:
A Plot of Land, an Average Neighborhood, and
the Systems That Make Our World Work

A DELICIOUS COUNTRY

Rediscovering the CAROLINAS

along the ROUTE of *John Lawson's*

1700 Expedition

SCOTT HULER

THE UNIVERSITY OF NORTH CAROLINA PRESS

Chapel Hill

*This book was published with the
assistance of the Blythe Family Fund of the
University of North Carolina Press.*

Manufactured in the United States of America

Set in Adobe Caslon
by Tseng Information Systems, Inc.

The University of North Carolina Press has been a
member of the Green Press Initiative since 2003.

Cover illustrations: map (background) from Christoph von Graffenried,
MSS.Mül. 466 (1), courtesy Burgerbibliothek Bern; marsh grass (top right)
and pup tent (bottom right) courtesy of the author; notebook paper
© shutterstock.com; canoe on lake © Victoria Park / Creative Market

Library of Congress Cataloging-in-Publication Data
Names: Huler, Scott, author.
Title: A delicious country : rediscovering the Carolinas along the
route of John Lawson's 1700 expedition / Scott Huler.
Description: Chapel Hill : The University of North Carolina Press, [2019] |
Includes bibliographical references and index.
Identifiers: LCCN 2018030741 | ISBN 9781469648286
(cloth : alk. paper) | ISBN 9781469648293 (ebook)
Subjects: LCSH: Lawson, John, 1674-1711—Travel. |
Huler, Scott—Travel. | North Carolina—Description and travel. |
South Carolina—Description and travel.
Classification: LCC F260 .H85 2019 | DDC 975.6—dc23
LC record available at https://lccn.loc.gov/2018030741

FOR LOUIS & GUS

CONTENTS

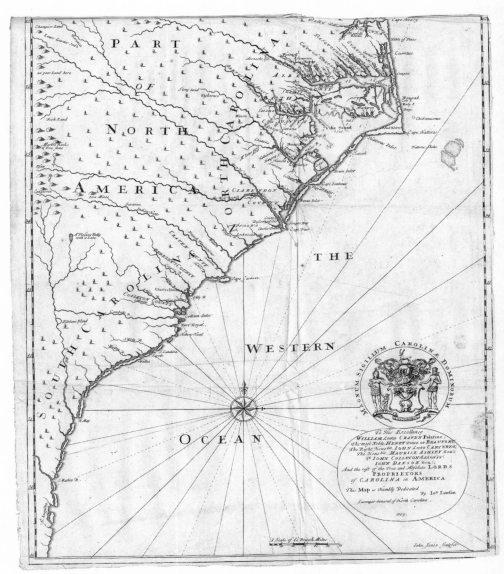

The map from John Lawson's A New Voyage to Carolina.

A DELICIOUS COUNTRY

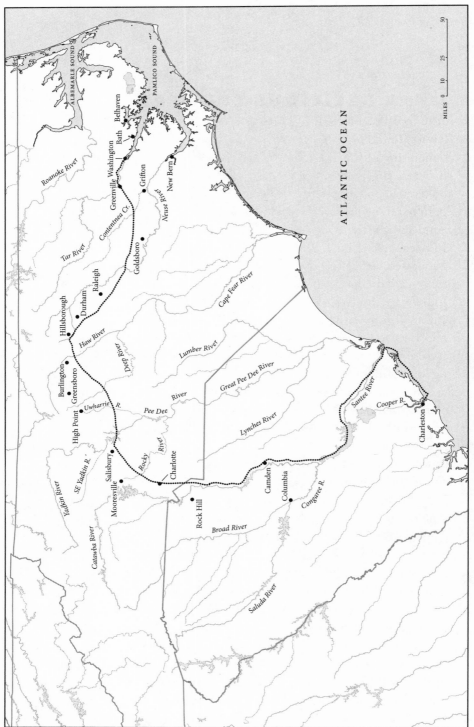

ALBEMARLE SOUND

PAMLICO SOUND

ATLANTIC OCEAN

Roanoke River

Belhaven
Bath
Washington
Greenville
Grifton
New Bern

Contentnea Cr.

Neuse River

Tar River

Goldsboro

Raleigh

Durham
Hillsborough

Haw River

Cape Fear River

Burlington
Greensboro
High Point
Uwharrie *R.*

Deep River

Lumber River

Pee Dee River

Great Pee Dee River

Santee River

Cooper R.

Charleston

Lynches River

SE Yadkin R.

Salisbury
Mooresville

Rocky River

Charlotte

Camden
Columbia

Congaree R.

Yadkin River

Catawba River

Rock Hill

Broad River

Saluda River

50

25

10

MILES

Approximate route of John Lawson's journey, December 28, 1700–February 24, 1701, with present-day place names.

INTRODUCTION
The Best Country I Could Go To

n the middle of a dark September night in 1711 in Carolina, John Lawson found himself captive, tied up and flung in the center of the council ring of the Tuscarora Indian town of Catechna. A wolf skin lay before him; next to him "stood an Indian in the most dignified and terrible posture that can be imagined. He did not leave the place. Ax in hand, he looked to be the executioner."

Around him in the flickering firelight the Tuscaroras who had captured him leaped and lunged, performing a dance that lasted hours. Next to Lawson, tied just as tightly, lay Baron Cristoph von Graffenried (also commonly called "de Graffenried"), whose words describe the scene. "The Indians themselves, when tired of dancing, would all run suddenly away into a forest with frightful cries and howling," von Graffenried went on, "but would soon come back out of the forest with faces striped black, white, and red. Part of them, besides this, would have their hair hanging loose, full of feathers, down, and some in the skins of all sorts of animals: In short in such monsterous shapes that they looked more like a troop of devils than like other creatures; if one represents the devil in the most terrible shape that can be thought of, running and dancing out of the forest."

That we can quote from von Graffenried's account tells you he survived the night. Lawson did not.

That night brought to a sudden end one of the great stories of European exploration and discovery in North America. John Lawson's extraordinary 1709 book, *A New Voyage to Carolina*, narrates his adventures and misadventures along a journey deep into the backcountry of what is now South Carolina and North Carolina (then a single colony, though beginning to split in two). In one of the most important early books to emerge from the colonial South, Lawson vividly describes the region's flora, fauna, landscape, and native inhabitants according to the principles of the emerging discipline we now call science. Few adventurers of his time had traveled as deeply—and successfully—among the Indians of Carolina.

Indeed, Lawson's description of Native American cultures are some of the best and most sensitive we have from the turn of the eighteenth

1

century. He spent a decade among the Indians in the earliest days of the Southeast's European settlement, and he documented native communities, buildings, agriculture, hunting, dance, trade, and culture through eyes clear, thorough, and respectful. Lawson depicts the natives as fully human—not some subspecies perceived only in comparison to European settlers. "They are really better to us than we are to them," he writes at the end of his book about them. "For all our Religion and Education, we possess more Moral Deformities, and Evils than these Savages do." Lawson described people and societies that were complex, rich, and multifaceted, and he did so with admiration and grace.

Yet for all of that, John Lawson lived at a time when cultures were mixing, populations transforming—North America was changing from its former life, supporting millions of Native people, to its new one, dominated by European settlers. And in that transformational time Lawson, despite his admiration of the Native peoples he met, lived a life that led the Tuscaroras to capture and execute him. And so instead of his own textured descriptions, we have of that final encounter only von Graffenried's cartoonish depictions of "monsterous shapes . . . a troop of devils." John Lawson's death was only the final in a stream of ironies and contradictions. The end of a life lived, quite literally, on the edge of the known world.

As one of Carolina's chief citizens in its earliest days, Lawson made dealing with Indians central to his life. Lawson also helped found North Carolina's first two cities—Bath and New Bern. He provided botanical and scientific specimens to one of the greatest collectors in London—specimens he gathered were part of the collection that founded the British Museum. He became surveyor general of the colony. And in 1709 he published his masterwork, *A New Voyage to Carolina*.

And yet today Lawson is almost unknown. Though he was one of the foremost explorers of the American South, his contributions to history and science are scarcely remembered, even his terrifying execution little remarked. Those who know of him generally know one thing only: that in late 1700, a few months after he arrived in North America, he took a walk of nearly two months and 600 miles. He left Charles-Town (today's Charleston), then the largest town in Carolina—fifth-largest in the British colonies—and ended up in what Carolinians now call "Little Washington," a tiny town where the Tar River enters the Pamlico Sound. Eventually he used that journey as the basis for his book, which provides

This is Lawson. We think. The portrait hangs in the home of a collector, the widow of a longtime Lawsonian. Its frame holds a bronze plate that says "Sir John Lawson," and though Lawson was not aristocracy, he strived toward that. Art historians tell us that it is from the proper time period. In any case, it's the only image we have.

entertaining and powerful observations of his surroundings and the finest written record of the Native cultures whose people he visited.

:::

Lawson documented a moment in which not just Carolina but the continent hung, poised, between Native and European, settlement and colony, old and new. In 1700 the Carolinas, like the rest of the East Coast of North America, were beginning to emerge as a European-style civilization: no longer mere outposts, they were colonies, with towns that could almost be called cities.

A few decades earlier, those exploring Carolina still wrote of hostile Indians and entirely new species. William Hilton was one of the earliest Carolina explorers, investigating the territory in 1664, soon after the first Carolina Charter granted the land to its new English owners (a second charter in 1665 expanded the territory's boundaries). "We presented to the [Indian] King a Hatchet and several Beads," Hilton relates of his meeting with Natives who had shot arrows at his men in canoes, "also Beads to the young women and to the chief men and to the rest of the Indians, as far as our Beads would go." This is the stuff of first contact—uncertain meetings, the constant threat of violence, descriptions of "Duck and Mallard, and innumerable of other water-Fowls, whose names we know not." Mere decades later, the colonies fought in the French and Indian War—part of what Europeans call the Seven Years War—as thoroughly integrated extensions of their parent nations. When Lawson came to Carolina, it was perched almost equidistant between "where the hell am I?" and "just another place in the world."

The Native societies too balanced on that knife edge. A century before Lawson, many Native populations lived as they had for centuries, though the smallpox that came with the Spanish explorers was spreading. A century after Lawson, Native southerners were dramatically reduced in number and on the verge of forced removal from the Southeast. Lawson, with an honesty rare among early explorers, recognized the precarious position of the people he met: "The Small-Pox and Rum have made such a Destruction amongst them, that, on good grounds, I do believe, there is not the sixth Savage living within two hundred Miles of all our Settlements, as there were fifty Years ago. These poor Creatures have so many Enemies to destroy them, that it's a wonder one of them is left alive near us."

Lawson documented that world-on-edge. And as observant, even prescient, as he was regarding the Tuscaroras and their fellow tribes, he could not have imagined how similarly, three centuries later, our world would teeter: a way of life dying in the countryside, implacable new forces once again balancing an entire civilization on a knife edge. What, I wondered when I first discovered his work, would Lawson make of the Carolina of our time? I ended up retracing Lawson's backcountry trip, so you may consider that foreshadowing.

:::

I first stumbled across Lawson's journey while seeking information about the history of my own piece of land in Raleigh. A relative newcomer to the place I had started calling home, I searched the historical record for accounts of the region before European settlement. I encountered Lawson's story and was amazed—less that he took the journey than that the journey seemed so largely forgotten. He bestrode the backcountry, treated with the Natives, wrote history, made scientific observations, founded towns. Given his various contributions he ought to be considered Carolina's William Penn—he ought to have a museum; his portrait ought to hang in schoolrooms. Yet no.

I began looking into Lawson's life but found, outside of his own book, only the barest biography. One obstacle to knowing Lawson is his mysterious British origins. We have no accurate recording of his birth or even agreement on his family background. Biographies vary based on conjecture and incomplete information. One interpretation, included in the preface to a 1967 edition of *A New Voyage to Carolina*, has him born in 1665 to one Andrew Lawson in London and apprenticed to an apothecary in 1675, after which we don't hear much until his book resumes the narrative. Another belief is that he was a member of the Lawsons of the Brough Hall, Yorkshire, though sons of baronets usually leave more of a paper trail than this fellow did. In a biological sketch from a 1951 edition of Lawson's book, historian Francis Latham Harriss says, "He appears to have flashed like a meteor across our ken, leaving behind him only this illuminating record of his presence and the tragic memory of his death."

His most recent biographer did better, though. The *Dictionary of North Carolina Biography* contains the tale most current Lawsonians—among whom I include myself—find most persuasive. This Lawson was born in 1674, the only son of a London doctor with some small influence: a relative on his father's side was Vice-Admiral Sir John Lawson—a special friend of Charles II—and on his mother's side his distant relatives included the archbishop of Canterbury. The *Dictionary of North Carolina*

Biography has him attending lectures at Gresham College in London, where in 1660 was founded the Royal Society of London for Improving Natural Knowledge, the world's first learned society, now generally known as the Royal Society. Not yet named scientists, these pioneers included Isaac Newton and Robert Hooke and called themselves natural philosophers. With the fireworks of Enlightenment principles exploding around him, one can imagine a young college man looking at the members of the Royal Society as future generations gazed at steamboat pilots, or at astronauts. Publishing Robert Hooke's *Micrographia* and Isaac Newton's *Principia*, inventing the academic journal with the *Philosophical Transactions*, the Royal Society must have dazzled the students at Gresham College.

That being the case, in 1700 Lawson would thus have been a footloose, inspired young man of twenty-five, with a questing mind and a college background, looking for a way to make a name for himself, perhaps in science. He tells us in his book that with no good reason to go anywhere else he was originally headed "to see the Solemnity of the Grand Jubilee at *Rome*"—a sort of World's Fair held by the Pope every quarter century—but then he made a chance acquaintance in London.

"I accidentally met with a Gentleman, who had been Abroad, and was very well acquainted with the Ways of Living in both *Indies*," Lawson says in the book that a decade later resulted from this chance meeting. "Of whom," he goes on, "having made Enquiry concerning them, he assur'd me that *Carolina* was the best Country I could go to; and, that there then lay a Ship in the *Thames*, in which I might have my Passage. I laid hold on this Opportunity, and was not long on Board before we fell down the River, and sail'd." It doesn't have quite the zing of "Go west, young man," but it was the same advice, if 150 years ahead of its time.

And now you know almost as much as anyone else in the world about John Lawson's background. Regarding his remarkable journey through what is now North and South Carolina, Lawson tells us he left London in April 1700, arrived in New York in July, and after a couple of weeks' stay headed to Charles-Town. He describes the city of 2,000 or so souls as having as "thriving Circumstances at this Time, as any Colony on the Continent of *English America*"—and remember, Lawson had just come from New York. Charles-Town was going places. Good and pleasant streets, buildings of wood and of brick, a fort and fortifications. Churches, where one could worship as one wished (the Fundamental Constitution of the colony actually provided for freedom of worship—provided it was Christian worship). Add in the many successful immigrants and the international reputation the city was building as a port of trade, and Charles-Town's many excellent qualities, Lawson tells us, had "drawn to them ingenious People of most Sciences, whereby they have Tutors amongst them that educate their Youth a-la-mode."

Charles-Town, that is, would have marketed itself exactly like the cities of the modern Southeast market themselves: world-class infrastructure, advantageous trade, a good education system, good employee stock, pleasant places to live and above all do business. Lawson stuck around for several months, doing nobody knows what—he is not mentioned in a single existing document—until December 28, when off he went on his journey, and again, for reasons nobody knows.

Historians have traditionally—and confidently—stated that his trek had some sort of official capacity, and, though there isn't a scrap of evidence to back that claim up, it's not implausible. With Lawson's London family connections it's possible that one of the eight Lords Proprietor of the colony—supporters of Charles II who for their loyalty were given total control of the land from the Virginia border to what is today about the border between Georgia and Florida—might have sent word to the locals to find him something to do, though one might expect a record of such an order to have survived. It's likely, however, that Lawson was just looking for opportunity, and that the journey was less Lewis and Clark than "Road trip!" That is, Lewis and Clark, a century later, had the backing and support of the U.S. government; Lawson had nothing of the sort. From what I can tell—and I am backed up by knowledgeable people on this—Lawson probably overheard some traders talking in a tavern and begged to come along. Maybe he was introduced to them more formally.

In any case, what we know is what Lawson tells us: "On *December* the 28th, 1700, I began my Voyage (for *North Carolina*) from *Charles-*Town, being six *English*-men in Company, with three *Indian*-men, and one Woman, Wife to our *Indian*-Guide."

They left by single canoe—an enormous dugout cypress trunk—and paddled along the coast to the mouth of the Santee River, some forty-five miles northeast. There they headed upriver, abandoning the canoe after a day and continuing on foot. The company varied as the journey continued: Indian guides came and went; English traders continued or dropped out, others joined. When Lawson emerged at the Pamlico Sound some fifty-seven days later, he had interacted with Huguenot settlers and had met the Sewee, Santee, Sugeree, Wateree, Catawba, Waxhaw, Occaneechi, and Tuscarora Indians. He stayed in their wigwams, ate their food, trusted their guides. And he emerged with their stories, for some of which he is the only source in the world.

When he ended his journey, he set up housekeeping with British settlers on the Pamlico and began making his way as a scientist, anthropologist, trader, and land developer. He was founder of the state's two first incorporated towns—Bath, in 1706, and, with von Graffenried, New Bern in 1710. He was part of the commission working to resolve the colony's border dispute with Virginia and served as surveyor general of the colony. He corresponded with and sent botanical samples to James Petiver in London, one of the great collectors—at the time called "vertuosi"—at the dawn of the age of science and collecting. Petiver's specimens, along with those of Sir Hans Sloane, formed the foundation of what is now the British Museum. Lawson has left behind no grave marker, but his gathered specimens remain to this day at the Natural History Museum in London, lovingly displayed among the contents of the *Hortus Siccus* ("dry garden") books of Sloane's collection.

And, of course, he met that grim fate among the Tuscaroras.

We do not know the exact circumstances of Lawson's death that night in 1711. Some say he was burned to death, others that he was hanged; von Graffenried's account raises those two possibilities and adds that some Indians had threatened to cut Lawson's throat with his own straight razor. In the end, von Graffenried says, "The savages keep it very secret how he was killed. May God have pity on his soul." Christopher Gale, North Carolina's first chief justice, said Indians told him Lawson was burned. Historians gravitate toward that claim because Lawson himself, in his vital descriptions of the Indians, describes the awful fate of an Indian captive:

> They strive to invent the most inhumane Butcheries for them, that the Devils themselves could invent, or hammer out of Hell; they esteeming Death no Punishment, but rather an Advantage to him, that is exported out of this into another World.
>
> Therefore, they inflict on them Torments, wherein they prolong Life in that miserable state as long as they can, and never miss Skulping of them, as they call it, which is, to cut off the Skin from the Temples, and taking the whole Head of Hair along with it, as is it was a Nightcap. Sometimes, they take the Top of the Skull along with it; all which they preserve, and carefully keep by them, for a Trophy of their Con-

quest over their Enemies. Others keep their Enemies Teeth, which are taken in War, whilst others split the Pitch-Pine into Splinters, and stick them into the Prisoners Body yet alive. Thus they light them, which burn like so many Torches; and in this manner, they make him dance round a great Fire, every one buffeting and deriding him, till he expires.

Yikes.

In any case, we know Lawson died that night. He left London in 1700 and departed Charleston on his epic journey later that year; he remained in Carolina after that until in 1709 he returned briefly to London to publish his book, returning to the colony in 1710. In 1711 his career came to a dead stop.

To remember him, we have the specimens he collected. We have descriptions of him by the people trying to organize the border with Virginia (they didn't like him much) and by von Graffenried (who didn't like him much). We even have a portrait, in private hands, that might be of Lawson.

But above all we have his book, filled with descriptions, tales, and observations in a cheerful, clever, and highly readable voice. In Lawson we have more than a delightful author. We have his record as a sort of prototypical southern colonist. Whatever religious freedom was provided in that original constitution, the Charles-Town Lawson arrived in was filled with people seeking not salvation but fortune. Lawson showed up looking for the same and for adventure, if such was to be had.

::::

In late 2014, I set out to, for the first time ever, retrace Lawson's entire journey and observe our own world-on-edge and compare it with his. It seems kind of a stupid idea, or at least a rash one, but if you give it some room, it made a kind of powerful sense. Lawson showed up in Carolina and, knowing nothing about the place, set off on the kind of adventure a young person loves to take: The hell with planning; this looks fun. Off we go, and where we end, well, there we'll be.

I was quite the opposite—in middle age, with home, wife, children—and yet with the same driving curiosity. By the time I stumbled onto Lawson I had lived in North Carolina for nearly two decades and pretended to myself that I in some ways knew the place—not utterly foolish, considering I had married a native and had populated the state with two more natives. I had taken many a car trip and many a forest hike in Carolina, and I would have had to be senseless not to see the changes occurring even in my own years here. The tobacco that I had once smelled in Durham factories was long gone; likewise much of the furniture and textile manufacture that had been the state's livelihood since not long after Lawson's time. The small towns, you could not avoid seeing on any visit or drive through, were at best struggling and more often dying, even as the cities prospered, with thousands of new residents arriving every month.

Some days, still with my Yankee roots, I felt like Lawson, trying to understand my adopted home and its residents' strange habits; other times, as that tide of new residents swamped the city I had come to know, I felt more like a native watching my cherished culture vanish around me. I make my living asking people questions and writing down what they tell me; I began to work on an idea. I wondered what I'd find if I, like Lawson, set out and took a journey—looked around and wrote about what I observed. I couldn't do what Lawson did—with nobody to care for and no work to leave behind, he could just set out into the bush and see what happened, popping back up a couple of months and half a thousand miles later. I'd have to do something a bit more circumscribed—I'd have to be a weekend explorer, planning my trips around summer camp and work holidays. That's the down side. On the up side, Lawson took a journey and wrote a book about it, and the book came out eight years later, which was about the speed of communication then. I, in contrast, could (and did) create a website, sharing my observations almost as I made them and asking for input from the locals. Before the trip was done I was updating my Instagram feed from a kayak, writing blog posts by firelight, uploading them via cell-phone hotspot.

A lot had changed since Lawson's day, but not the value of travel, of walking the earth, of breathing the air, of moving your body through fresh terrain and allowing it to make its impressions upon you, of candidly sharing those impressions. When Lawson did that he made a lasting contribution to the understanding of this place, of Carolina—and somehow, when I stumbled on his story, nobody had ever retraced that journey to connect it to our own world, centuries later.

I thought it was about time somebody had, so I started by doing the same thing he did. I went to Charleston. And I found a place in a canoe.

1 : Spartina, Mon Amour

For a week, I see almost nothing but *Spartina alterniflora*.

Tall, green stalks stretch several feet above the surface of the water. For hour upon hour, mile after mile, my canoe slides quietly along the edge of the saltwater marsh. And what grows in the marsh? Mainly one thing: *Spartina alterniflora*.

Marsh grass. Acres upon acres of marsh grass. If I stray a bit farther into the Intracoastal Waterway, I can see it spread in waves of green shoot and brown husk, whispering with wind, rustling and swaying with waves. When I paddle closer, right along the edge, I hear it hiss as my canoe rubs up against it. When, as I occasionally do, I paddle into a winding tidal creek, it all but closes above my head, and I look around and see nothing but marsh grass, look above and see only blue sky and high, white clouds. For all the difference I see in my environment from what John Lawson would have seen, it could be 1700.

:::

It's not, though. It's 2014, and if my canoe strays too far from the border of the salt marsh I'm quickly in danger of being run over by one of the yachts speeding down the Intracoastal Waterway. The "Intercoastal," as locally known, is the I-95 of coastal boat traffic and about as far from 1700 as you can get. It's October, and all the people who own fancy boats are moving them—or having them moved—down the waterway to take up winter residence in Florida. I am paddling a heavy, fat canoe—a big, friendly, accommodating pack mule of a craft, and just as streamlined and responsive as a pack mule, too. Loaded with a cooler of food, a seven-gallon water container, a tent, flares, an emergency satellite phone, and dry-bags full of clothes, books, maps, and electronics, I need to stay close to the edge of the marsh for safety.

"If you see a boat that doesn't see you—and they won't see you," says my first-day guide, Ed Deal, who skitters along beside me in a kayak, "pull into the marsh. It'll deaden the wake." Just as marshes and other coastal wetlands do to hurricanes, the spartina will do to the waves from speedier and larger craft. It'll calm the waters and keep me afloat. Ed says

A view that Lawson himself could have seen: acre after acre of marsh grass.

the edge of the marsh is the place to be anyhow. "That's where the action is." He means that the salt marsh is the great preschool of the coast, filled with juvenile fish and crustaceans. Apart from the riot of bird life that frequents the marsh, all kinds of larger fish patrol the periphery, looking for lunch. Then things even bigger await them. The adult menhaden hang around the edge; the bottlenose dolphins, working as a team, round up the menhaden into thick schools and feast. Circle of life and all that.

The marsh, the spartina, spreads for miles, as it has for centuries. And the reason I can see this spread of marsh grass is because South Carolina is fortunate in three ways. First, it has a mucky coastline, full of shifting barrier islands that harbor the pluff mud that will suck the shoe right off your foot if you step in it — Carolina Quicksand, the locals call it. It is not especially accommodating for human development, but spartina loves it. A second stroke of good fortune for South Carolina's coast is how much of it remains in the hands of the original families who took charge of it all the way back in Lawson's time. Long-term residents like to keep things

SPARTINA, MON AMOUR

as they have been. Finally, the Cape Romain National Wildlife Refuge, the Santee Coastal Wildlife Management Area, and a half-dozen other national- or state-managed reserves have meant that the South Carolina coast north of Charleston, with its barrier islands, salt marshes, and seemingly endless winding tidal creeks, has remained as protected as any in the Southeast—perhaps any on the East Coast.

"Much of the South Carolina coast is unspoiled," James Morris, director of the Baruch Institute of Marine and Coastal Sciences at the University of South Carolina, told me. "South Carolina is unique in that regard in that we have so much protected coastline." In 1700, before slaves cleared the tidal swamps and freshwater marshes for the rice and indigo plantations that first made South Carolina rich, "it still would have been really, really wild." And whereas freshwater marshes, further in on the coastline, are riots of different plant species, the salt marshes are monospecific, Morris said. *Spartina alterniflora* is perfectly adapted to this place, and there it remains. "He would have smelled rotten eggs," Morris said of Lawson. "You'll smell it too. That rotten egg odor is hydrogen sulfide, and it's a natural byproduct of the decay of leaves and roots in a salt marsh marine environment." I smelled it. To me it smelled great.

The Carolina coasts—the Cape Hatteras and Cape Lookout National Seashores in North and the many refuges of South—have for decades been held as examples of how to preserve a natural coastline, in comparison with the treatment of those further north. The coastlines of Connecticut and New Jersey are largely hardened—stabilized with seawalls, jetties, and groins, all of which resist the natural movements of sand, mud, and marsh along with sea and tide. South Carolina's unstabilized coastline results in about 350,000 acres of salt marsh—30 percent of all remaining tidal salt marsh on the entire eastern seaboard. The total on the East Coast is something less than half of what would have been there in Lawson's time.

Like Morris said, a salt marsh is a monoculture, at least in its vegetation: spartina is a magician of nature, slowly and patiently creating the land beneath its roots. Designed to prosper in the tidal zone where sediments accumulate and sea and soil meet, it has learned to excrete excess salt, not only making it able to withstand the salty tidal water but making it attractive to species like periwinkle snails, which come by to lap up the delicious minerals the spartina doesn't want. The snails, using rows of replaceable hook-like sharp teeth in a mouth-like thing called a radula, also help decompose the dead spartina. That decomposing marsh grass begins to create mud, which of course becomes matrix for more spartina, which spreads through long, hollow rhizomes, or underground stems.

What's more, the marsh also attracts microscopic diatoms and other phytoplankton. When the tide goes out, these organisms form a surface scum that helps stabilize the mud, further encouraging spartina growth and sustaining things like snails, oysters, clams, and other filter feeders, to say nothing of the fiddler and ghost crabs so plentiful along the shoreline. Those animals form the base of an incredibly rich habitat. The spartina stabilizes the shoreline with its rhizomes, allowing oysters to get—literally—a foothold. The Spartina and the oysters clean the water and improve the habitat. Oyster shells create shoals that further stabilize the coastline. Sponges come along and eat the whelk, snails, and other invertebrates by drilling into them (those tiny holes you see in found shells? Sponge-sign), after which the shells slowly dissolve back into the water, their calcium carbonate just what new baby oysters need. Nothing wasted.

Lots of little fish equals lots of big fish who like to eat them, and lots of shorebirds who like to eat the big and little fish. In one five-day period of canoeing north up the coast I saw local brown and migrating white pelicans, herons (great blue, little blue, and tricolor), egrets (snowy and great), ibises, oystercatchers, black skippers, black skimmers, bald eagles, osprey, willets, short-billed dowagers, the no-longer-as-endangered brown woodstork, and an enormous variety of gulls and the plovers, sandpipers, and sanderlings that, like grandparents with grandchildren, even guides can't always tell apart (though my second-day guide Elizabeth Anderegg pointed out spotted sandpipers, identifiable by their stuttery wingbeats: b-r-r-r, coast; b-r-r-r, coast). One night I slept on the front porch of a cabin and heard in the silence all three common eastern owls: screech, barred, and great horned. At this point in his journey Lawson is so overwhelmed by birds that he simply lists "Plenty of Fowl, as Curleus, Gulls, Gannets, and Pellicans, besides Duck and Mallard, Geese, Swans, Teal, Widgeon, &c." Of the owls I heard Lawson says the "scritch" is "much the same as in *Europe*," though he describes one other, surely the great horned, which he says "is as big as a middling Goose, and has a prodigious Head. They make a fearful Hollowing in the Night-time, like a Man, whereby they often make Strangers lose their way in the Woods."

With my fine guide I kept my way. Elizabeth even pointed out a pair of roseate spoonbills, who were just then coming in on their migratory path. Elizabeth also explained why the double-crested cormorants we saw

The view for a week: oyster shoal, Spartina alterniflora, *overpacked canoe.*

tended to stand stoic atop pier pilings, wings open, as though doing sun salutations. The cormorant's feathers are not particularly oily, she says — this gives it less buoyancy and enables it to compete by diving deeper for fish. But that means the feathers get wet, so the bird is heavy and needs to dry off before it can again fly well. If one was not yet dry when we came upon it, as it flew away from us it descended right to the surface of the channel, where—whap! whap! whap!—it patty-caked its feet along the surface until it had enough speed to rise. We saw bottlenose dolphins engaging in various hunting habits for the menhaden, rising manta and stingrays, and other fish that came and went too quickly for us to recognize.

Go further in toward shore and you get smaller spartina (less able to grow above the tide), then black needlerush and goldenrod and other plants more suited to brackish or freshwater. Trees like loblolly pines and salt cedar become common, along with the omnipresent palmetto. We saw yaupons and holly on the natural shoals, and buckthorns that

Elizabeth said grow mostly on islands of dredging spoils. So Lawson would have seen the yaupons—he described them, in fact, including the medicinal and ceremonial purpose for which the Indians used them—but maybe not the buckthorns.

Which reminds me: I'm ahead of myself. We were talking about Lawson. I paddled north in an overburdened canoe through the South Carolina salt marsh because Lawson did the same 300 years ago.

:::

In response to Morris's observation that the salt marshes hadn't changed much in 300 years, guide Ed Deal raised an eyebrow. "Well," he said, "you *are* taking a shortcut." He referred to the Intracoastal Waterway, the series of bays, canals, and dredged channels that's been growing since the early 1800s. So once we paddled across Charleston Harbor, we did not have to do what Lawson did, and snake our way through tidal creeks along Sullivan's Island and then ride the tide across a treacherous inlet called "the Breach" (almost a century later, British troops tried and failed to cross it during the Revolutionary War Battle of Sullivan's Island). Instead we crossed the harbor, headed north into a broad opening 300 feet wide, and could have paddled pretty much straight for forty miles or so to the mouth of the Santee. Very different from the tidal creeks and inlets that Lawson described as "the most difficult Way I ever saw, occasion'd by Reason of the multitude of Creeks lying along the Main, keeping their Course thro' the Marshes, turning and winding like a Labyrinth, having the Tide of Ebb and Flood twenty Times in less than three Leagues going."

Lawson describes leaving Charleston thus: "At 4 in the Afternoon, (at half Flood) we pass'd with our Canoe over the Breach." He and his nine companions threaded their way into what would then have been called the Inland Passage, the web of tidal creeks, inlets, and channels by which one paddled along the coast. If ten people—plus guns, journals, and whatever other provisions they would have carried—seems rather a lot for a canoe, let me explain that canoe. Made most likely of a single cypress trunk, the canoe would have been made as Indians had been making canoes for centuries. Bud Hill, of the Village Museum in tiny McClellanville, halfway between Charleston and the mouth of the Santee River, used an ancient canoe the museum owns to demonstrate (the canoes, made of cypress and buried in mud, last pretty much forever; ones from the 1600s and 1700s dot museums up and down the Carolina coast). Indians would have felled the tree, laid it down, and lit fires along the top the trunk. When the fires died down they'd scrape the char away with oyster shells, then light new fires. In a couple of weeks you could make your way all the way through a large trunk.

Europeans brought drills and dowels and improved the construction. For example, leaving unburned buttresses along the side, they could drill down for seats into those buttresses, and presto—instead of pushing the canoe apart and encouraging split, the seat held it together. They'd also drill into the bottom of the canoe a dowel of whatever measure they wanted the hull to remain. Then they'd scrape until they hit the end of the dowel and know they had their hull at exactly the right thickness. And as for big, ten people was hardly the limit: Lawson describes canoes that hold "fifty or sixty Barrels."

Lawson's first destination was the community of French Huguenots at the mouth of the Santee, about forty miles north of Charleston. After a night on a neighboring island with a Bermudian—the island had no freshwater, so Lawson says "our Entertainment was very indifferent"— Lawson spent the rest of the week in the winding tidal streams. The next night the party stayed on Dix's Island (likely today's DeWee's Island) with a Scotsman who entertained them well with supplies he had scavenged from a ship that had foundered during a hurricane on September 5, 1700. Lawson describes enjoying "Oat-meal and several other Effects," but since the ship was Scottish, one hopes the other effects were more entertaining than oatmeal. Lawson also describes nearly losing the canoe—and their lives—in the waves at the northern tip of the island, where they went to spend the night.

Day three took the travelers to Bull's Island, on the southern edge of Bull's Bay, about halfway to the mouth of the Santee. There too the company struggled, heading across the bay toward Raccoon Island until "there sprung up a tart Gale at *N.W.* which put us in some Danger of being cast away." Despite rough seas on Bull's Bay, they safely returned to Bull's Island, spending another day there—Lawson visited the ocean side, "having very fair sandy Beeches, pav'd with innumerable Sorts of curious pretty Shells, very pleasant to the Eye." There Lawson also encountered his first jellyfish: "a muciligmous slimy Substance, though living, and very aptly mov'd at their first Appearance; yet, being left on the dry Sand, (by the Beams of the Sun) soon exhale and vanish." For provision the Indian guides hunted deer, raccoon, and wild hogs, which the party augmented with "great Store of Oysters, Conks, and Clanns [clams]."

The whelk is done with this shell, so sponges have been using it to supply calcium they need. Nothing wasted in nature.

From Bull's Island, Lawson continued "thro' the Creeks which lie between the Bay and the Main Land," sleeping at an abandoned Indian settlement he called Avendaughbough, a name almost surely retained in today's tiny Awendaw. The next day they reached the mouth of the Santee, then one of the greatest river mouths on the East Coast—they found it in flood, and it took all they could do to paddle upstream a few miles. Hearing noises Lawson feared were gunshots, the party encountered a band of Sewee Indians firing a canebrake to drive out wildlife for hunting—the popping noise was segments of cane bursting from internal pressure as they burned.

Lawson spends a couple of pages telling stories about the Santee, then describes arriving at the Huguenot community, after which, Lawson tells us, they resolved "to go the Remainder of our Voyage by Land."

So ended his voyage by canoe—about fifty-five miles along the coast and up the Santee. He seemed glad to get out of the boat. By the time I was done I couldn't blame him.

SPARTINA, MON AMOUR

:::

When I looked at a map of the South Carolina coast as I planned the beginning of my trip, I confidently determined that all I needed to do was rent a canoe, throw my gear in it, and paddle a week or so up the Intracoastal Waterway, stopping at this island or that one as I grew tired. A confident paddler, I blithely called an outfitter in Charleston and reached Kathie Livingston—guide, outfitter, and coastal Carolinian. "Exactly what," she asked, "are you planning to do?" I explained. The line went quiet as she thought a moment.

"I got this," she then said. And like Lawson, I was suddenly in very good hands, no thanks to myself. Kathie ended up sort of signing on as my Lawson sponsor and guide. She put me in a canoe, found me places to camp along the coast for five nights, made sure I had all the safety equipment I might need, and filled me up with maps and contacts. She provided me a guide for each day—including herself, on the final day—and pointed out places along the route I was simply not to miss. I called her a Hero of the Lawson Trek, and I was far from the coast and several journeys up the road before I stopped calling her for help and she stopped rescuing me.

Kathie first matched me with Ed Deal, who puttered around Charleston Bay in his kayak while Kathie and I loaded my canoe and my family watched. I pushed off from the dock at the Charleston Maritime Center, a public dock about a mile north of Oyster Point, Charleston's southern tip, at the meeting of the Cooper and Ashley Rivers. We left in early morning—the tide was coming in, which Kathie said would not hinder us much as we crossed the harbor and made for the Intracoastal. Given that Lawson in his introduction speaks at length about "their Roads, with great Industry,... made very good and pleasant" and describes Charlestonians making "a considerable Number of Vessels" with which to conduct island trade, I had no reason to believe some sort of dock hadn't stood on that spot 314 years before, when Lawson set off.

Kathie told me later Ed didn't relax until he saw I could comfortably paddle; he had feared, I think, having to drag me along, through uncertain waters, on his own. Bottlenose dolphins investigated us as we pushed off. It seemed like a good omen. My children waved. We have pictures.

Ed and I paddled easily enough across the harbor—it wasn't windy, and if the tide was pushing in it met the river flowing out and caused us no trouble. That said, by the end of the day I felt that I had learned my first important truth about Lawson: I do not believe he paddled his canoe. That is, something Lawson never did mention was the horror of paddling a heavy canoe upcurrent or, worse, upwind—which leads me to believe that of the ten sets of hands in Lawson's canoe, at most nine were paddling. I think Lawson sat and took notes. He was too observant not to have noted his own blisters, sore muscles, exhaustion. Anyhow, I certainly noticed mine.

We ran into a light headwind late in the day, and pushing that heavy canoe upwind (and also, as it happened, against one of those unpredictable currents) exhausted me to the brink of tears. "Your canoe is like a sailboat," Ed told me. "And you're the sail." Then he would skitter across the channel in his low-sitting kayak looking for less wind, skittering back to me, crossing the channel twice in the time it would have taken me to forge ten or fifteen feet into that headwind. We ended up hugging the west shore, paddling beneath piers to scrub off the wind. And we got to my first night's shelter, on Goat Island, which Kathie had organized with a fellow named Jimmy, whose house could be recognized by the ten-foot plastic smiley face that marked its front porch.

Goat Island is a tiny barrier island between the Intracoastal and the mainland. In the first half of the twentieth century it was populated only by feral goats and an equally feral human couple who apparently lived in a palm-frond lean-to. Too small for cars or even a paved road, the island started gaining residents in the 1960s and 1970s and now hosts descendants of the hippies and back-to-nature types who came then. Jimmy now rents his home to visitors—you must arrive by boat, there's no bridge—but he let me set up my tent in the backyard.

Lawson spent his first night complaining about the "thousands of Musketoes, and other troublesome Insects, tormenting both Man and Beast." It was December, but Carolina even then was Carolina. Lawson also noted the palmettos, South Carolina's state tree. Lawson likely slept on an island now known as Isle of Palms, and though Goat Island is across the Intracoastal, Jimmy's yard was full of palmettos.

After I cooked and ate my standard camping-fare macaroni dinner, we sat in the evening and chatted about Goat Island history while the sun went down. When it got dark enough Jimmy flipped a switch and Christmas lights came on, winding their way around the palmetto trunks. Lawson was interested in the palmetto, as one can imagine—it fairly radiates tropicality, with its fan fronds, spiky "bootjack" bark, and porous, stringy wood. Lawson noted that locals made brooms and fans out of the leaves and shipped leaves to the islands and northern colonies, where people wove them into baskets and boxes. The weavers making sweetgrass baskets in the Charleston City Market still sometimes use palmetto leaves in their weaving. Lawson wrote that the palmetto grows so slowly that "the Growth of the Tree is not perceivable in the Age of any Man," which is of course a vast exaggeration. What impressed me most was how nice a palmetto looks wrapped in white Christmas lights, the fronds reduced to silhouette under the a fading blue of an autumn Carolina sky.

Next morning I broke camp, reloaded the canoe, and repeated the day with a new guide. The days in the canoe soon developed a rhythm. I used a kayak paddle, pushing the canoe along as spartina and other marsh grasses flowed by; a guide kayaked next to me, identifying birds and fish, islands and shoals, and making sure I didn't get lost or run over by yachts. Each day I would break camp and paddle to a nearby put-in, where I would meet the guide Kathie Livingston had organized for me. Late in the day that guide and I would part at the boat ramp nearest my night's destination. So I paddled alone every morning and evening and before long became confident in my ability to move along, even exploring little tidal creeks and side channels off the Intracoastal. Each night after my guide paddled off I would find my home. This was my first journey following Lawson, and like Lawson I was trying to figure out what I was doing.

:::

Like Lawson, I learned most when I listened to my hosts. Lawson mentions the scavenged foodstuffs from the *Rising Sun*, destroyed in the great hurricane that preceded him, which tells me that something besides the spartina remains unchanged from Lawson's time to ours. In my first weeks following Lawson, in the coast and the lowlands, I found that everyone on the South Carolina coast has a story of Hurricane Hugo, the devastating storm of 1989. Jimmy told me about what people called the Goat Island Yacht Club—the crush of pleasure boats washed up on the island's shore in Hugo's wake. The storm hit nearly three decades before my visit, a legendarily devastating category four storm that plowed into Charleston and the coast, drowning dozens and leaving a path of forests turned into matchsticks. They still talk about Hugo in Charlotte, for that matter, which gives you a sense of how strong it was.

From Jimmy I heard tales not just of Hugo but of the history of the area's growth, with development pouring northward out of Charlestown.

Not unlike the Native peoples Lawson met, who surely feared that the new arrivals would overwhelm them, current locals fear what the rising tide of retirees, Yankees, and footloose young people might do to the coast they loved—a theme I frequently encountered on my journey. And I couldn't help wondering whether I, like Lawson, wouldn't end up just another voice advertising how lovely Carolina was, and how ripe for migration. I tried not to worry; I just paid attention.

My guides pointed out fish and birds—and brought their understanding of their local landscape into mine. My first-day guide, Ed, talked about the fish and the spartina, which he called one of the most important plants in the world. My second-day guide, Elizabeth Anderegg, joined me at a boat ramp a half-mile north of Jimmy's, and her cheerful stories entertained me all day. She especially pointed out the musicality of the shores, covered with thin shells and translucent fragments that, once you knew to listen, played a tinkling melody as the water rose and fell. "You've heard of jingle bells? These are jingle shells," she said. "People make wind chimes out of them. I love the way they sound, especially when it's really quiet and the tide is just . . ." She waved her hands and shoulders, swaying like a hula dancer, ". . . just a little bit, and you can hear them jingling. You can hear the shells kind of tinkling. It's just really musical to me." The hiss of the water lifting them, the jingle as they settled back down became a constant backdrop for the week I spent on the coast. Kathie Livingston later went into even more depth, noting that you could distinguish between the shell music of a rising and a lowering tide: "On the way out, it laps," she told me, "it's kind of a water-washed jingle; on the way in it's more of a rush." By the time I was done I had convinced myself I could tell the difference.

After Elizabeth paddled to a boat ramp near the end of the day, I was to keep heading north and then, according to one of the waterproof maps Kathie had outfitted me with, turn toward the sea after I passed dozens of tidal creeks and came to the wide turnoff that would obviously be the Price Inlet, which led southeast between Capers Island and Bulls Island. She was sure I couldn't miss it, and, despite the uncertainty that came with paddling on my own among the trackless tidal marshes, I paddled on and found that she was right. Creeks to the left, to the right, but when the inlet appeared it would have been obvious even without the green and red markers put up to guide boats. I headed toward the ocean, recognizing Capers Island and the official camping area on its northeast tip when I arrived. Again, I had paddled to an official camping area,

SPARTINA, MON AMOUR

guided by enormous boating markers planted by the government—but the selfie I took when I got there shows me looking like I had just summited Everest.

I spent two nights alone on Capers Island, part of the Cape Romain National Wildlife Refuge. A beach on the seaward edge of the island goes by the name Boneyard for its dead trees, weathered into stark monuments as they die as the sea erodes the shore. The shells on that beach were just as pretty as they were in Lawson's day—sand dollars and whelks mixed in much more liberally than usual with the clams and oysters. The next day I paddled across the inlet to Bulls Island, where I spent a day hiking in maritime forest, among live oaks and Spanish moss, loblolly pines and magnolias. I saw no alligators but plenty of gulls. The island gets its name from Stephen Bull, one of the original settlers of Charleston in 1670. Those settlers landed on this island, then called Oneiscau, and met with the Sewee Indians, for whom things did not go very well thereafter, though about them more in a moment. Returning to Capers was a simple paddle across an inlet about a thousand feet wide. I knew from my tide charts that the current would be flowing out at the end of the day, when I was heading back, and I took my paddling seriously. All I can tell you is that I set my sights straight inward, upcurrent toward the coast, and it took everything I had to cross the thousand yards and end up back on Capers Island only a little bit further out toward the sea than I was on Bulls. The currents are not to be trifled with.

Lawson mentions his fear of being cast away by "a tart Gale at *N.W.*" near Bulls Island, and my little campsite on Capers that night endured a late-season tropical storm. I upended the canoe over my supplies, put the electronics in waterproof bags, and zipped up my tent, which as the storm passed overnight bent and swayed as though it were trying to catch its breath. One stake pulled out and another bent, but otherwise the tent was a champion. The upturned canoe protected the rest of my supplies, and after a morning spent in sunshine allowing items to dry I rode the incoming tide up the inlet to the Intracoastal, where at a nearby put-in I met my next guide, Eddie Stroman, a lean, affable ex–Forest Service guy (he used to work controlled burns and still does some as a freelance) who as we paddled told me about farming clams, which he does, starting with clam seeds. Clam seeds are of course tiny baby clams, but I found the image of clam seeds delightful.

With their readings of the landscape, their descriptions of the menhaden and spoonbills, of spartina and yaupon, my guides were like the storytellers Lawson met, telling him what lived where, how the water flowed in the uncountable channels of the Inland Passage. The maps Kathie gave me, with their depths and longitudes, their dotted lines and icons, laid another layer of information on the landscape, another story on top of Lawson's, on top even of the stories Lawson heard. One friend called my trip a "geographical palimpsest"—a layering of my trip atop Lawson's, of current conditions atop those of times before, of stories onto maps.

With Eddie I left the Intracoastal and paddled into a tidal creek I could not have identified on my own in 10,000 years. As beautiful as I found the grasses along the Intracoastal, when I paddled along inlets or up creeks, in their winding silence I felt like I was truly seeing nature at her ease, going about her business as she had done for centuries. One of my main goals on this undertaking was to compare what Lawson would have seen with what I could see, and it was a pleasure so soon after the start to find myself in a place where I could imagine we were seeing the same things.

At the end of this creek Eddie and I found ourselves at the Sewee Shell Ring, a 4,000-year-old circular mound made of oyster, clam, and other shells, long since covered with earth and grasses. Archaeologists debate what such rings, which dot the coasts and barrier islands of Florida, Georgia, and South Carolina (the Sewee ring being the northernmost), indicate. Egalitarian societies, living in circular camps and tossing their shell waste behind their huts? The mounding of feast remains? Purpose-built sites surrounding a central plaza for ceremonies? Nobody is quite sure. Nobody, that is, except Billy Baldwin, who had a story.

:::

Billy Baldwin is sort of the poet laureate of McClellanville, South Carolina—a well-published writer of everything from local histories to travel guides to novels to poems, and a beloved personality in McClellanville, which is something of a haven for beloved personalities. Once Sewee hunting and fishing grounds, McClellanville grew into being in the 1850s as a fishing village around the mouth of Jeremy Creek, still an active boating and fishing dock. It has a store, a restaurant, a museum, around 500 highly individual residents, and the Deerhead Oak, a live oak some thousand-plus years old that from certain angles looks like the head of a deer with antlers. It was once the capital of terrapin fishing in the United States and boasted a strong shrimp fishery as well, and like the entire

Carolina coast had a vast oyster industry. (Charleston itself was once called Oyster Point.) I met Baldwin, a cheerful man in his sixties with a button-down shirt and a huge bushy beard, at the Sewee Shell Ring, where he and a few others had come when news spread that Eddie and I would be docking there to visit. We tied up at a boardwalk overlooking the shell ring, clambered up, and read the government information cards speculating about the ring, which is about 6 feet high and 225 feet or so in diameter.

When we had learned all the foolishness the cards had to share, the time came for Billy. He had worked there one summer in his youth, building a vacation house for a local family (Hugo destroyed it). He'd knock off each day and watch the sun go down over nearby clam middens. He grew interested enough to quit his job and dedicate himself to the shell ring: "I read everything Lévi-Strauss had written about foods and totems in the South American Indians. I decided that the clams had a totemic significance. All of it did." He concluded, in what he describes as a vision—"one day this whole thing for a split second arched, as a universe, with lines"—that he was looking at a calendar, with clam middens marking spots where the sun went down, visible from the shell ring, at the solstices and equinoxes. He gave me copies of his calculations.

The archaeological people he reached out to were not impressed. Was I convinced? I don't know; I almost don't care. The point is twofold: First, like Lawson, I never felt happier than when I was fortunate enough to have the locals tell me things. I learned about the oyster industry from mentions and books, but hearing Eddie tell me about clam farming brought it home to me. Eddie also taught me about the local industry harvesting horseshoe crabs, whose blue blood, useful in detecting impurities in pharmaceuticals, sells for $15,000 a pint after it is extracted; the crabs are then replaced to their spawning beds, from which they are grabbed up overnight. He talked about running into locals when he was out clam farming or oystering. "They're out there in the middle of the night, in short pants, feeling for horseshoe crabs." For Lawson, as for me, this I think is why you journey out among people you do not know. For stories like this.

Perhaps Lawson's most significant story is one that comes down to us, as far as I can tell, from him alone. Lawson describes running into the Sewees once his canoe had headed inland, up the Santee River. The Sewees, from all accounts, were a coastal people—the name perhaps means "island"—and Lawson found them in their home territory. The

Sewees, in fact, were the people who greeted the first British settlers of Carolina in 1670 when their ship came to the barrier islands. (And by the way—settlers naturally associated the shell ring with the Natives they met. It probably predates them by a good 3,000 years; the Sewees probably settled in the area sometime after 1000 CE.)

"These *Sewees* have been formerly a large Nation," Lawson says, "though now very much decreas'd." The Sewees, according to the tale Lawson spins, early on esteemed "the *English* that were among them, no better than Cheats," and thought the furs and skins they traded could fetch much higher prices if they took them directly to England themselves. Right on both counts. "Some of the craftiest of them had observ'd, that the Ships came always in at one Place, which made them very confident that Way was the exact Road to *England*," Lawson goes on, and the Sewee drew the conclusion that they could go from thence directly to England and trade with "a better Sort of People than those sent amongst them, that then they should purchase twenty times the Value for every Pelt they sold Abroad." So the Sewees set about a plan. They agreed to build a fleet of canoes to carry their wares to England. Some built enormous canoes; others hunted to build up an inventory; others prepared supplies for the voyage. Once they had prepared, they "set Sail, leaving only the Old, Impotent, and Minors at Home."

Off they went—"and were scarce out of Sight, when there rose a Tempest," which upset the fleet and killed many of the Indians. "The others were taken up at Sea by an *English* Ship, and sold for Slaves to the Islands." The remaining Sewees—again, the old, the young, and the infirm—recognized the undertaking as the most terrible mistake their tribe had ever made, "nothing affronting them more, than to rehearse their Voyage to *England*." The saddest summation comes in Lawson's book, which like many of the time has occasional italic text summaries in the margins. At the end of this tale runs the phrase, hanging stark in the margin, "*They never hearing more of their fleet.*"

With this story Lawson begins his unparalleled descriptions of the Indian tribes he encountered. Among most modern Carolinians Lawson is all but unknown; those who know him know of his lurid death, or perhaps of his trail. Among historians and ethnographers, though, his Indian descriptions are remembered and rightfully praised. In Lawson's time, two narratives seemed to compete for primacy regarding the New World: First was that North America was in essence empty, a virgin country awaiting European settlers. The other was that the Indians were savages to be swept aside. Lawson saw things differently. He recognized that the Indians had been treated terribly by the European settlers—"They are really better to us, than we are to them," he says late in his book. "We reckon them Slaves in Comparison to us, and Intruders, as oft as they enter our Houses, or hunt near our Dwellings. But if we will admit Reason to be our Guide, she will inform us, that these *Indians* are the freest People in the World, and so far from being Intruders upon us, that we have abandon'd our own Native Soil, to drive them out and possess theirs." What of those other stories of Indians that Lawson's contemporaries had heard, which portrayed them as simpletons or savages? "Those that generally write Histories of this new World, are such as Interest, Preferment, and Merchandize, drew thither, and know no more of that People than I do of the *Laplanders*."

Lawson's tales of the Indians portray, as does his story of the Sewees, the ragged end of a dying, once-great civilization that spread across continents. Lawson at the time of his journey was just beginning to learn of the Indians. During my journey and research I too learned things about the Indians, their treatment at the hands of the Europeans, and the history of their descendants that I had heard no place else.

:::

Eddie paddled with me to the Buck Hall Recreation Area, where on a two-wheeled cart that Kathie had dropped off I pulled my canoe to an asphalt parking spot designed for an enormous RV; the lot was full of them, housing families participating in the shrimping season. Eddie had told me to be prepared for numerous invitations to shrimp boils, but by seven that evening every one of those RVs was shut tight against the bugs, generators rumbling away and air conditioners whirring, the flickering of television glowing through closed curtains. My little tent huddled on the grass under some pines at the edge of a lawn, looking appropriately out of place. I was just glad for a campground with a warm shower.

The next morning Eddie met me back there and chatted cheerfully through a day of paddling, which ended at the dock of Jana, another friend of Kathie's, whose family beach house stood in a marsh on a plantation their family had owned for "thirteen, fourteen generations," though Jana admitted she could be off by a generation or two. I slept on the screen porch, to protect me from the bugs. Jana laughed at the idea that my town of Raleigh had mosquitoes, at least compared with the clouds of mosquitoes, gnats, and no-see-ums that plague the plantation, surrounded by marsh and swamp. She recommended B-12 and endurance. I was glad for the screens. I heard whippoorwills and owls.

The next morning Kathie Livingston herself joined me in my canoe to guide me home. For the first time the canoe thus had two engines instead of just one, and it felt like being in a speedboat. I awoke that day in a pure coastal ecosystem: as we paddled we heard the cackle of marsh hens from the spartina; ospreys and bald eagles flew overhead. Then a mile or so up the Intracoastal we hit the mouth of the Santee, which Lawson noted stayed freshwater because of its huge flow. Nowadays its flow is far lower, given the lakes built upstream by the Army Corps of Engineers. Eddie told me the first work by the Corps slowed the flow down so much that the salt and brackish water crept up some ten miles, and an oyster fishery blossomed. But the lakes caused trouble and the Corps directed more water back into the Santee, which pushed the saltwater boundary further down again, which was probably good for the ecosystem but was lousy for the oyster fishers. Kathie and I saw manta rays and bottlenose dolphins as we turned upriver.

At that point the ecosystem changed quickly. Alligators, for one thing—on the shore, basking or raising their eyes and nostrils from the water. Red-winged blackbirds rose en masse from canebrakes with a furious beating of wings as we paddled by, and we began seeing cypress, the spreading trunks reminding us we were heading out of the marsh and into the swamp. With the omnipresent Spanish moss dripping from cypress branches, the trip now officially looked like the Hollywood representation of the Mysterious South.

I was glad Kathie was in the canoe—her experienced eyes easily picked out little Hampton Creek, which sidled into the Santee from a mouth I'd have never caught. When we stepped out into the sticky mud at the Hampton Plantation, we were, according to local Huguenot historians, within a mile or so of where Lawson himself "lay all that Night at Mons. *Eugee's*," that being Lawson's transcription of Monsieur Daniel Huger, a French Huguenot settler who was deeded the land in 1696 but probably arrived sooner. After his night with Monsieur Huger, Lawson and his companions set out "to go the Remainder of our Voyage by Land."

Kathie and I, stepping out of our canoe at Hampton, were met by among others Martha Zierden, archaeologist and wife of my guide Eddie. She and Eddie had invited me to stay with them in McClellanville as I digested my experience following Lawson by water, and I was thus introduced to perhaps the best guestroom in history, an upstairs bedroom in their old unheated house, in which the four-poster single bed nestled beneath a dormer window, making my first view in the morning the growing light reflected on whitewashed beadboard ceiling. I recommend this experience.

Again in McClellanville, I learned that the two original landowners, the McClellans and the Morrisons, disputed some over the name of the town. The McClellans evidently won out, though some bad feeling is said to remain. About the capacity of such feelings to remain, I will paraphrase once again Billy Baldwin. He shared a story told by his own family, who remembered generations before of another family that the patriarch had been seen riding a mule down the main street of town during the day— without, shockingly, a collar. When a delegation went to the man's home to inform his wife, she came to the door not only barefoot but holding a broom. When many decades later, in the 1960s, members of that family were arrested for selling drugs, Billy's mother shook her head, saying, "It was only a matter of time." And the reader will note that I share this story without names. Feelings, Billy assures me, are still raw.

:::

And thus, among stories generations old, seemingly running in the blood of the people who have never left, ended the first journey of the Lawson Trek. Regarding the landscape, much, astonishingly, has remained the same, at least along the fifty miles we traveled, though things aren't looking up. Another 30 percent of our remaining salt marsh is threatened by runoff, by sea level rise, by attempts to control mosquitoes, and above all by development. This is far from a southern problem. In New England in the nineteenth and twentieth centuries salt marsh area declined by approximately two-thirds; in San Francisco in the same time period it declined by 79 percent. And with it go ecosystems, filter feeders that clean water, and the storm protection marshes naturally provide. Ask New Orleans how it's doing without the marshes that used to protect it.

The people living along the coast, from Kathie Livingston and my guides to the Huguenot descendants, retain a love of their land- and waterscape that does not die. Of Lawson many of them knew little; yet to me they showed the same hospitality their forebears had shown him. I hoped to see more of the same when, starting my next segment, I would walk rather than paddle.

2 : Coffee with the Huguenots

Douglas Guerry's mother, Jean, bustles around her immaculate dining room the way mothers do, setting out cups, saucers, a covered cake stand with a Bundt cake, from which ecologist Katie Winsett and I cut slices large enough that one might avert one's eyes in embarrassment—and then slightly smaller seconds. Having covered many miles carrying heavy backpacks, slogging through swamps in drenching rain, we are damp, we are tired, and we are hungry. But in the Guerry home, a neat and trim house in tiny Jamestown, South Carolina—"population 74; when Mark and I come home it goes up to 76," Douglas says—we feel warm, welcome, and grateful.

And not just for the food. We are thrilled because by enjoying coffee and cake with the Guerrys we are following Lawson as perfectly as we can. We have trudged through two days' worth of cypress-tupelo swamps, camping in parkland, examining enormous plantations and tiny slime molds, enduring cold and rain and blisters on our feet instead of hands as instead of paddling a canoe we walk. More, we have been welcomed by people who are descendants of the very Huguenots who welcomed Lawson three centuries before. The swamps in the protected Francis Marion National Forest don't seem to have changed much. Nor has the hospitality, though to be fair Lawson never specifically mentioned Bundt cake.

I met Katie, a ready-for-anything ecologist then teaching at North Carolina State University, through a book club. When she heard about Lawson she quickly began providing me with information about swamps and ecosystems and then gamely agreed to join the trek for a spell, driving down to South Carolina, getting dropped off with me where my first trip ended, near the site of the home of Monsieur Eugee. We then made a circuitous progress northwest, along much the same winding trails and pathways through the swamp that Lawson would have followed. The Guerrys, for their part, came from the internet. That is, the Guerrys were the first proof that when, like Lawson, I used the tools at my disposal to share my story, I had good results.

Lawson took a long trip, gathered information, and then eight years later took a ship to London and printed a book. But I bet that if Law-

Even with open water under a layer of duckweed, a cypress-hickory swamp never fails to radiate an aura of mystery.

son had access to Twitter and Instagram and Facebook he would have gladly used them—to share what he saw, to try to get the best information about the terrain and the locals, and, probably, to pelt the homepage of the Royal Society with little observed details—and requests for membership. For my part, with a website, an Instagram feed, and the attention of the local press, I did everything I could to let people know: the Lawson Trek was coming through and wanted to meet the locals and learn what it could, whether about multigenerational family history or swamp flora and fauna or the best place to get a pizza. So naturally one day, after the canoe trip was over, I got an email through the Lawson Trek website from one Douglas Guerry, who offered, "My family are descendants of the original Huguenots that landed at James Towne [North Carolina]. We currently still live in Jamestown. If you have an interest in visiting the original site, please let us know, if you have not already passed through town."

Well, this was the stuff. A brief email correspondence, exchange of mobile numbers, and we had an agreement: Katie and I expected to emerge from the swamps of the Francis Marion National Forest on such-and-such a date, and we would call or text as we approached their house. As it happened we emerged from the forest a couple of miles from their house, during a daylong rain, and when the family Guerry offered to pick us up where we stood and save us two miles of road slog we did not turn them down. Katie and I changed into dry clothes under the tiny shelter at a roadside Used Oil Recycling station, waited for our benefactors, and headed to the Guerrys' for entertainment.

The Guerrys, mind you, were not our first Huguenots. Like Lawson, we found the Santee River area infested with them, and they treated us like royalty. My first interaction came at the end of the canoe portion of my journey, when as I planned the trek through the swamp I called Cheves Leland, archivist for the Huguenot Society of South Carolina. She and her cousin Susan Bates were then working on a book, *French Santee: A Huguenot Settlement in Colonial South Carolina*, which gave details on more than 100 of the Huguenots among whom Lawson walked. Cheves said when she and Bates heard of my Lawson retracing, their first question, considering the swampy mess of the Francis Marion, was simple: "We were curious to know if you understood exactly what kind of terrain you were getting into." Don't forget, Francis Marion, for whom the forest is named, was called the Swamp Fox because he could famously disappear into the trackless swamp during the Revolution, frustrating the British. Well, no, I didn't know the terrain—that's why I called.

At the end of the canoe trip, Cheves joined archaeologist Martha Zierden and me for a walk in the woods of the Francis Marion next to Hampton Plantation, the state landmark where my canoe, and Lawson's, had come to ground. Just across the Wambaw Creek from the plantation, we parked at the end of a forest road and roamed the woods there, looking for a spot that might have been Monsieur Huger's house. The house, the two told me, would have likely been wattle-and-daub, which is in essence lath-and-plaster using what you find: sticks, mud, sand, and grasses. (Something different would be worthy of mention: Lawson notes that he spent his second night among the Huguenots in a "very curious contriv'd House," curious because it was built of brick and stone. Brick became an important local industry, but stone in the silty flats of a coastal plain is hard to come by.) Lawson spent two days traversing the fifteen miles of Huguenot settlement along the Santee. Cheves noted that when I did the same I'd either need passage across the many creeks in the swamp or I'd have to stick with the forest roads that have emerged. One of the first things I did on that trip was secret a little inflatable boat at a spot where I hoped we'd paddle across a creek, but as it turned out we didn't use it. Katie and I ended up sticking to the roads, though we found the going plenty messy even so.

:::

Lawson describes his time among the Huguenots briskly. Leaving their original Indian guides with their canoe, he and his compatriots "hir'd a *Sewee-Indian*, a tall, lusty Fellow"—lusty enough that though they loaded him down with a pack of the party's clothes, "we had much a-do to keep pace with him." Creeks crisscross the swampy area, across which Lawson notes the French gladly ferry them in dories. He says that the French get along well, functioning almost as a tribe or commune, looking out for one another and in general concord—he regularly notes that the English settlers are not nearly as assiduous (the French "give Examples of Industry," he says later, "which is much wanted in this Country"). Everyone he meets invites him to stay, but he and his fellows are moving forward; they spend their second night in that curious contriv'd house, with Monsieur Gallian, the elder, very near the road from Charles-Town. Lawson describes this as a very good road, which leaves in question why the group suffered through the trip by canoe. The only sensible explanation I have encountered is that they might have planned to stay in the canoe up the Santee all the way to modern-day Charlotte but were overwhelmed by the flood of the Santee, which Lawson describes as "risen perpendicular 36 Foot, always making a Breach from her Banks, this Season of the Year." Given that Jamestown itself, the settlement Lawson clearly visited, is barely forty feet above sea level, this must be an enormous exaggeration. Just the same, Lawson says the woods "seem'd like some great Lake, except here and there a Knowl of high Land ... appear'd above the Water," and notes that on their way to the home of Monsieur Gallian the younger even their guide became lost, "altho the *Indian* was born in that Country, it having receiv'd so strange a *Metamorphosis*."

Lawson favors us with a delightful bit of mansplaining here ("Are you listening, Royal Society?" one can almost hear him cry), explaining that the floods are caused by the snow in the mountains, far from saltwater, suddenly melting because of breezes from the southwest, "coming down with Impetuosity." One hears in this possibly some vague misunderstanding of freezing-point depression of salt in water, or something, though it simply makes no sense. It probably gets real rainy, which causes flooding. January is a rainy month in upstate South Carolina, and in the rainier summer months the rain falls on warmer, more absorbent soil, but frankly that's as speculative as Lawson's explanation. Let's just say this: Lawson found the Santee in flood, and he and his party got out and hoofed it.

After the night in the curious contriv'd house, the party the next morning crossed to the northwest shore of the Santee with the help of their Sewee guide, the Sewees being "excellent Artists in managing these small Canoes." Lost, the party broke in two, leaving Lawson and two others behind on a dry spot with "but one Gun amongst us, one Load of Ammunition and no Provision," while the guide and the other four went looking for their host for the night. Six hours later the guide returned, "being half drunk," and the group made it to the home of Monsieur Gallian the younger, where Lawson found "our Comrades in the same Trim the *Indian* was in." The French, "a very kind, loving, and affable People," marveled at their voyage "thro' a Country inhabited by none but Savages" but wished them well. Hearing of a party of Santee Indians nearby, the travelers set off to spend the night with them. One member of the gang, trying to cross a creek on a single-pole bridge, was drunk enough to fall in; "my self laughing at the Accident, and not taking good Heed to my Steps, came to the same Misfortune: All our Bedding was wet," Lawson tells us. "The Wind being at N.W. it froze very hard, which prepar'd such a Night's Lodging for me, that I never desire to have the like again." They were miserable until the next morning, when they reached the party of welcoming Santee and, as Lawson says, "recruited ourselves before a large Fire of the Indians."

They left their Sewee guide there drunk, while they spent the day hiking forward through swampland made barely passable by the flood, ending up "at a House ... built for the Indian Trade" and spending the night by leave of its owner, whom they had met when they stopped at Jamestown. The next day they traversed swamps so deep they had to disrobe to pass through, spending the night "in one *Scipio's* Hutt, a famous Hunter." Scipio, the famous Roman, is a name Lawson sometimes gives to Indians he doesn't care to assign a particular name; Indians are often otherwise simply called Jack—Santee Jack, Keyauwees Jack, and so forth. Different times, to be sure, but still one cringes; Lawson may have had a higher regard for the Natives than most of his fellow settlers, but I would not nominate him for the Nobel Peace Prize.

He mentions passing the patch of forest demolished by the September hurricane, and in these pages he begins talking in detail about the Indians and their habits. The Indians farmed corn in the bottomlands along the rivers and kept stores of grain. Lawson sings the praises of their grain cribs—"daub'd within and without upon Laths, with Loom or Clay, which makes them tight, and fit to keep out the smallest Insect," even with latchable doors. He describes the practice among Indian traders of staying in any Indian hut they encounter and availing themselves of supplies like nuts, corn, peas, and beans, "the *Indians* allowing it practicable to the *English* Traders, to take out of their Houses what they need in their Absence, in Lieu whereof they most commonly leave some small Gratuity of Tobacco, Paint, Beads, &c." In the one they stay in, "the Wind being at *N.W.*, . . . being very intent upon our Cookery, we set the Dwelling on Fire, and with much ado, put it out, tho' with the Loss of Part of the Roof." Hey, what's a camping trip without a little adventure? Sorry, uh . . . Jack! Yeah, Jack—here's a couple extra beads. He says of the Santees that they are "a well-humour'd and affable People; and living near the English, are become very tractable." He also notes that among themselves the Indians are trustworthy, "theft to each other being altogether unpractis'd, never receiving Spoils but from Foreigners."

::::

Like Lawson, I started out this segment in the swamps, on foot; unlike Lawson, I had an ecologist with me, so instead of a confused wander in the flood my first days in the swamps felt like a graduate course not just in swamp ecosystems but in paying attention. Katie reads a landscape like a sea captain staring at clouds. "That drops off quickly," she would say, looking at land that to me read as purely flat or at most just gently sloped; then she'd lead me off the sand road on which we walked, and, leaving the trail, in a minute we'd descend into a cypress-tupelo swamp, the defining ecosystem of the Francis Marion. "See there? There's the swamp. You see the land descending, then you see the palmettos, then you see the trees with the flaring bottoms." Both cypress and tupelos have that flaring bottom, which Katie explained is largely engineering: they're wide to keep the trees standing in swampy soil. Cypress knees, the spooky knobbles rising up from the roots, are less certain in function: some scientists believe them to be further engineering, others think they offer an opportunity for the roots to get oxygen in anaerobic soil, rising high so that they stick out even above rising water.

Relax the focus of your eyes and you can see the fire line where the darkness ends on the trunks of these longleaf pines.

Speaking of water level, Katie taught me to gently relax the focus of my eyes; when you do that, the swamp's high-water line fairly leaps out at you: the tree trunks are dark up to a certain level, above which they're merely gray. That's the level to which the swamp water occasionally but regularly rises. If the water was low and you want to know its usual level, just look for where the moss at the base of the trees suddenly leaves off. You can use the same trick in longleaf pine forests, which thrive only where there is regular fire, to find the fire line: the height of the flames during one of the spooky, smoky orange controlled burns necessary to the life cycle of longleaf, whose seeds germinate only after fire, and thrive only when fire has cleared the underbrush of competitors. For an afternoon a half-dozen men wearing hard hats and fire-retardant clothing wander among the trees carrying 1.5-gallon tanks with wands, squirting flame at pine straw and emerging from banks of smoke only to disappear again across road or path. Then for a few days the trunks are blackened, but after the first rain or anyway a few days it fades, and then only when you fuzz your eyesight or remove your glasses can you see the line, as clear as the line of high tide.

A cypress-tupelo swamp radiates a kind of gloomy magnificence that Lawson barely mentions but that I could not stop noticing. The Spanish moss dangling from the bald cypress boughs, the trunks of the tupelos spreading into the tea-colored, tannin-stained waters of the swamps, the pointy spread leaves of the saw palmettos, low to the ground, their leaves poking up through the ground like a splayed hand with a dozen or so fingers, had a right-from-central-casting feel. Katie and I would walk along a sand road—all the roads we followed in the swamp were sand—and our eyes would almost glaze over. With the sameness of sight I concentrated instead on the sounds. Air whispered through the bald cypress—bald, by the way, because like deciduous trees they drop their needles in the winter. Water trickled and birds sang, especially the pileated woodpecker, one of the swamp's indicator species, whose loud laughing call seemed to find us every night when we set up our tents.

Katie explained how the ecosystems within the swamps changed almost inch by inch—open water would host one group of microorganisms, water a foot away with decaying leaves floating would host another. When we walked back up the almost unnoticeable slope from one swamp she pointed out how we left standing water behind and then found our way back to dry ground. With the elevation came loblolly pines and various oaks, often with resurrection ferns, which shrivel up and look like dead things when it's dry but can come back from almost completely desiccated when it rains. "You see?" Katie said of the change in forest over maybe a foot or two in altitude. "We climbed a mountain—an ecological one, anyways." She poked around in rotting logs to discover slime molds, a special interest of hers, and we took pictures of them—they're tiny enough that they just look like a spray of yellow on decaying wood until you look at them up close—with a magnifying glass or, as we did, with a macro lens for my phone. "See? It's not just a longleaf pine forest," she said as we walked through one parklike stand of longleafs and she pointed out ferns. "The interesting stuff is the small stuff."

We walked often through longleaf pine forest, where various conservation programs have been working to restore what was once part of a 92 million-acre forest that covered pretty much the entire Southeast. The loss from overharvesting has been catastrophic, "equal in scale and impact to the loss of chestnut from Appalachian forests by blight," according to a text published in 1993. Bertram Whittier "B. W." Wells, North

Carolina ecologist and author of the 1932 *Natural Gardens of North Carolina*, said, "The complete destruction of this forest constitutes one of the major social crimes of American history."

What happened to the longleaf? Simple: we did. Lawson notes that throughout the coastal colonies, "As for Pitch and Tar, none of the Plantations are comparable for affording the vast Quantities of Naval Stores, as this Place does," the longleaf having not only turpentine and tar to offer but its straight trunk, useful for masts and other construction tasks. Add to that the forestry practice of clearcutting, which works fine with loblollies and slash pines, which reseed effortlessly, but not with longleafs. The result was that longleaf stands were clear cut and replaced with the omnipresent loblollies throughout the Southeast. The 92 million acres of longleafs Lawson and his fellow early European settlers found have been reduced to around 3.5 million now, and that's already a significant improvement from its lowest point.

Lawson never mentions the longleaf by name. He speaks throughout his book of pines, though they are so common that he rarely goes into detail. Long past his description of his journey, in a later section of his book he does mention several species, including "the white Pine with long Leaves," clearly the longleaf. Late in his journey he mentions "pleasant Savanna Ground, high and dry, having very few Trees upon it, and those standing at a great distance," which many have noted also sounds like a growth of longleaf. In any case, Lawrence Earley, in his *Looking for Longleaf*, describes a stand of longleaf as a "rolling, parklike landscape of randomly spaced trees," and Earley quotes earlier observers like John Muir, noting "the pines wide apart," and E. W. Hilgard, who in 1860 wrote, "The pine forest is almost destitute of shrubby undergrowth, and during the growing season appears like a park."

As Katie taught me, the longleaf has learned to cooperate with fire: its seeds germinate only after the cones pass through fire, and they then burrow down into the soil thus cleared of brush. (I strongly recommend the chapter "Built by Fire" in *Ecology of a Cracker Childhood* by Janisse Ray, upon which some of this description is based.) More amazingly, as each year pine needles struck by lightning would burn again, the seedlings spend most of their energy developing a deep, strong taproot, and protect their tender buds with those long, green needles. Then, when they have survived a couple of years, the trees suddenly sprout, growing as much as a yard in a single season, still protecting themselves with bright needles, poking straight up. In the Francis Marion National Forest, the

U.S. Department of Agriculture reckons that its efforts—planting, controlled burns, and other forms of maintenance—have helped return some 45,000 acres to longleaf domination; the USDA figures local longleaf acreage would have been closer to 145,000 back when Lawson walked through. Various other environmental strategies—including work to preserve habitat of the endangered red cockaded woodpecker—have helped rebuild longleaf stands. Katie and I thought the young longleafs, three feet high or so and perfectly straight, with no branches (another antifire strategy), with their green needle haircuts poking straight up, looked like creatures from some Dr. Seuss book. We both tended to pat them on the head as we walked by. Longleaf has been through a catastrophe, but you never know—perhaps we've caught it in time and we'll be able to slowly regenerate its enormous range. You cannot help rooting for it.

:::

Longleaf pine is the greatest lost ecosystem Lawson would have encountered, and it was thrilling, if a little bit sad, to encounter at least a little bit of it. But the other ecosystem Lawson would have encountered surrounded us in the Francis Marion National Forest: wetlands.

And wet the lands are. Sand roads follow tiny natural ridges in the once trackless swamps. Tiny creeks trace the landscape, identifying low places and hollows. As Katie had pointed out, we'd be walking along among pines and live oaks, then the sandy track would dip, not even noticeably, and suddenly we'd be among palmettos and tupelos and cypress knees. Periodically we'd run into small areas dry enough that a few trailers or small houses would make up a tiny neighborhood; we almost never saw people, but roving dogs kept us moving through briskly. At the end of one long road we stumbled onto a cleared acreage, whose green metal gates, marked with an enormous "G," we had no trouble circumventing. We found a dammed pond, with a pier and a sink for cleaning fish, and a sandy loop road through the clearing. It looked like a private campground—we had clearly stumbled into a weekend retreat, belonging to someone who needed a big iron fence marked with an initial to make his presence known.

That was near the end of a day, and from there we went off the pavement, over pineland on a little-used forest road that we hoped led to another road that would take us further on our way. Our old friend Kathie Livingston had told us that not far from where we were we could find springs feeding the Echaw Creek, whose branches run all through the forest. We set up camp among a healthy stand of pines and, low on water, tried to find the springs. No luck, and by the time we found them the next morning, with further help from Kathie and from Google Maps, we enjoyed a few minutes in one of the most beautiful swamps we encountered. Then more up and down, in and out; with no Huguenots to paddle us across creeks, we made a longer route to stay dry—and I understood what Cheves Leland had meant when she wondered if we understood the country we were walking into. From maps I had sketched out a nice, Lawsonian, straight-ish line, not far from the Santee, figuring we could ford small creeks as necessary and even leaving my little rubber boat near one we thought would be bigger. The laughable arrogance of the uninformed, of course. A small creek might be a blue line on a map, but encountered in person it was surrounded by acres of mushy swamp that would have been hard to press through for even the well-versed, which we were manifestly not.

Add in a steady daylong rain and you will understand why, by the time Katie and I had made our way through most of the Francis Marion, we were glad to avoid a two-mile walk along a paved road when the family Guerry offered to pick us up.

:::

The Guerrys were only the next in an unbroken stream of volunteer Heroes of the Lawson Trek. And the funny thing was, though I met Douglas when he offered to help me visit the original site of Jamestown, along the Santee River, it turned out that was the one place Douglas could not take me. The tiny riverside site is owned by the Huguenot Society of South Carolina, and it's surrounded on three sides by other properties—so even the owners need permission to cross to it unless they access it directly from the Santee. We had no powerboat, and Douglas sadly told us the owner of the surrounding property was refusing access. Exactly why nobody would say, though one is commonly told that some people in the Francis Marion run moonshine stills, which might make a property owner nervous about unvetted visitors.

In any case the Guerrys more than made up for our lack of access by taking us to their home, where Jean, age eighty-five, brought us that coffee and Bundt cake, and she and Douglas talked with us about the Huguenots. The Huguenots were French Protestant dissenters who, though despised, had been treated with something like fairness as a result of the Edict of Nantes, signed by the French king Henry IV in 1598, giving them civil rights in a mostly Catholic nation. After nearly a century of erosion, those rights utterly vanished when Louis XIV revoked the edict, rendering Protestantism illegal in France. Fifty thousand families fled the country, though over the centuries of persecution some half a million French citizens had left, many of them tradespeople and guild members—a severe brain drain for the French, and a win for the European nations and their colonies where the Huguenots landed. "France had opened her own veins and spilt her best blood when she drained herself of her Huguenots," says historian Esther Forbes when discussing the enormous contribution Huguenots (among them Alexander Hamilton's grandfather) made to the American Revolution. "And everywhere, in every country that would receive them," continues Forbes, "this amazing strain acted as a yeast."

Lawson quite agreed. "The *French* being a temperate industrious People, some of them bringing very little of Effects, yet by their Endeavours and mutual Assistance amongst themselves, (which is highly to be commended) have out-stript our *English*, who brought with 'em larger Fortunes, though (as it seems) less endeavour to manage their Talent to the best Advantage."

The British colonies, we are commonly told, were founded on the principles of religious freedom, though we like to forget that the Massachusetts Bay Colony was hanging Quakers by 1659. The Fundamental Constitutions of Carolina, written in 1669 by no less a personage than John Locke, guaranteed, in point 97 (of 116) that "Jews, heathens, and other dissenters from the purity of Christian religion may not be scared and kept at a distance from it . . . ; therefore, any seven or more persons agreeing in any religion, shall constitute a church or profession, to which they shall give some name, to distinguish it from others." This must have sounded attractive to people used to religious persecution, especially when point 111 continued, "No person whatsoever shall disturb, molest, or persecute another for his speculative opinions in religion, or his way of worship." Of course, in other points the constitutions admit that you can't be free in Carolina unless you believe in God, and that once the colony had enough people to make church-building an issue, the government would obviously build churches according to the Church of England, that "being the only true and orthodox and the national religion of all the King's dominions." So Carolina was far from a religious Utopia (and anyway the constitutions, far too complicated for settlers, were revised as early as 1670 and suspended in 1693). Just the same, in addition to good land, a temperate climate, and the "delicious country" that Lawson described, Carolina could claim it offered religious freedom.

So the Huguenots came, they prospered—and they stuck around. Douglas Guerry counts himself a ninth-generation Jamestownian ("the Guerrys are long-lived," Jean said when Katie and I tried to figure how nine generations took you all the way back to the 1680s). Over cake and coffee we talked about Lawson, the people he'd have walked among, and the changes to the lower Santee since then. We know Lawson visited Jamestown in 1700 only because he mentions, of the night his party spent in "a House which was built for the *Indian* Trade," that they had parted with its owner "at the *French* town." Whether the owner was a member of Lawson's party who had stayed behind in Jamestown or someone they just met there Lawson doesn't say, and he also doesn't say a word about what Jamestown was like.

Hardly surprising—though the Huguenots worked hard and built plantations growing indigo and rice, Carolina's earliest export crops, Jamestown never developed as a town. Charleston, sixty miles away, prospered enormously as a trade center, and as the colony grew in the early 1700s Georgetown, on the coast just north of the Santee, became another town with a port to offer. Modern Jamestown, where the Guerrys live, is a crossroads about a mile and a half from the Santee, and the original spot that we didn't get a chance to see is a bluff overlooking the river, where a church and graveyard once stood.

The Guerrys, after the manner of people long resident in their place, knew the names and background of everyone we had spoken with so far; they told us the plantation behind the green fence with the enormous "G" in the forest belonged to a high-profile attorney in Charleston. When I mentioned my guide Eddie Stroman, who had kayaked with me in an earlier segment of my journey, Jean knew not only the Stroman name but also the names of Eddie's forbears. "Oh, they're not old," she said of one such family. "I know. . . . I can get into the Daughters of the American Revolution, but I can't get in the Huguenot Society." She can trace her own ancestry to 1720, but the Huguenots demand one more generation. Douglas is a member, but through his daddy; the Guerry name (spelled "Guerri") shows up in the very earliest records of Huguenot settlement, and Lawson would likely have met them, though I feel sure that if they'd have given him Bundt cake he'd have made note. The church that once stood at the site of old Jamestown is long gone, as are others built near Echaw Creek, along which Katie and I had walked. The third church, called the Old Brick Church by the locals or the Wambaw Church, after a nearby creek, was built in 1768 and still stands lonely on the sandy Old Georgetown Highway through the forest, notable not only for its circular columns of locally made brick but also for its history.

When it was built, at a time of growing population, limited church space, and remaining suspicion between the English and French settlers, the church managed to serve everyone who needed it. "The Huguenots used the back door," Jean told us. "The English used the front." Church has been essential from the first days of French Santee, which the community was once called. The first clergy arrived in 1687, and Lawson, in praising the French for their helping his party across rivers in their dories, mentions they were all dressed up nicely, "coming from their church."

We talked about other lost buildings—"I have lived long enough that I was photographed in some of the plantations that were drowned," Jean said, referring to the damming of the Santee and the creation of nearby Lake Moultrie and Lake Marion by the Army Corps in 1941. Her family used to take car rides into the area sited for the lake to have a look at what would be lost. She remembered also visiting Hampton Plantation, which was built in the 1740s near where Lawson left his canoe and began walking, as did I; the restored home now serves as a museum, though Jean had visited when it was still occupied by its last private owner, South Carolina poet laureate Archibald Rutledge. George Washington had visited the home in his southern tour in 1791, at which time he urged the owners to save an oak they had planned to cut down. Now called the Washington Oak, it still stands. If you look at the plantation history you find that it was owned at one point by Daniel Huger Horry, a descendant of the Monsieur Eugee (Huger) Lawson mentioned, and as the Guerrys spoke it was impossible not to feel the connection in place, in blood, in community they had with the very first European settlers. As it happens, the connection might be quite literally in the blood of my hosts. That is, my various Huguenot historians told me that Lawson spent the evening of his third night among the Huguenots—the night everybody got drunk—at the home of what he calls "Mons. *Galliar's jun*," that is the younger Gaillard. This refers to one Barthelemy Gaillard, who sometime after his drunken revelry married a daughter of the family Guerri, into whose hands the house eventually passed. Which is to say it's perfectly believable that in the veins of my host ran some of the same blood that ran in the veins of Lawson's host. A small point, but it spoke to me.

Jean may not have a long enough local history for the Huguenot Society, but to me it felt like her roots dug down as deep in the South Carolina coastal plain as those of the Washington Oak. In 2014, the Carolina Demography Center at the University of North Carolina investigated state "stickiness"—the degree to which adults born in one of the United States still live in that state. According to its data, North Carolina was second only to Texas (South Carolina also was in the top ten for stickiness). Carolinians just stick around. I've lived all over the world; Lawson in 1700 left London and moved to what was, quite literally, the edge of what he'd have called civilization. Douglas Guerry still lives within a couple of miles of the place where his great-great-great-great-great-great-great-grandfather was born.

Jean wasn't done. She told us of the steamboats that plied the Santee as late as the early 1940s, before the Corps got involved with the river. "My husband used to read the river gauge for the depth," Jean said. "It would be ten, twelve feet. Sixteen, seventeen feet was high." Not anymore: the gauge at Santee near Jamestown currently reads about three feet, and its discharge and velocity both daily dip into the negative numbers—showing its interaction with the tides.

I could have talked with the Guerrys all night, but, like Lawson, Katie and I had places to go. The Guerrys belong to the St. James United Methodist Church, a simple little white clapboard church in an enormous grass clearing to which they gladly opened the door so that Katie and I had a warm and dry place for the night. We spread maps and books out on the plastic tables in the common room and slept in sleeping bags on nicely padded pews.

:::

The next day we crossed the Santee on foot, on the U.S. Route 17 bridge, which was my first interaction as a pedestrian with major road traffic. This I do not recommend. We were very glad to return almost instantly to side roads that, if no longer sand roads, were at least somewhat winding two-lanes and much less traveled. The land remained utterly flat, but now on the north side of the Santee and a little further from Charleston and the coast, the terrain shifted to a sort of backwoodsy feel—still large stands of pines, though mostly monocultural loblollies prepared for harvest rather than for ecosystem. Sit in a mixed pine and hardwood forest and you'll see squirrels and deer, you'll see nuthatches and bobwhites and red-headed woodpeckers; keep quiet for a moment until everybody gets used to you and the world comes alive around your ears. Try the same thing in a monoculture stand of loblollies and it just stays quiet.

The roads don't, though. The further away from the Francis Marion National Forest I walked, the more often the walking was interrupted by the rumble of logging trucks, either rattling empty toward a harvest site or toiling in the other direction, pulling a trailer stacked with fresh trunks. As I walked along the road I would suddenly notice, at the edge of perception, a grinding sound. I would walk toward it as it swelled into a roar, and then I could creep down an entryway into a forest where a clearcutting harvest was under way. Clearing is done almost entirely by machine—a guy in a machine cuts the trees down; a guy in a machine uses a giant crane arm to pluck the cut trees up, drag them through a machine that strips them of branches, and load them into those trucks that go grinding away. And once Katie and I left the swamp and began following rural two-lanes through lowland South Carolina, it was loblolly farms we walked by. South Carolina has about 13 million acres of forest, which is 68 percent of its land area; almost half of that is loblolly pine forest planted for harvest. It's billions of dollars of economic activity every year; wood products are even the largest export by volume out of the port of Charleston. It's sustainable—you don't have to fertilize or even pull stumps; you just let the root systems rot in the ground and feed the next generation. It's one of South Carolina's most important industries, and that's all good. The regeneration of those southeastern pine forests, albeit with loblolly instead of longleaf, has been called, in a USDA monograph, "the premier story of forest conservation the world over."

So I may be being churlish, but I can't help noting that the most powerful observation I carry with me is the silence of those loblolly stands, and the numbing regularity of row after row of loblolly as I walked—or drove—by. Just the same, Katie, slime mold expert that she was, didn't feel as oppressed as I did by the monotony. In the first place, she said, "you can't tell a forest by its edge." There may have been more going on deeper in was her point; we were out by the road, and we might have been missing a lot of the fun stuff. In fact, she was sure we were. "It's not just about deer and squirrels. It's not just a pine forest," she said one night. "I think it's more interesting what's going on down in the soil. On the level of the microorganisms." She talked about her students liking to break the world into three sizes: regular size, giant size, and microscopic. "But nature doesn't work that way," she said. "I like that it's all more complex than we can really organize in our minds." So there's lots to know—and lots that Lawson never even thought about.

:::

The other observation Katie and I couldn't avoid making about road walking was the enormous roadside ditch popularity of Bud Light, which is evidently the official beer of the South Carolina Littering Community. I mean, we saw more Bud Light—cans, mostly—than everything else combined. We saw a lot of trash in ditches (and we saw the machines the highway maintenance people use to clear out those ditches). And speaking of clean ditches, Katie told me an ecologist secret for reading the terrain when you're in a flat area like the South Carolina coastal plain. If you can't figure out which way the terrain slopes, if it slopes at all, there's a simple lay-of-the-land cheat: "Check which way the water's flowing in the ditches."

During the rainy part of this segment of my journey Katie and I were in the swamp, and that flat water just rose; the ditch was just the edge of the swamp. Our road walking all took place in clear, sunny days, so there was no water to check. But I could say—after about five days of total walking, as the Lawson Trek approached the dam across the Santee River that created Lakes Moultrie and Marion—that a stretch of asphalt two-lane struck me as somehow different than I had expected. I took a look backward, and then a look forward, and then I looked down. And to be sure, I stood on a little rise. No more than a few feet, certainly not a dozen, and ahead it went back down and flat again ahead as far as I could see, but we had climbed our first hill. At the top, at the end of a little stretch of sandy two-track, was the Cantey Family Cemetery, established in 1739, according to a roadside sign; Francis Marion evidently kicked around with the Canteys some. We poked around the cemetery among dried leaves and the straight trunks of oaks—not the live oaks of the swamp territory, we noticed, but dry-land oaks. We admired thin marble tombstones of various long-ago Canteys, including Joseph, born in 1765, who might have been underfoot when Marion, staying at the plantation, learned that General Cornwallis had surrendered at Yorktown.

I took out my little notebook and jotted it down. The Lawson Trek had left the marshes of the coast and had passed through the swamps. We were heading for the hills.

3 : The Corps's Work Is Never Done

My cell phone buzzes and I snatch at it hopefully: is it Val? It is Val. "Do you want to meet me where Lawson met the Santee King?" The answer is of course yes. Rob Waters, my companion for this segment of hike, and I set out for a place Val Green has told me about many times. It's a spot in one of the four separate puzzle pieces of the Santee National Wildlife Refuge, all strung along the northern shore of Lake Marion, one of two lakes created in 1941 when the Army Corps of Engineers dammed the Santee River. Hearing from Val is terrific news—it means we'll know exactly where we are related to Lawson. And it means we'll be swamped with information, a process that borders on constant when Val Green begins talking about his favorite subject: the inspiration for my trek.

Rob and I have been walking only a day or so on this segment of the journey, and already I have worn him out talking about Val. Val taught me everything I know about Lawson. Val knows where the Indians lived. Val has figured out where Lawson slept almost every night of his journey. On and on, and Rob is now looking forward to meeting Val, perhaps for no other reason than to hear from Val rather than about Val. So we're set for our meeting on the following day, and for the current one Rob and I continue walking. Picking up where Katie and I left off on the previous segment, Rob and I had dropped a car at Randolph's Landing, a combination fish camp, greasy spoon, down-at-the-heels brick motel, and end-of-the-line that sits on a mud and gravel parking lot at the Santee Dam, where even the "Road Ends" sign hangs at an angle, and roosters strut among the four-wheelers in the lot. Two days' road walk had taken us along the far edge of territory that though still somewhat swampy was mostly dry. Without the dam, however, it would look a lot more like the cypress-tupelo swamps further south. One swamp we did pass disturbed us with a rainbow film covering the surface, pinks, yellows, and purples swirling among the grasses and floating leaves, reflecting the clouds between the spreading cypress boughs. It was very pretty—it stopped us by the side of the road to gawk—but we couldn't help wondering what kind of pollutant caused that lovely but obviously awful effect. We shared an

I took notes all the time, but never so much as when
Val Green shared his limitless knowledge of Lawson and his path.
Photo by Rob Waters.

image on Instagram and wondered as much. It looked like the gas or oil rainbows we used to love to see swirling on puddles as kids.

We learned, to our delight, that the film was entirely natural—and not unlike those oil slicks. That is, the film comes from bacteria in the anaerobic mud underwater in the swamp. Aerobic bacteria at the surface release CO_2, like we do; anaerobes in the muck release methane, and some of it does what hydrocarbons do and makes a film on the surface. Thing one: you just never get tired of swamps. Thing two: Instagram makes a dandy tool for interpreting your surroundings on the fly.

A few weeks earlier, on the evening before Katie and I started our previous segment, we had driven the same stretch to get the lay of the land and had seen pickup after pickup parked on the edge of the pines, a lone camouflage-clad hunter idling against most trucks. It had been the last night of dog hunting season—when hunters loose dogs and hope they flush deer in the right direction. We had congratulated ourselves on taking the advice to postpone any hiking until after that season. Forget stray shots: the hunters trying to regain control of the loose dogs, we were told, were a danger and a chaos in which we would not enjoy camping.

The territory Rob and I traversed was rural pretty, not nature pretty. We saw long rows of pines as we passed omnipresent farming operations, and sand roads off to the left and right as we walked north along two-lane blacktop. Vultures and hawks circled in thermals; Rob can tell the difference at a glance. "No, that's a soaring bird," he said of one speck, then pulled out his binoculars. "That's a red-shouldered hawk. Thank you. Thank you for the show." He also identified cooper's hawks and an osprey—we were getting near the big lakes. Logging trucks would grind by, with a dozen or so stripped trunks between the posts on the trailer bed, piled high at one end, their pointy tops like a bunch of carrots at the other. Rob worked a summer logging old-growth forests in the Pacific Northwest in his youth, and he remembered seeing those same trucks go by, with their high posts keeping trunks from rolling off, but each trailer could fit only a single trunk.

On the asphalt two-lane we passed the occasional plantation, now no longer a place to raise crops but rather a weekend retreat for a wealthy family. The Carpenters, who once owned the Philadelphia Phillies, owned one lovely home called Longlands, whose white double-decker columned porch we viewed from afar down a lovely allée of live oaks—among a grove of signs assuring us that were we there after sundown we could expect canine patrols. We moved right along. And were glad when Lawson's path took us off the asphalt onto sand roads leading directly toward the dam and Lake Marion. With Spanish moss swaying in live oaks lining the berms a good couple of feet above the road surface, we felt sure we were on routes that, if not walked directly by Lawson, weren't much younger. You can walk roads like that in companionable silence for hours. We passed at one point a small boxy house with that homiest of details, laundry hanging from the line in the yard. No signs told us to beware of dogs.

:::

The early part of Lawson's walk through this territory described how ours would have looked if not for the damming of the Santee River. "Within half a Mile of the House, we pass'd over a prodigious wide and deep Swamp, being forc'd to strip stark-naked; and much ado to save our selves from drowning in this Fatiegue," Lawson says about one day. Soon, though, Lawson begins to leave the lowland swamps as the terrain slowly rises. "The next Morning early we pursu'd our Voyage, finding the Land to improve it self in Pleasantness and Richness of soil." A little further along he notes that the land has become "high and dry, very few Swamps, and those dry and a little Way through." At about that time his party loses one of its English members: "one of our company tir'd, being not able to travel any farther; so we went forward, leaving the poor dejected Traveller with Tears in his eyes, to return to *Charles*-Town, over so much bad Way, we having pass'd thro' the worst of our Journey." Rob and I passed that point and recognized it (on a previous reconnaissance trip Val Green had directed me to it).

At this point in Lawson's journey he notes that once again he and his remaining troupe are led by a sure-footed and strong Indian guide, this one named Santee Jack. In payment for his services Lawson's party gave him "a Stroud-water Blew, to make his Wife an *Indian* Petticoat, who went with her Husband." A Stroudwater blue was a coarse blue blanket from the British town of Stroud, already emerging as a textile center before its growth in the Industrial Revolution. And it brings up a point of enormous importance. Lawson has mentioned his Indian guides before, and he has told the story of the Sewees and their disastrous trading voyage. But with the Santees Lawson begins describing the Indian communities he visits in detail, and it is for this detail that his work is most remembered.

In his visit with the Santees he describes the way they prepare and serve their food. He describes their trade practices, their family and sexual customs, their burial and religious rites, their medicine. Lawson provides a view into indigenous society that is one of the most thorough, wide-eyed, and frank in all of early colonial literature. And his unabashed perceptions help fill out an understanding of the relationship between the European settlers and the Indians that is far more complex and, frankly, far more disturbing than what most Americans—certainly more than what I—have been taught.

One of Lawson's most famous comments is the one I mentioned in the introduction to this book—that "the Small-Pox and Rum have made such a Destruction amongst them, that . . . there is not the sixth Savage living within two hundred Miles of all our Settlements, as there were fifty Years ago." He notes in his journey along the coast the abandoned village of Avendaughbough. Lawson, that is, understands he's traveling through the residue of something, not the healthy thing itself. We are all familiar with the depredations of the Europeans toward the Native cultures they encountered—dispossession goes without saying; the diseases Europeans brought, like smallpox, were far more devastating than the diseases they encountered from the North Americans, like syphilis; the distilled alcohol that European society had been learning to manage for millennia hit the Indians just the way you'd expect. But the thing that I found most shocking as I learned about Lawson's trip was Indian slavery.

Until I began researching this project I did not know that Indian slavery was even a thing. And yet I share with you this quotation, from Alan Gallay's *The Indian Slave Trade: The Rise of the English Empire in the American South*: "The drive to control Indian labor . . . was inextricably connected to the growth of the plantations, and . . . the trade in Indian slaves was at the center of the English empire's development in the American South."

Now listen to this, from the same source, about the great slave port of Charleston. According to Gallay, about the half century from Charleston's founding in 1670 to 1715, a few years after Lawson's death: "[Indian slavery] existed on such a vast scale that more Indians were exported through Charles Town than Africans were imported during this period."

Please pause to let that sink in. We all know about Charleston's horrific legacy as the port of entry of nearly half of all slaves imported to provide labor on the American plantations, run on the inhuman chattel slavery system developed in Barbados and the other Caribbean islands. We are taught about its horrors and we cope daily with its results down the centuries. And though I knew settlers had dispossessed, infected, and killed Indians, still I had no idea their enslavement had been so vast. And yet it was. British settlers, not allowed to capture and enslave Indians but allowed by law to purchase slaves from other Indians, encouraged intertribal wars, after which Indians would sell their captives to the settlers. Indians made terrible slaves in their home territory—escape was simple and rescue always a possibility—so settlers extracted their value by selling them to island plantations where escape or rescue was not possible. And they did so to the degree that they were sending more enslaved Native Americans out to a brief, terrible life cutting sugarcane than they were importing the Africans we all know about, sentenced to the same fate on rice or cotton plantations.

I tried to process this information as I followed Lawson and took walks among the Natives.

Lawson's account explodes with detail when he describes the Santee. He describes their corn cribs at length, set off the ground on posts and daubed with clay, "which makes them tight, and fit to keep out the smallest Insect." Though it must be protected from insects, the corn is safe from theft, Lawson says, since among Indians theft is "altogether unpractis'd, never receiving Spoils but from Foreigners."

Lawson shares hunting stories. The Santees cleverly hunt deer by creeping toward them in deer hides with the heads preserved, he says. He avers that these costumes are so realistic that Indians have so often accidentally killed disguised hunters mistaken for deer that they do not use the costumes when a tribe is numerous. It's an awesome story, and the reader cannot help but imagine the snickers of Indian hunters getting the credulous Lawson to believe it.

And yes, Lawson discusses the great Carolina tradition of barbecue. His hosts, he said, "made us very welcome with fat barbacu'd Venison, which the Woman of the Cabin took and tore in Pieces with her Teeth, so put it into a Mortar, beating it to Rags, afterward stews it with Water, and other Ingredients, which makes a very savoury Dish." Modern Carolinians will nod with approval that shredded, not diced, meat is proper for barbecue, though it sounds like those Santee were combining a little Brunswick Stew in with the main dish.

Lawson also details Santee burial customs: "a Mole or Pyramid of Earth is rais'd," atop which is a sort of house, about which "is hung Gourds Feathers, and other such like Trophies, plac'd there by the dead Man's Relations, in Respect to him in the Grave." The corpse is laid on bark in the sun, as the tribe anoints it with powdered roots and bear's oil. Kin surrounds the body with "all the temporal Estate he was possess'd of at his Death, as Guns, Bows, and Arrows, Beads, Feathers, Match-coat, &c." Chief among relations is the mourner who, "his Face being black with the Smoak of Pitch, Pine, Mingl'd with Bear's Oil," keens by the body, telling stories of the dead man's life to anyone who will listen — much like a wake or the Jewish custom of sitting shivah. When the flesh begins rotting, Lawson explains, the Santees clean it off the bones and burn it, preserving the bones in a box and cleaning and oiling them every year. Indians thus often have the bones of their ancestors with them,

This Santee burial mound is likely a thousand years old or so and is considered the furthest-east of all Mississippian mounds.

Lawson says. Where an Indian is killed, "in that very Place they make a Heap of Stones, ... to this Memorial, every *Indian* that passes by, adds a Stone to augment the Heap, in Respect to the deceas'd Hero."

Lawson's detailed description of Santee burials will be familiar to anyone who has looked into the Mississippian Indian cultures that dominated the Native South before contact. They were called Mound Builders for a reason. And right on the shore of Lake Marion, a few steps north of I-95 and directly along the path Lawson would have trod, is the Santee Indian Mound, managed by the U.S. Fish and Wildlife Service as part of the Santee National Wildlife Refuge. Located in the refuge's Bluff Unit, the mound is said to be the furthest-east mound built by the Mississippian peoples before European contact. It stands about twenty-five feet high, a four-sided truncated pyramid covered in grasses and shrubs. A wooden stairway mounts to the top, where you can scan all around the territory—the mound overlooks the lake to the south and east and commands a view of the neck of land it now sits on, though in its day it would have been on a high and dry spot near the swamp, not on an isthmus. Signs atop the mound tell of the Santee, who probably began inhabiting the site around 1200 CE and stuck around until the diseases and other catastrophes brought by the settlers killed them or until they merged with other tribes. The mound itself was incorporated into Fort Watson during the Revolutionary War, during which it was captured by the British and recaptured by the patriots, under our old friend the Swamp Fox, Francis Marion, and Light Horse Harry Lee.

On his journey Lawson encountered Indians of the three major eastern language groups, all names familiar even to modern Americans: Iroquoian, Algonquian, and Siouan. The Santees, who belonged to the Siouan language group of tribes that predominated in northern coastal South Carolina, probably numbered a thousand or so when they first encountered European explorers in the 1600s. By the time Lawson came through they were likely down to a little over a hundred; by the time of the Tuscarora War (1711) and the Yamasee War (1715) they had dwindled to around eighty.

But as years of illness, conflict, dispossession, and abuse caused a coastal tribe to collapse, those remaining did not always act in concert. The Santee, for example, are believed to have been absorbed by the Catawbas, a Siouan-speaking nation to the west, around modern-day Charlotte. True for many, perhaps, though others surely did as the dispossessed have always done in times of great change: they melted into the landscape right where they were. Remnants of Indian tribes found refuge in the swamps that had proven so useful to Francis Marion, along with escaped slaves and fugitive indentured European migrants. For generations cultures have mixed and mingled in these southeastern swamps, in poverty out on the edges. In the last century or so the Santees have reemerged; Santee communities exist in several places in southeastern South Carolina, including one near the town of Holly Hill, near the edge of Lake Marion. There the 800 or so identified members of the tribe have for the first time in centuries a piece of land to call their own—the site of an unused fire tower, donated to the tribe by the South Carolina Department of Natural Resources. A large steel building, erected with a grant from Orangeburg County, sits on the site and hosts powwows, dances, and other gatherings. The poverty in the surrounding community is great, but this is an enormous step forward for a group that, though recognized by the state of South Carolina, remains unrecognized by the U.S. government.

"We're the only race to have to prove who you are," said Vice Chief Peggy Scott of the Santee tribe, when she met me in a cabin Rob and I had rented in the state park named for her people. She spoke of American Indians as a minority group and she made a significant point. You can be African American or Japanese American or Jewish or Muslim or a member of any group you choose. But if you want to be an American Indian, you've got a lot of hurdles to clear. "Even as a child it used to irk me," she recalls. "You came here, you tell us we're savages," she says. And then, when she tries to get recognition for her tribe, "now, hundreds of years later, they say go find your history, your heritage—that we took from you."

I had originally invited Peggy to join in and walk some of Lawson's path, but Peggy had recovered from an accident requiring spinal surgery, so instead of walking we met and talked. Lawson says the Santees came out to meet him with barbecued venison; when Peggy emerged from her little red Mustang, a small but strong woman in a purple T-shirt with images of wolves, she welcomed us with stories—which was what we had come for. We felt grateful to an almost absurd degree.

Peggy herself started with gratitude—to Lawson. "When you are not educated, when you do not understand your history," she says, "you're lost." She talks about discovering *A New Voyage to Carolina* in college: "He is like a huge part of my life," she says of Lawson, who described her ancestors kindly and with admiration. "It's like the whole world opened up when you have access to your history." She always knows where her copy of Lawson's narrative is now. "He gave me my history back."

She recounts that in her younger days she was mostly uneducated, growing up as the third group in a southern culture segregated into two—whites and blacks. Of Indians, she says, "We were identified as a derogatory name, that I don't choose to repeat." She attended an Indian school, denied resources to the point where she says, "I didn't know what a gymnasium was. I didn't even know what a library was." A couple of her friends went to the local public high school but were treated so badly they left. She says when she was in fourth grade the Indian school closed and she moved into the public middle school, where she describes a segregated system with white and black drinking fountains. If an Indian child was thirsty? "The teacher or principal would go get you a paper cup of water."

Among the fugitives living for centuries on the fringes, origins are hard to trace, but Scott has no doubts. "I was born in the middle of my tribe," she says. "My father and the elders delivered me in my mother's bedroom." The relation between tribe and the rest of the culture remains complex, of course. For example, she has a son. "The old saying is you have to have one to put in this world and one to put in the other world," she says—a child for the tribe and a child for the greater society. For her part, she has embraced all aspects of her complicated background, though not everyone does so. She talks of tribe members who feel no need of tribal culture, seemingly buying into the old image of Indians as uncivilized. When her son was born, her father urged him to take advantage of his light skin, but Peggy smiles. "I raised him differently." He lives in Charleston, fully integrated into the world at large. But now engaged, he wants to be married on tribal land and include Santee tribal customs in his wedding.

Peggy has worked much of her life for the betterment of her tribe. She's taken the special training you have to take as you try to work your tribe toward federal recognition, she's traveled to powwows far and wide, and she has spent years of her life helping her tribe get, literally, back on the map, with that piece of old Forest Service land. Scott also told a story about recovery from her accident and surgery, and how she finally felt whole again through dancing with her tribe on their first powwow on their own land in modern times.

Today's powwows, scholars may tell you, draw from a wide array of indigenous traditions. But dancing has mattered for centuries, as Lawson's account of his time among the Waxhaws makes clear:

> The Company was summon'd by Beat of Drum; the Musick being made of a dress'd Deer's Skin, tied hard upon an Earthen Porridge-Pot. Presently in came fine Men dress'd up with Feathers, their Faces being covered with Vizards made of Gourds; round their Ancles and Knees, were hung Bells of several sorts, having Wooden Falchions in their Hands, (such as Stage-Fencers commonly use;) in this Dress they danced about an Hour, shewing many strange Gestures, and brandishing their Wooden Weapons, as if they were going to fight each other; oftentimes walking very nimbly round the Room, without making the least Noise with their Bells, (a thing I much admired at;) again, turning their Bodies, Arms and Legs, into such frightful Postures, that you would have guess'd they had been quite raving mad: At last, they

cut two or three high Capers, and left the Room. In their stead, came in a parcel of Women and Girls, to the Number of Thirty odd; every one taking place according to her Degree of Stature, the tallest leading the Dance, and the least of all being plac'd last; with these they made a circular Dance, like a Ring, representing the Shape of the Fire they danced about: Many of these had great Horse-Bells about their Legs, and small Hawk's Bells about their Necks. They had Musicians, who were two Old Men, one of whom beat a Drum, while the other rattled with a Gourd, that had Corn in it, to make a Noise withal: To these Instruments, they both sung a mournful Ditty; the Burthen of their Song was, in Remembrance of their former Greatness, and Numbers of their Nation, the famous Exploits of their Renowned Ancestors, and all Actions of Moment that had (in former Days) been perform'd by their Forefathers. At these Festivals it is, that they give a Traditional Relation of what hath pass'd amongst them, to the younger Fry. These verbal Deliveries being always publish'd in their most Publick Assemblies, serve instead of our Traditional Notes, by the use of Letters.

Peggy Scott told us about that first dance with her people on their own land—symbolizing her own recovery and that of her tribe. She had the honor of opening the powwow, stepping into the circle of dancers with her shawl and staff and tribal colors of black, red, and white. It was an honor dance, she said, which meant she had to keep her head down. So when a bird flew over the assembly—when people cried out, "An eagle! An eagle!"—she could not look up. "That was my blessing," she said. "It was one of the happiest moments of my life."

Peggy has about given up trying to clear the hurdles necessary for national tribal recognition, but she'll never stop working for the Santee. Lawson came among the Santees as the tribe neared its lowest moment. Recent centuries have not been kind to the Santee—or to any Native American tribe. But as it was for Lawson, it was an honor for us to hear Scott tell her story.

:::

But we were talking about the Santee king, or anyhow Val Green was. The spot where Lawson met the Santee chief he described as a king—and the "no-nos'd doctor"—who was his sidekick—lay in another portion of the Santee National Wildlife Refuge, south of the portion with the mound. The morning Val called, my friend Rob and I were walking in a third segment, between the two, where we had taken a hike around Dingle Pond, a Carolina bay, or pocosin (Lawson calls these "percoarsins"), one of a half million or so such small swamps sprinkled in the coastal plain between Virginia and Florida (though most are in South and, especially, North Carolina). Low places in the land where water settles and has little or no place to drain, pocosins become homes to either peat bogs or swampy areas. Pines and turkey oaks surround them, as do tiny rims of sand, probably generated by the action of floating ice in colder times. Carolina bays, a particular subset of pocosins, have long been subjects of myth in eastern North Carolina; many have a characteristic teardrop shape, with the round part of the tear to the east. Scientists think this is simply the result of predominant winds coming from the west, but local mythology has blamed everything from meteor showers to, no kidding, the action of fish tails. The bays get their name not because they open onto the ocean but because of the sweet, loblolly, and red bay trees that tend to fill them. Most Carolina bays are wetlands; some are utterly dry, but larger ones—like Dingle—stay filled. Rob and I had lunch on a little viewing platform at Dingle Pond, where we squinted to see a flock of vultures riding thermals in the distance and tried to distinguish between the hiss of the wind through the pines and the low rush of I-95 in the distance.

The path around Dingle Pond, a sandy little two-track, could very easily have followed the very route that Lawson walked. The Santee National Wildlife Refuge, that is, follows the shore of Lake Marion, and when it was filled, the lake spread over the lower places up to where the terrain rose enough to remain generally dry—which is exactly where the Indian path that Lawson followed would have lain. This makes total sense—you put the path where it'll stay dry even in rainy times when the swamp is high—but it's not the type of thing I would have thought much about had it not been for Val Green.

So: What to say about Val Green, whom Rob and I met in the Cuddo Unit of the Refuge, where beneath a high sky striped with altocirrus clouds Val drove up in his pickup, let down the tailgate, and spread out his scrapbooks, maps, and photographs dedicated to Lawson's path. This was far from the first time Val Green schooled me regarding Lawson, whom Val calls "Uncle John," and far from the last. I have spent the last several years learning everything there is to know about John Lawson and his journey, and Val Green knows more about John Lawson than anyone else alive—and probably more than anyone else ever, at least since 1711.

Here's the story. Val, a stocky, ambling man of around seventy whose

Indian heritage often shows in a baseball cap identified with one tribe or another, is a retired sewer engineer, and he lives in South Carolina. I met him because in my early days of research about Lawson I found an old story in the *Charlotte Observer* that mentioned his pursuit of Lawson's path, at that time generally sketched but not completely known. So I poked around until I found him, and my understanding of Lawson would never be the same.

In 1970, Val's (then-) wife gave him a copy of *A New Voyage to Carolina* as a gift, and he made his way through it, enjoying as he went. Two weeks into the voyage, Lawson describes being awakened:

> When we were all asleep, in the Beginning of the Night, we were awaken'd with the dismall'st and most hideous Noise that ever pierc'd my Ears: This sudden Surprizal incapacitated us of guessing what this threatning Noise might proceed from; but our Indian Pilot (who knew these Parts very well) acquainted us, that it was customary to hear such Musick along that Swamp-side, there being endless Numbers of Panthers, Tygers, Wolves, and other Beasts of Prey, which take this Swamp for their Abode in the Day, coming in whole Droves to hunt the Deer in the Night, making this frightful Ditty 'till Day appears, then all is still as in other Places.

Val loved the sound of the place—Tygers! Wolves!—and thought he'd like to visit. Which brought up, of course, where might that place be? Well, at the time of the entry Lawson had been gone from Charleston a couple of weeks, and according to his journal he'd been going up the Santee River for about a week. He had described the day before seeing "the most amazing Prospect I had seen since I had been in Carolina," a view from a hilltop over a swamp, looking toward far hills. Being from South Carolina himself, and knowing the terrain along the Santee River, Val suspected that Lawson must have been describing the top of the biggest hill in Poinsett State Park, which overlooks the Wateree River. In the distance from there you can see the Congaree, where the two join to form the Santee. Val visited the spot and it checked out. Further investigation to the south identified creeks that perfectly correlated to Lawson's descriptions of the terrain he had traveled to reach that hill. Val had found his spot—and something to keep him busy the next four decades or so.

As the next years—and decades—passed, Val spent more and more time chasing down spots that correlated with Lawson's descriptions.

Many weren't terribly hard—Lawson, guided by Indian traders and Indians, kept to well-worn Indian paths, like the famous Trading Path that runs from Georgia to Virginia, running northeast through the Piedmont from Charlotte toward Hillsborough. It got to Charlotte from the south in two parts—the part Lawson followed came up from Camden, and another fork came from somewhat further west, toward what is now Augusta, Georgia. Other spots required serious investigation. Val has pawed through colonial papers, gone up to his armpits in plats, deeds, maps, and property records. He's worn out many DeLorme *Atlas & Gazetteers* of South Carolina and North Carolina as he has traced, retraced, and improved his route. His scrapbooks bulge with maps, photographs, deeds, plats, and drawings. And by the end of his work, Val had understood, pretty much exactly, where Lawson had gone, though like any good researcher he's always willing to reconsider in the light of further evidence. Over the course of my journey Val visited me on the trail at least a half-dozen times, more than once taking me by the hand and guiding me. I make no exaggeration when I say that without Val I simply would not have been able to undertake this project.

And then Val's interests moved on. Lawson led him to the Spaniards—Hernando de Soto and Juan Pardo—who had wandered the same general area a century and a half before. In some cases the Spaniards used the same paths Lawson eventually used, and Lawson's trail is what led Val to the Spaniards. He has now mapped de Soto's journeys and the journeys of Pardo after him, and has strong opinions on those of several other explorers of the early colonial Southeast.

Though not interested in walking along, Val supported the enterprise of retracing Lawson's journey and met me regularly, sitting in Waffle Houses and telling stories of Lawson, meeting me at campsites or highway crossings, and once my journey began regularly visiting me as I traveled, alone or with companions. Of Lawson he told me once, "I think I know the old boy pretty good."

:::

At the Santee Refuge with me and Rob, he talked with us about Lawson's visit from Santee royalty. "At these Cabins came to visit us the King of the Santee Nation," Lawson writes. "He brought with him their chief Doctor or Physician, who was warmly and neatly clad with a Match-Coat, made of Turkies Feathers, which makes a pretty Shew, seeming as if it was a Garment of the deepest silk Shag. This Doctor had the Misfortune to lose his Nose by the Pox."

The pox was of course syphilis, which in its tertiary stage attacks the soft palate and septum, and which the North American indigenes gave to the European explorers much the way smallpox traveled in the other direction. Nobody much won by the exchange, though since smallpox spreads and kills faster and more widely, the Europeans came out on top. Lawson spends a couple of pages detailing the spread of syphilis through Europe, and he shares the Santee doctor's claim that he had traded his nose to "the white Man above, (meaning God Almighty) . . . he being much pleas'd with their Ways, and had promis'd to make their Capacities equal with the white People in making Guns, Ammunition, &c. In Retalliation of which, they had given him their Noses." Returning to his journey Lawson says the group slept in an Indian cabin a few miles on from the Santees called a *hickerau*, or "black house," on a bluff. Lawson talks about getting fleas from sleeping in Indian huts, but Val focused more on how the Taw Caw Creek, once a tributary but now a stretching arm of the lake just east of where Val met us, was the spot just past Lawson's meeting with the king and the "no-nos'd doctor" where his party had to strip to cross, and how the *hickerau* was near the mound just past I-95.

Sitting under that high sky on the shore of the lake, with Rob paging through Val's scrapbooks and Val telling us thing after thing about Lawson's trek—where the swamps would have extended, where the water would have been high, where the pocosins would have been (and where the early Spanish explorers, Val's current obsession, would have gone on their treks)—we felt like we were in the presence of royalty ourselves.

:::

The real story, finally, was the lakes. We had to guess what the swamps Lawson would have edged along would have looked like—because they're now underwater. We had to wonder whether other mounds accompany the Santee Mound we climbed (Val is sure they do)—because the surrounding land is underwater. The two lakes that dominate the land north and west of the Francis Marion National Forest, Lake Marion and Lake Moultrie, exist because the Army Corps of Engineers in 1941 continued an obsession that people have long had with "fixing" the watersheds of the Santee and Cooper Rivers. The Santee, as Lawson describes, was a flooding mess. Freshets caused it to spread over the swampy territory several times a year—it had the fourth-greatest discharge of any river on the U.S. East Coast, but the silt it carried barred the river and made it useless as a port. Still, residents upstream, where it was more navigable, saw that it offered access to farms and settlements in inner Carolina. Meanwhile, the source of the deep Cooper River, which flows by Charleston, rose not far from the Santee, across a single ridge. In fact, in 1800 North America's first summit canal connected the rivers, allowing river traffic to go up the Cooper, over to the Santee, and deep into Carolina (though the canal languished after the railroads came).

But people couldn't quite give up on fixing what Mother Nature hadn't thought was broken. "The Corps's work is never done," Bob Morgan, heritage program manager for the Francis Marion National Forest, told me. In the 1930s, planners had the idea that if they combined the two rivers—the Santee and the Cooper—they could kind of get a two-for-one along with the electrification projects being undertaken all over the eastern portion of the country. They could dam both rivers, build a diversion canal connecting them, and run the flow of the Santee into the Cooper watershed, which dropped much more steeply, enabling the generation of electric power. Plus all the extra water would sluice out pollution from the Cooper, and meanwhile the Santee, made much smaller in flow, would putter along as a milder, more tractable version of its former self, the unruly beast that Lawson knew. As yet another result of the dams holding water for electricity production, the region would get two beautiful lakes for fishing.

Right. Dam two rivers, combine their flow, and send it the wrong way. What could possibly go wrong? Well, almost immediately after the rivers were dammed and combined, the enormous flow carried down the Cooper all the silt that used to fill up the Santee, "with extensive shoaling of Charleston Harbor beginning immediately following diversion," according to the book *Estuarine Processes*. This somehow surprised the people who had moved heaven and a lot of earth to make it do exactly that. And with its vastly diminished flow, the Santee ecosystem shifted from fresh (Lawson describes it as fresh all the way to the sea) to salt. Barrier islands began eroding. Trees died. On the positive side were the new clam and oyster beds my kayak guide Eddie Stroman told me about working.

For a while. Because what was that Bob Morgan said? Oh, yeah: the Corps's work is never done. By the late 1970s the Corps decided to unfix what was never un . . . whatever. It decided much of the water needed to go back down the Santee. Cool enough, but instead of just opening the hole on the Lake Marion dam bigger, it dug an entirely new canal, called the Cooper River Rediversion Project, and the Corps's page about it crows that it saves $14 million per year in dredging costs in Charleston Harbor, which, being honest, is exactly like the money a protection racket saves you in avoiding arson costs. Oh, yeah—the renewed freshwater flow destroyed the clam and oyster industry that had grown up, too, as the freshwater moved further downstream again toward the sea. What's more, the Santee National Wildlife Refuge, which has grown and shrunk in size, now has the job, through considerable human management, of providing what the rivers and swamps used to provide naturally: habitat and wetlands for migrating birds, whose natural stops were destroyed when the lakes filled up. Henry Savage Jr., whose 1956 book *River of the Carolinas* is not just a history of but a love letter to the Santee River, writes that "the whole project was a monstrous error, the product of anachronistic enthusiasms." Far from the river that had seen steamboat traffic in Jean Guerry's childhood, Savage called the Santee afterward "an abandoned river." No disrespect to the Corps—you win some, you lose some.

But the ecological catastrophe was hardly the worst of it.

:::

"It was a cultural and ecological abomination," says author Richard Porcher. You get that cultural came first, right? He's involved in a project right now, trying to document the history of the people, mostly African American, who lived on the land before it was drowned, especially beneath Lake Moultrie. Ecologically, he compares the area beneath Moultrie to the famous ACE Basin, a portion of South Carolina near Beaufort protected from development and considered a natural treasure. "This would have been the equivalent," he says. "You lost 150,000 acres of longleaf pineland, riverland, creek land.

"But the main thing is the history of the people was not recorded."

He recites place names like Raccoon Hills and Hog Swamp, the names all that's left of places that, because of the poverty and excluded nature of their inhabitants, never even made it onto the map. "Santee-Cooper did not document one African American settlement, not one interview, not one photograph," Porcher says. Jean Guerry had suggested this earlier in the journey, when she told us of her daddy driving her through the area so that she could see what was going to be lost. Homes and plantations and other buildings were disassembled and sold for parts. Others nobody disassembled; they just ended up drowned in the lakes.

The drought of 2007–8 brought a spate of articles about the drowned lumber town of Ferguson, whose foundations rose to the surface when the water level dipped, and people still canoe and kayak to places where wreckage of lumber kilns or other artifacts of the lost towns and hamlets remain; a graveyard even still sits on tiny Church Island, resolutely above the waterline. Interred there is one Joseph Simons, who vigorously fought the process by which the Santee-Cooper tried to acquire his Pond Bluff Plantation—property once owned by Francis Marion himself. When in 1939 the project finally resorted to the eminent domain process, Simons returned to his home, put a handgun to his heart, and killed himself. As the resident of one of the final graves dug on what is now Church Island, Simons made the most powerful statement he could about the creation of the two lakes. Savage Jr. called them "a monstrous white elephant," and even the people who benefit from the sport-fishing industry (which all agree is the only benefit the lakes have yielded) recognize that the lakes are a catastrophe on every level. Like the people I spoke with at the Pack's Landing fish camp that provides docks, food, bait, gas, and parking way up near the top of Lake Marion. We stood in the parking lot, watching a special boat unload a cargo of invasive aquatic plants it had cut, an endless process Pack's undergoes to keep its docks clear enough for its fishermen's boats. Pack's has been there, in and out of the Pack family, since soon after the lakes opened, but the Packs know as well as anyone else that the lakes are a mess. "Nobody's going to step up to a billion-dollar mistake," said Stevie Pack, of the current ownership. Good point. I went out and watched the sort of waterwheel weed-cutting boat dump load after load of lake salad on the dock.

:::

But wait there's more—or there almost was. Soon after completion of Lakes Marion and Moultrie the Corps contemplated a dam just downstream from where the Congaree and the Wateree join to form the Santee. Their goals were the usual variety of reasons best summed up by Savage Jr.: "A remarkable proportion of the Wateree, Congaree, and Santee swamp lands . . . would have been protected from flood damage by being permanently inundated." Fortunately, the people of the South

Carolina coastal plain had about as many lakes as they wanted, and they stood up and hollered and the Corps went away. Which meant that the Congaree, coming in from the northwest, and the Wateree, coming in from the east and considered the main source of the Santee, continued to converge in peace. And, not coincidentally, the trees that had proven most difficult to fell during peak timber years in the late 1800s and early 1900s ended up still standing.

Even heading toward the late 1800s, South Carolina still had about a million acres of floodplain forests—bottomlands where pines mixed with live oaks and the cypress and tupelo swamps Lawson came to know so well. Some of that remained untimbered in the Francis Marion National Forest, but, for large stretches, the woods that had survived the naval stores industry that destroyed the longleaf pines were mostly cleared during a lumber boom in the years surrounding the turn of the twentieth century. The land at the confluence of the rivers sat in floodplain where the water level, park rangers told us, could vary by ten feet or more, so even during the boom times getting men and equipment to function in loose, swampy soils like that was mostly more trouble than it was worth. Still, as the National Park pamphlet notes, "many remnants that survived the ax and plow were drowned by reservoirs." Logging in the Congaree area stopped in 1914, and when it looked ready to start up in midcentury a conservation movement sprang up in response. In 1976 the Congaree Swamp National Monument was formed, and it became a national park in 2003. Rob and I drove up there—it's just northeast of the top of Lake Marion, not far from Pack's Landing, but it couldn't look more different.

::::

Walking the boardwalk trails of Congaree felt like stepping back into Lawson's time. Bald cypress and tupelo there grow to enormous sizes: there are cypress trees of up to 26 feet in circumference and 127 feet high. On what amounts to rises—a few inches above where the floodwaters usually stop—loblollies grow to 160 feet or more, and it almost hurts your brain to look at them. Rob and I walked along mostly in silence—in low areas seas of cypress knees spread as far as we could see, and a few feet higher hollies, oaks, maples, hickories, gums, and of course loblollies rose to almost absurd heights, the highest in the eastern United States. Rob suggested that those steps we took might be the most Lawsonian moments I would experience on the entire trek, and in a way he was right:

this terrain was, like the moments canoeing among the *Spartina alterni-flora* on the coast, the closest I'd come to experiencing an ecosystem like the one Lawson would have experienced.

But—okay, does that make it the most Lawsonian moment? I guess that brings up what I was out there to do, and what Lawson did. Yes, it's amazing to see what Lawson would have seen ecologically. But I was really out there to see what I could see now, so at that point I thought of the most Lawsonian moment of my trip so far as walking up S.C. highway 375 from the tiny town of Gourdin to the Lake Marion dam, where we had left our car in the parking lot of Randolph's Landing, Motel, Campground, Fishing Pier, and World's Filthiest Restroom, with a sand parking lot and a chain-link fence and a magnolia tree with a truck parked under it and roosters that crowed when you walk up. I mean, that's what Lawson did—see what was out there and talk about it. I got a lot of satisfaction out of buying a caffeine-free Diet Coke there and using that awful restroom (it was the women's—the men's was closed off).

That is, much of this enterprise involved road walking, and when you walk along roads designed for you not to walk along them, you see the country in a way that it's not quite prepared for you to see. You see the unprettified underpinnings of our world: electrical substations behind chain-link fences, and cable pedestals in front of houses set far back from the highway. Orange plastic pylons announced where, beneath us, communications cables ran, and above us we never lacked for electrical wires and cable. We learned a lot about the town of Santee when we noticed that a restaurant, less than sixty miles from the coast, served us linguini with shrimp that clearly came frozen in a bag from Food Lion, but made sure it had what it called a Gentlemen's Club but you and I would call a strip joint attached to the back. That's what you do when you're walking through the country: you observe and you learn. I loved to see the metal building Peggy Scott and the Santee tribe had worked so hard to create, but I could not fail to notice that the town of Holly Hill near which it lay comprised empty building after empty building. Away from the coast the Lawson Trek began encountering little towns without the ocean to serve as an economic driver, and the news wasn't good. Every little town seems all but empty; such business as the main-street strip hosts usually involves services—tanning beds, hair salons, pet grooming—or stores selling used stuff. Government services for senior citizens and the poverty-stricken usually made an appearance. Beyond that and an occasional restaurant the Holly Hills and Santees and Lanes and Pinevilles are drying up.

Same with the churches. There was a little church every five miles or so—remnants of the time when you needed a church close enough to walk to, the locals told us—but those churches served aging and dwindling congregations. Congregations of people who could never do enough for us, mind you—allow us to park, give us water, welcome us to use their facilities—but dwindling nonetheless.

The Congaree felt a little like a reminder of that overwhelming change. The enormous trees, the acres of preserved forest were thrilling and lovely. But even in the reserve feral pigs showed up, rooting through the soil, reminding us that things weren't quite what they had been. The Spanish explorers brought hogs with them for food in the 1500s, and they've been roaming the countryside ever since. Outside the national park the terrain was a mixed bag of monoculture pine plantations, enormous farms, plantations that were playgrounds for the rich, and dying small towns. Lawson knew that he was walking through a terrain that represented the end of a way of life. It was hard not to begin feeling the same way.

We could see the dying towns as we walked through; we could feel the paved surfaces; we could see the farms and crops where forest once was. But of all the changes from Lawson's time to our own, I think the least noticed—and yet terribly important—was the stars. Lawson on occasion includes latitude and longitude measurements in his book, and before all was done for him he was the surveyor general of the North Carolina colony, so stars would have been of great importance to him. The difference between his day and ours of course is that he could have seen them just by looking up. If we live, as I do, in urban or suburban or even exurban areas, we cannot. Light pollution has spread across our nation and our world until even the Dippers, even the planets, are hard to pick out in a sky that is never quite dark, never black.

Which made all the more satisfying one of the few benefits of Lake Marion. Our deluxe rented cabin backed right up to the lake, and I still had in the trunk of my car the little inflatable boat I had bought in the vain hope that it might help us cross some of the creeks in the swamps near the coast. That never happened, but when I saw the lake I dragged it out, inflated it, left the cabin porch light on for guidance, and rowed out into the blackness. The biggest nearby town was Santee, population 740, so what light pollution the lake had to dispel stayed very low to the southern horizon. Above me: stars.

Orion, kneeling and shooting not as five or seven of maybe fifteen visible stars but against a backdrop of powdered sugar. Jupiter not as a lone beacon but as a brighter light than its thousands of neighbors. Sirius. Polaris. The Little Dipper pouring into the Big Dipper. And the swath of the Milky Way like a smudge across the screen of the sky. And even this was surely nothing compared with the nightly sky display Lawson would have taken for granted.

While I took my quest NASA had its flyby of Pluto, which I heard a scientist involved describe as the last first-view of anything that our solar system could afford. He had a good point: We've sent cameras flying by everything in this world and all worlds without our reach now, which to me made returning to Lawson's own first glimpse all the more worthy. And at a time when we see what's remarkable by looking at our screens—by looking down, not by looking up—I was grateful for the opportunity to lie on my back, look up, and, as my raft turned in the current, watch the stars whirl above me. Dogs barked and occasionally a car whispered by on the highway a few miles away, but otherwise silence— and the trickle of water off my paddles.

I can't say I saw what Lawson saw. But for a moment, alone in the blackness, opening my eyes to light waves landing on my eyes from trillions of miles away, I knew I was doing as Lawson had done. I opened my eyes.

And I looked around.

4 : The Most Amazing Prospect

At the intersection of swamp and "no trespassing," the trail ran out. No sign, no further blazes, no marking: nothing.

So I did what hikers do, wandering and poking and eventually finding *a* path, which was going sort of in the right direction. Eventually it hooked up with *the* path, a quarter mile away or so, and along I went on my way. It wasn't much of a challenge—I was looking for a poorly marked hiking trail, and I had a map, actually a few maps. Just the same, I wouldn't have minded one of Lawson's local guides. It helps to have someone who knows the country.

:::

The trail started, of course, at the end of a road—the road leading to Pack's Landing, where I met the Pack family, who had owned the Lake Marion fish camp and store on and off for decades. Pack's Landing Road leaves the Old River Road—about which more in a bit—just past a place called Halfway Swamp. And just before Pack's Landing Road is Elliot Pond, an atmospheric spot of epic stillness: Spanish moss sways from the boughs of cypress and tupelo, which poke out of an utterly serene pond completely covered with light green duckweed. The pond is left over from Elliot Mill, yet another casualty when the Army Corps of Engineers demanded some 300 acres of the Elliots' land to fill Lake Marion. The Elliot family runs a landing of its own just south of Pack's, and the decaying old mill building on the pond still carries a sign offering pond fishing for five dollars per day.

Pack's Landing was a lovely place to start a segment of the journey that finally left the coastal swamps and headed for the hills. My focus, though, was the Old River Road along which I walked. When you hear "old," please think in the neighborhood of a thousand years. My guide and chief Lawsonian Val Green had once toured me around on a car trip in this part of the world, and he believes that the Old River Road follows what was essentially a foot-traffic superhighway in the days of the Mississippian peoples. Some call it the Catawba Path, others the Waxhaw Path, either referring to the Indian peoples who lived near present-day Charlotte, where the path led. It stretched all the way to the Santee Mound near the bottom of Lake Marion, considered the easternmost edge of the Mississippian Indian culture. The Indians walked it for generations before European contact. Lawson and his group walked it. Later, revolutionary armies walked it. "There aren't too many roads in America that are a thousand years old," Val said. "But this one is."

The first couple of miles up from Pack's Landing had followed the Palmetto Trail, a modern trail project meant to cross the state of South Carolina, from the seacoast to the mountains. It starts from the Buck Hall recreation area near Awendaw, where I camped with my canoe, and ends in the town of Walhalla, in the Blue Ridge escarpment. The trail needs more maintenance than it gets (common for projects managed by small nonprofits), and it commonly runs through areas prone to sudden change when one tree farm or another marks an acreage for harvest. That's how I ended up at the end of the trail and had to make my own way. Without much trouble, but it's a point worth remembering if you're the exploring type.

I once attended a small seminar on how to find old roads. Dale Loberger, the man giving the talk, explained that a road is a fairly simple thing: it starts someplace travelers are, and it leads someplace travelers wish to be. Whether those travelers are animals, Native Americans, colonists, carts, railroad trains, or automobiles—or, as in many cases, each of those in succession—a road is a connector. Perhaps not the shortest but the best way between two points.

Look at an old map, Loberger told us, and the drawings of roads worried less about exact representations of twists and turns than on connections: from the Indian town to the good place to ford the river; from the trading post to the harbor; from the town to the good pass through the mountain. The way up or down the hill that kept to a 5 or 6 percent grade, beyond which a wagon, just like an eighteen-wheeler, became unsafe. A road in some way invented itself. It partook, I like to think, of what Platonists might call roadness.

Not far from where I abandoned the Palmetto Trail I rejoined that Old River Road, which had changed names a time or two before devolving, in the Manchester State Forest, into a sand track that actually felt like it had been trodden by human feet for a thousand years or more. That Mississippian Indian path lay, naturally, on the far edge of what before the lakes would have been the Santee swamp—the route that could have been depended on to be dry most times, regardless of the state of the river or swamp.

I loved the natural feeling of the dirt roads of the state forest—more correctly sand roads, since as we exited the coastal plain we entered sand-hills, the residue of what was once the floor of an ancient sea near its shore. As I walked those sandy miles, every step radiated roadness. A stand of holly—a ton of holly in these hills—to the left, commonly a pine farm to the other side. Dips down to creeks, rises to plateaus, and occasionally a home site or church, a graveyard, a stand of deciduous trees showing that once upon a time a home stood nearby. It's a lovely kind of walking that makes you feel that you simply are where you ought to be. To be sure, Route 261, the state asphalt two-lane that generally follows the same path only more smoothly and faster, was a half-mile to the west, and the windings of the Palmetto Trail were next to the road. But this sand road, skirting the edge of the swamp, exuded a kind of patient as-suredness that its adolescent asphalt cousin cannot duplicate.

:::

Lawson describes this path, mentioning camping "by a small swift Run of Water, which was pav'd at the Bottom with a Sort of Stone much like to Tripoli," a kind of silica schist often called rottenstone or fuller's earth (you or I would call it natural Kitty Litter). While walking this segment I passed the Tavern Creek, whose banks are covered with just that, and it flows just as swiftly as ever. When Lawson and his friends told their Indian guide, Santee Jack, that they'd like to hang around the creek an-other day, he assured them they'd be happier half a day further. So they went on—as did I—and a half day further we were all rewarded with the view from the overlook at Poinsett State Park. (The park is named for Joel Poinsett, the South Carolinian for whom we name the Poinsettia). Atop a genuine hill—it's several hundred feet up, and you notice it when you climb—you look to the west, down across the swamp the road has skirted for miles. And you get a view: "We mov'd forwards, and about twelve a Clock came to the most amazing Prospect I had seen since I had been in Carolina," Lawson says; "we travell'd by a Swamp-side, which Swamp I believe to be no less than twenty Miles over, the other Side being as far as I could well discern, there appearing great Ridges of Mountains, bear-ing from us. W.N.W."

I rented a cabin for the night at Poinsett. At the top of the highest hill in the park there is an overlook shelter, a little gazebo atop the park's high

Lawson calls this view "the most amazing Prospect I had seen since I had been in Carolina," and it's hard to disagree. A lovely spot in Poinsett State Park.

point. And from it, looking west and northwest, you have a view over the swamps that is, truly, the first great prospect you'll find as you travel into the Carolina midlands.

Val Green kept in touch with me on my travels and visited when he could—he roared up behind me in his white pickup as I trudged from my cabin to the lookout, and I thus had a first-rate guide to this particular point of land. Val pointed out that if you look west you easily see the ridge of pines on the far edge of the Wateree Swamp, which is several miles distant. But if you look very carefully—I brought binoculars against just such a possibility—you can see, in distant, faded blue, the line of hills on the far side of the Congaree swamp, a good twenty miles distant. The region is called the High Hills of Santee, and though they barely hit 300 feet, they do feel as though they tower above the swamp; the trails hug the hillside, and you can see for miles.

I have been on much higher prospects, but in contrast to trudging through lowland swamp, the view was somewhat awe-inspiring—I actually took a picture through the lens of my binoculars. Lawson mentions that "One Alp, with a Top like a Sugar-loaf, advanc'd its Head above all the rest very considerably," and until recent years, both Val and park manager Zabo McCants told me, you could see Cook's Mountain, ten or so miles away to the north-northwest. Timber has grown up to block the view, and since a paper mill now stands in that direction too, Zabo says he's loath to cut down the screening woods, because exposing the charming Cook's Mountain would expose much that is less lovely. Later on, on the steep trails leading north from the park, I found a break in the trees to the north-northwest, and viewed the mountain from there. It poked up like a little cone and stood just where it was supposed to be.

I stood atop a ridge where Lawson stood and saw what he saw, though I had a state park gazebo to keep the sun off my head. And I had left tracks in the sand along the same path trodden by Lawson, by Val, by traders and colonists and Indians—and by hunters and timber farmers and locals today. I don't think many asphalt roads can equal this.

:::

The night before I reached the park I slept, in a tent, in the Mill Creek County Park, a lovely park in Clarendon County that contained a mill pond, green areas for camping, overnight lodgings for horses, and little else. Poinsett State Park, in contrast, an easy day's walk away, boasted deluxe cabins, piers, developed trails, and a stone lake house and welcoming lodge. And not for nothing does Mill Creek suffer by comparison: it was the supposedly "separate but equal" facility maintained, until a few decades ago, by Poinsett staff for black families, who were until 1964 restricted from most state parks. In fact, when a 1963 court case required South Carolina to open its parks to all, the state closed all the parks for a year rather than, as state senator Rembert Dennis said, "have integration thrust upon us."

Walking through this countryside where hills have begun to gently roll, where cardinals, chickadees, and titmice zip through the forest on

The Lenoir Store lacked the ham biscuit I craved, but Beverly Johnson told me stories.

either side of the road, can be lovely and peaceful, and you can lose yourself, like Lawson did, in the zen of observation. From beginning to end of the Lawson Trek I met people who told me, from one perspective or another, about segregation and parks, flags and lynching, guns and freedom. The empty houses and churches, the drowned towns beneath the lake, and the once-segregated parks tell their own tales, too.

Mind you, Mill Creek Park was a lovely place to camp a chilly February weeknight. I cooked my obligatory macaroni and tuna fish at a picnic table, started a pleasing fire, listened to a barred owl and a pileated woodpecker converse, slept cold. I awoke in the morning to a convocation of blackbirds so noisy I wondered whether there was a problem (there was not). I noted my own camping routine—hot, cold, rain, shine, alone or with companions, in a tent campsite or a cabin, I wake at seven and am on the trail at nine. I took a picture of the park's mill pond on my way out. And rejoined the old Indian path after a while on a track called, lest one begin to forget, Milford Plantation Road. I even stopped at the plantation house, where the caretakers, though not offering tours, cheerfully allowed me to peep in the windows of the beautiful house. I have lived in the South for a quarter century. I have never found a way to process the existence of these works built by slaves. I bear witness and I move on.

:::

The night after the cabin in the park I carried a tent again, and I did something Lawson and his companions would have done—and that I had long wanted to do: I simply wandered. I woke in the morning, fixed my meal and packed my pack, and set out. I walked for a day, stopping to eat when I was hungry or rest when I was weary. I walked for a long time along an abandoned railroad, which is clear for seeing but bad for stumbling—railroad ties just never space out to meet your stride. This one had been abandoned long enough that saplings grew between the ties. I scurried across a major road and carried on the Horatio-Hagood Road. When the sun began to lower in the sky and the air grew cold, I spent my last mile looking for a comfortable and secluded spot. I found one in a little copse of pines at a bend in the road. I took off my pack and set up my tent. No park, no fences, no forms, no rules. And, of greater importance, no yard, no crops, no buildings. I was out some damn where, where nobody was paying me any mind. I made my little dinner, slept very cold—it went below 10 degrees Fahrenheit; a water bottle I had put in the bottom of my sleeping bag to stay liquid for breakfast had crusts of ice in it—and got up in the morning, at which point I packed up and was on my way. Just, I thought, like Lawson. I stayed in no hut, so I left behind no beads or tobacco. When my gray tent was up, you would not have noticed it from the road (I checked); when I left I roughed up the grasses, so you wouldn't have been able to find the flat spot where I slept. I took only photographs and left not even footprints.

It was one of the most satisfying nights of my life. Lawson and his companions mostly stayed with Indians or in trader lodgings left expressly for the purpose of travelers like them, not unlike the shelters you find along the Appalachian Trail. But on occasion they slept rough, and Lawson liked to complain about it: "lying all Night in a swampy Piece of Ground," he says of one night, "the Weather being so cold all that Time, we were almost frozen ere Morning, leaving the Impressions of our Bodies on the wet Ground." Another night, he mentioned that frozen northwest wind that "prepar'd such a Night's Lodging for me, that I never desire to have the like again." For Lawson, a rough night just meant they had failed to find welcome among the locals. For me, rough nights were part of what I was out there for. Lawson walked the land in a time when on foot was pretty much how you got places. For me spending my days traversing the land was a rare pleasure. Sleeping outdoors, finding such shelter and space as nature provided (augmented of course by Gore-Tex and nylon and fiberfill), and awakening to the sounds of birds rather than traffic—or the heating system clicking on—never lost its charm.

I packed up quickly that morning, as much to clear up my contraband campsite as to get out of the cold, though it was plenty cold. But in fact Val Green had informed me that barely a couple of miles from where I ended up sleeping lay a delightful old country store, in the barely there town of Horatio, and I walked toward it. After less than an hour's cold walk I came to a crossroads and found the Lenoir Store, a one-story white clapboard building with a false front top like something out of the Old West. A store by that name has stood at the crossroads since at the very least before 1808, though how long before that nobody knows—it pops up in the historical record in the will of one Isaac Lenoir that year, and it's been in the family ever since, represented on a map from 1825 and another from 1878, by which point the current building stood. It turns out to be the longest-standing continuously run business in Sumter County and probably the whole state, according to my eventual guide, Bubba Lenoir.

: : :

The Lenoir name is far from unknown in the South—Lenoirs in South Carolina, North Carolina, and Tennessee all trace their line back to mariner and tobacco farmer Thomas Lenoir (the French name gives a clue that he, like the Huguenots Lawson first visited, came to the colony seeking the religious freedom Carolina supposedly offered). Thomas Lenoir lived first in Virginia before finally settling in North Carolina. Of his sons, Isaac was a soldier in the Revolutionary War and brother to General William Lenoir, who has a namesake city and county in North Carolina. South Carolina has this store.

I learned much of this from Beverly Johnson (née Lenoir), tending the store when I walked into tiny Horatio, with great expectations of a warm ham biscuit that would probably change my life. No such luck. Like many of South Carolina's small towns, Horatio is losing population, and left behind are large corporate farms and retired people—not much population to keep a store running. A sad little bunch of bananas, a wall of soda pop and chips and pastries in plastic. Toilet paper and paper towels. Given that the store didn't even have central heat—Beverly stood in front of a space heater and smoked wearing gloves—I was glad at least for the shelter, the company, and the surroundings. Lowering breakfast expectations, I bought an orange juice and absorbed the atmosphere.

And the story. Beverly clued me in, walking me around on creaking wooden floors, beneath whitewashed beadboard ceilings, among hanging single-bulb lamps. She gave a tour of the portraits on the wall (everything from generations of Lenoirs to horse carts) and various old objects still on the store shelves, reading labels aloud and filling me in on family lore. The store contains one of the oldest post offices in the country—a corner filled with little bronze post boxes with those alphabet combination locks—and is the subject of considerable resistance when the Postal Service periodically considers closing it. There was a story in *Parade* tacked up about it.

As much as I loved the Lenoir Store, I didn't want to move in, especially without a ham biscuit. So having reached the end of a planned segment of my trek, I reached out for my ride. But when I called thirty miles south back to Pack's Landing, where I had left my car days before, I found that nobody was prepared at that moment to come get me.

So by mutual agreement I went looking for another ride while I waited, and I found it at the tidy brick house not fifty feet away. There, behind the wheel of a white Chevy pickup that had driven from the front door to the mailbox in the frigid weather I met Bubba Lenoir, Beverly's cousin. Bubba not only ferried me back to Pack's Landing but on the way gave me a historical tour of that segment of Sumter County.

The house Bubba had emerged from was built in 1954, and Bubba told me its predecessor, built in 1760, burned on Thanksgiving morning 1953: "Daddy said, 'Don't grab nothing, just get out.' The whole house was built out of fat lighter"—pitch pine, which burns like a candle; the same stuff the Tuscaroras eventually poked Lawson full of. "We just did get out."

The lesson continued when on the road back through the state forest Bubba stopped to show off the tiny St. Mark's Episcopal Church, to which he had the keys. We explored the cemetery and the church itself, established in 1757 and currently in a trim white gothic building, built a century later of bricks made of local clay. Like most of the churches I encountered, it serves an aging and dwindling congregation.

"There were a lot of Richardsons around here," Bubba said as we looked through the graveyard. The Richardson cemetery is a few miles away, and there is buried Richard Richardson, perhaps the most important of all colonial South Carolinians—born in 1704, a Revolutionary War hero and the progenitor of a family that has provided South Carolina with six governors, all of whom worshipped at this church. Young Richard Richardson would have gamboled around the yard of his parents' home in Virginia while John Lawson lived in North Carolina, not many miles south. Little means more in South Carolina than the name Richardson—when my new friend Zabo McCants, manager of Poinsett State Park, told me about himself, he mentioned that "my grandmother is actually a Richardson." The South Carolina state song is the Richardson Waltz, passed down for 300 years by ear from Richardson to Richardson.

Anyhow, between the Richardsons and the Lenoirs and the store and Packs Landing and the abandoned railroad I had camped near I got to feeling I had really managed to learn a bit about Sumter County, to say nothing of the route Lawson would have trod. The Lenoir Store only stood where it did because the old Mississippian Indian trail to the Santee Indian Mound ran by there. That became a settlers' trail that became the dirt road along which I had walked, and that had given rise to the railroad—since abandoned—and then the asphalt Horatio-Hagood Road on which I'd finished my trek segment.

Bubba and I cheerfully conversed until we pulled into Pack's Landing, where talk instantly turned to the kind of good-natured foolery that makes places like Pack's Landing—and the Lenoir Store, and for that matter Sumter County—the wonderful places they are. "What's the population of Horatio?" needled a fellow named Duck in overalls and a knit hat with a little brim, who would have eventually come to pick me up had I been more patient. He pronounced it HO-ratio. "Well, this morning it's about twenty-five, since I'm down here," Bubba said, and off they went. They got into game wardens and how to manage them. They teased me about sleeping outdoors the night before in 10-degree weather ("You didn't have to worry about no mosquito bugs," Duck said, meaning me and Lawson at this time of year). By the time I left they were standing around the woodstove in the middle of the store, hands in pockets, talking about someone Bubba had played football against in high school.

Lawson took his long walk, basically, to see what was out there—to meet the inhabitants and see the country. Me too.

:::

I started my next segment of Lawson's journey by leaving a car parked near the Lenoir Store. This once again brings up a significant difference between Lawson's undertaking and mine. Lawson was twenty-six, unattached, and an ocean away from even the slightest whisper of responsibility. For him to walk into the woods with a bunch of newfound friends and not be heard from for a couple of months was a great adventure. Lawson, I remind people, did not have Sunday school carpool and Mighty Mites basketball to manage. So I never disappeared into the bush for longer than a week at a time, and planting cars in places like church parking lots at the end of planned segments or finding rides back to places like Pack's Landing where I had left them at the beginning became essential elements of this project.

In this case I walked for a few days with Michael, an old camping friend, and Katie Winsett, my ecologist friend from the swamp who rejoined the project for another hike. We set out along the Horatio-Hagood Road, another road that probably lay right on top of the old Indian trail, passing the Wateree River Correctional Institution not far up the road. A white sandwich sign stood out front, red letters stenciled, "Now Hiring," eloquently summing up the economics of that patch of rural South Carolina. The Wateree River—which at the top of Lake Marion joins the Congaree to form the Santee—lay a couple of miles to our west as we walked north, surrounded by swamp as it wiggled and flowed. Despite the rising land and my travels of the previous section in the High Hills of Santee, the low coastal plain had not yet started to feel far in our past— maps still showed swamp, though we rarely encountered it anymore. We looked instead at the wildflowers by the road—Katie identified lamium, which has purple flowers and square stems, and lifted her eyes to the trees and shrubs lining the road. "You can see the haze of green where the leaves are popping out," she said. Spring was approaching. Not long after we passed the prison, we passed another business: "Coastal Stoneworks," in a small wood-frame building. Lawson mentions of this area that "here begins to appear a very good Marble, which continues more and less for the space of 500 miles," so the stoneworks made sense: we were beginning to rise from the coastal plain into the Piedmont, and stone entered the makeup of the soil. We began to encounter little stones of quartz and granite when we left the roadside.

Lawson also says of this part of his trek, "From the Nation of Indians, until such Time as you come to the Turkeiruros in North Carolina, you will see no long Moss upon the Trees; which Space of Ground contains above five hundred Miles." When I had stepped onto the Palmetto Trail from Pack's Landing on Lake Marion, some thirty miles south, I swept thick Spanish moss aside as I walked along the trail. But Lawson was right—that was about the end of it. We noticed as we walked along the road—the swamps were gone, and so was the moss. It reappeared for Lawson near Little Washington when the swamps returned; months after this we would have the same experience, right on schedule.

:::

As the trek left the lakes and parks behind, the land we passed still included trees, but we started to see more crops, like cotton and soybeans. Traces of cotton lined the sides of the road—soggy, soiled bolls at field edges, where the harvesters missed the plants. We regularly passed enormous bales—picked and formed by machine—covered in tarps still in the fields, but it was spring, so we saw tending, not harvesting. At the center of one field we saw a copse of trees, undergrowth, and vines and realized that in the middle of that brushy spot was a two-story house, abandoned. Once we had left the state forest, abandoned houses had become a commonplace along the trail—as powerful evidence of the changing world around us as the paved roads and empty churches. I photographed many of those houses, and this one looked too good to miss, so we headed up a double-track that ran between rows of the field.

We quickly encountered a tractor that we hadn't noticed was occupied. As we stood and talked near the trees, considering whether to approach the gray house within, behind us the tractor suddenly rumbled to life, spindly brown steel trusses of a spraying mechanism unfolding and spreading outward, like the wings of some great wading bird. It began herkily rolling up rows of cotton, spraying as it went. Nitrogen, Katie explained; fertilizer. Michael said when he saw it he thought, "praying mantis"; Katie, ever the ecologist, thought, "threat behavior."

The machine trundled off, and we crept through the jungly undergrowth to the abandoned house—probably the home of the family that once farmed those acres. Up brick stairs, across a rotting porch, and into the decaying living room of a silent ruin. Once a room of color, the broad parlor was a place of pale blotchy greens and washed-out grays. Paint peeled from the ceiling, fallen fragments curled among the dead leaves

Its occupants long gone, this farmhouse tells a tale with its emptiness.

on the floor like late snow. The bay window bulged into matted under-growth, a wide archway opened onto the rest of the dead house, wallpaper seemingly rotting on the walls. Black smoke traces around a painted brick fireplace betrayed despairing final owners or careless squatters. A stair-way led up but we did not climb it, less from caution than from sorrow. A family had lived here once and its traces barely clung to the walls.

Empty houses. The town of Jamestown was little more than a gas sta-tion and a church; the little crossroads of Horatio with its store was barely there, and Hagood simply was not. The farms the people once worked be-longed to corporations now, most of the jobs done by machines. We were getting our first sense that, like Lawson, we were seeing not a culture in flower. We were seeing the end of something, shells, like those Lawson had seen on Capers Island or the ghost trees of Boneyard Beach—or the empty town of Awendaw, the silent record of a vanished tribe. The life that sustained them was gone.

Though not entirely. Continuing north we passed into the tiny hamlet of Boykin, which though it barely exists does include a little roadside collection of log buildings, some moved from hither and yon, including a restaurant, a little church, and most important the Broom Place, housed in a relocated slave cabin from 1740 into which we ducked to get out of the rain. There we passed an agreeable hour talking with Susan Simpson, who makes brooms by hand, using equipment a century old or more. She told us stories about Boykin: site of a Civil War battle, one of the last of the war (reportedly it was a draw); the church is almost, and the mill pond is more than, 200 years old; a bunch of people drowned in the mill pond once; Boykin has a Christmas parade that draws people from miles around. While she told stories her hands, wise in the ways of brooms, cut and filed straw and wound and crimped wire and hammered tacks as she tried to catch up to the years' worth of orders she's behind on. Colored straw and handles and twine filled shelves and buckets and hung from the wooden walls. Simpson worked on a Johnson Improved Broom Sewing Vise. No Boykin native, she grew up the daughter of an itinerant minister and has been making brooms for decades—she ended up in Boykin in 1972 and figures to stay. "I've already picked out my spot under the live oak tree," she laughed. "They're stuck with me now."

Simpson had found a way to make rural South Carolina work for her—she practiced an old-time craft and sold brooms to tour buses. Camden, about nine miles north of Boykin and the first real town we hit on the trek, has mostly chosen history as well. "History, horses, and Hagler," was how Joanna Craig, director of Historic Camden, described her town's current economy. History was baked into the town's bones—founded in 1730, it was the first inland Carolina town settled by Europeans, as King George II, looking to force the Indians off prime riverside land and spread English colonization, chartered almost a dozen new settlements. The town was first planned as Fredericksburg, right on the Wateree River, then moved to a low part of the current town and called Pine Tree Hill (actually rather swampy; it still floods, Joanna assured us). It began to prosper in 1758, when one Joseph Kershaw arrived from England, established a store, and got things going. In 1768 Kershaw renamed the town after Lord Camden, a supporter of colonial rights. The revolutionaries lost the Battle of Camden in 1780, by the way. General Cornwallis took over the stately manse Kershaw had built and imprisoned its owner for the duration; "hundreds of unhappy prisoners" of the revolutionaries met the same fate penned in the yard, wrote one Mrs. Thomas McCalla, the wife of one of them, according to a sign in front of the rebuilt house—it survived the Revolution but not the Civil War (Sherman; you know the drill) and was rebuilt in 1977 on its original brick foundations. With white clapboard sides and columned porches on the ground and second floor, it radiates colonial gentility. The revolutionaries did only somewhat better in 1781 at the battle of Hobkirk's Hill, along the Indian trail just north of town—another loss, after which the British were so annoyed that they decamped from Camden and pretty much burned it.

The town was rebuilt up a hill from the old revolutionary-era site, which is now a park, including the rebuilt Kershaw House. Camden's current downtown main street—Broad Street; Lawson would have walked the Indian trail along which it's laid—is filled with neoclassical buildings designed by Robert Mills, who was the designer of the Washington Monument, not to mention the author of the 1825 *Mills Atlas of South Carolina*, a vital historical map resource from which Val Green drew a lot of information in figuring out Lawson's path. (Though the atlas came out more than a century after Lawson had passed through, the passages between settlements, towns, and Indian territories would have had little reason to move.) Modern Camden is probably very near the center of the town of Cofitachequi, an Indian polity visited by de Soto, Pardo, and, as late as 1670, Henry Woodward, the first British colonist of South Carolina. By the time Lawson came through the territory was just the southern reach of the Catawba people.

Joanna Craig insisted we stay in the basement of the Kershaw House, which we gladly did, remaining dry and cheerful on a damp and drizzly weekend. Camden grew over the years as a travel destination for northerners looking to escape harsh winters, and the equestrian pastimes of the wealthy became central to Camden's culture. Joanna assured us they still are: the National Steeplechase Museum is housed in Camden, and it hosts famous steeplechase races each fall and spring.

That all came long after Lawson, of course, as did Hagler, a colonial era "king" of the Catawbas, whose territory stretched southward to this area. Hagler signed a treaty with the Iroquois Confederacy, with whom the Catawbas had historic troubles, and he signed the Treaty of Pine Tree Hill in 1760 that established a small reservation for the Catawbas. The reservation did as much good for the Catawbas as most deals with colonials did (settlers swiped it, first bit by bit and eventually wholly and governmentally; the resurgent Catawbas didn't gain federal recognition until 1993). Hagler himself would have been an infant when Lawson passed through—maybe Lawson chucked him under the chin, though he doesn't mention it. Hagler is sometimes called the patron saint of Camden, and his image shows up everywhere—on windvanes atop both the city hall and the former opera house as well as on newel posts, wall hangings, and garden columns everywhere in the city.

:::

Again—Hagler came long after Lawson, as did the colonial architecture and the horse culture that define Camden now. Our most significant resource in Camden beyond Joanna was a bakery (Mulberry Market, if you must know, and you must) that provided pastries that made our Kershaw House basement breakfasts things of luxury.

And, to be honest, Camden was a resource itself. Simply existing as a city—the first inland city in the colony—brought things like interstate highways into the picture, which were jarring and unsettling. "You don't realize how fast cars go until you walk along a road like this," Michael said as we walked along U.S. 521, the major road into which our peaceful little two-lane fed a couple of miles before Camden. We had left a car just there and drove the rest of the way; the next morning they dropped me back so I could continue walking like Lawson had, and for the first time along the trek I felt myself to be in a truly alien environment.

As I approached town, where I-20 crossed 521, I noticed two things.

First, the mounds that provided support for interstate overpasses were almost the exact size and shape as the Indian mound we had visited and Lawson had described. The same slopes, the same general design. One used for burying chiefs and erecting temples, the other used to bury costs and erect temples to automobiles, but still. Once people get up to building earth mounds, it turns out they're going to look about the same.

I checked with an engineer who works with highways and he said that's right on. You can have a slope of four or even three to one (that's run to rise, so the smaller the first number, the steeper the slope) and you're okay. But go any higher and you need special reinforcement—you can't even get grass to grow, to say nothing of the kind of erosion that a slope that steep will suffer. So whatever their purpose, our mounds look exactly like those of our predecessors. Maybe future archaeologists will think of us as mound builders too, except that we'll be remembered for roads it's dangerous to walk along.

Because the second thing I noticed—could not fail to notice—on my way into Camden was that the roads I walked on had utterly no interest in my passage. I did not belong there, and nobody thought about my needs, my safety, or my experience. That intersection was for cars, not for people, and if you happened to be a person trying to cross it, too bad.

I wondered what the people in cars would make of me, teetering along with my knapsack and my camping hat. Double-takes from windshields? Delighted children waving from the back seats? Nope—worse. Nobody noticed me at all. In an environment designed for big things moving at machine speeds, not a single driver even glanced at me, a small thing moving at human speed. I scurried across lanes of traffic one direction at a time, and I crossed exit and entrance ramps only when I could see nobody was near; drivers slowing down or speeding up appear especially preoccupied with things other than vulnerable pedestrians.

The interstate highway itself gave a moment of shelter from the rain— and a drip line where the bridge shed its water. Along the west side of the road, once I passed the interstate, was what the map called Big Pine Tree Creek, and behind one of several vast parking lots with a little gas station and convenience store in the center the Big Pine Tree was entered by a nameless tributary. As ever I loved seeing the way tiny little microclimates set themselves up: creekside, by the pipes in ditches were tufts of grasses; a dirt road entered 521 that I could have driven be 200 times without ever noticing; the post and pylons of infrastructure systems were everywhere.

You cannot help wondering, even as you walk into a lovely little town like Camden, rich with history and filled with kindness: what kind of culture erects roads on which people cannot walk? Along which you travel without noticing … anything? Just walking the surface of the earth fills you with questions and ideas minute by minute. Driving puts you in a fugue state. I was sorry to see that we all zoom by so quickly.

:::

Leaving Camden the next day we headed north, toward Lancaster. We left our brick basement in the Kershaw House and headed north on Broad Street—the old Catawba Trail—through the town square, past the little fencepost effigies of Hagler. Many of the trim, well-maintained front porches had ceilings covered by the light-blue paint of Carolina porch tradition: keeps the haints away, according to Gullah myths that have spread through the South that haints—ghosts—can't cross water, so the light-blue paint protects the house, ghosts evidently among their other problems not knowing which way is up. With haints in mind we walked through a lovely morning fog that reminded us of the lay of the land. We might not have noticed that we were gently rising and descending, but the fog let us know when we were in a hollow. We had truly left the coastal plain behind and now walked through rolling hills, either green with cover crops and winter wheat, which Katie pointed out, or brown with last year's grasses. Ahead we could see the humps of hills, some green with pines, others bearing still-brown deciduous trees. In the distance they looked like buffalo.

We heard roosters when we passed farms—"hobby farms," we had heard them called in Camden: not really businesses producing food as much as something to occupy their wealthy or retired owners. When as we left town we entered exurban territory and were separated by a fence from fiercely barking dogs, Michael wondered whether we were passing a hobby junkyard. On the chimney of one white brick building a black vulture perched, wings spread, waiting for the sun to dry the fog off its wings. I remembered seeing cormorants doing the same thing off the coast. The vulture looked to be doing sun salutations.

Soon enough we were back on a country two-lane, in this case called Flat Rock Road, which hugs a ridge that strays to the east, away from the Wateree River while still following it generally northward. Lawson, in his delicious prose, describes the surrounding terrain: "The Land here is pleasantly seated, with pretty little Hills and Valleys, the rising Sun at once shewing his glorious reflecting Rays on a great many of these little Mountains."

Exactly my own feelings as I traversed this lovely Piedmont terrain. Just north of Camden we had passed the Battle of Camden National Historic Landmark, which apart from the information about the battle itself preserved a segment of pine-straw covered sand road. "See that flat depression in the ground?" a sign asked. "That's the surviving imprint of the Great Wagon Road"—which, starting in the 1740s or so, is what they started calling the Catawba Trail, or the Great Trading Path, or whatever name it had wherever you were along its hundreds of miles. By then it stretched from Philadelphia to Georgia, but in Lawson's time it was still the Trading Path. It was unmistakable in the park, an easily recognized path through the pines. I was consciously following Lawson, and I had the most knowledgeable people in the nation telling me where to go, explaining how the old trails followed the animal paths, and the railroads and roads followed the old trails, and so the rural roads we walked were Lawson's path. Just the same, when I could stand not on pavement but on earth, and say to myself, "Three hundred years ago, Lawson and his gang walked along this path, and they stood right here," I loved it. And when Lawson walked through, he noted not just the hilliness of the terrain but the stone beneath the surface that is responsible for the hills.

"These Parts likewise affords good free Stone, fit for Building, and of several Sorts." Which we saw everywhere starting at this point—Hanging Rock Battleground, site of a Revolutionary War battle (the good guys won, on August 6, 1780; unlike the Battle of Camden ten days later), lay barely ten miles north. More interesting than the battle to me—and to Lawsonians, given that Lawson passed through three-quarters of a century before the war—are the enormous rocks that give the field its name.

In fact, Lawson describes a specific spot nearby where he stopped and had lunch: "At Noon we halted, getting our Dinner upon a Marble-Stone, that rose it self half a Foot above the Surface of the Earth, and might contain the Compass of a Quarter of an Acre of Land, being very even." This specific spot is, of course, the protrusion from which Flat Rock Road gets its name, about ten miles north of Camden. The flat rock that remains is a broad, parking-lot-sized spread of stone, and though mostly even with the turf it's plainly the broad, flat rock Lawson described: I sat on that rock and had lunch, like Lawson did. Meanwhile, across from the road is a quarry, and down the road a bit I had passed a monuments business. We had entered stone territory.

The clean chips that littered the Georgia Stone Industries quarry were white and pink, with the salt-and-pepper inclusions that define granite. The flat stone that Lawson mentioned probably had been the protruding top of that granite; the stone surface I ate on still resisted the covering grass, though lichens abounded on it. I had my lunch there, alone—Michael and Katie had headed home, depositing my car nearby. I sat in the quiet, listening to crows and the occasional midday rooster as the wind whooshed through the pines. Another indication: you hear that kind of wind up in the hills, not in the plains. The Lawson Trek was climbing.

I later visited Hanging Rock Battlefield, and even by there, barely ten miles further along, we were no longer talking about protrusions or flat areas: those were boulders; the change in the territory was astonishingly rapid. Here's the story, according to sources more modern than Lawson (I trust *Exploring the Geology of the Carolinas*, by Kevin Steward and

Mary-Russell Roberson, for my info). We had begun encountering rock and hills because we were crossing the fall line between the flat coastal plain and the hilly Piedmont. "Granite forms when a body of magma rich in silica cools slowly deep underground," *Exploring* tells me. And some 300 million years ago, Gondwana, containing parts of what are now Africa and South America, banged into Laurentia, which contained what is now North America. What with all the pressure and heat of two such enormous bodies you end up smashing and heating the Earth's crust, which, "rich in silica," cooled to form granite—in this case, what's called Pageland granite, after the nearby town of Pageland. Because the granite is so tough, it weathers much more slowly than the surrounding earth and you get big pieces of it sticking out—like here on Flat Rock Road. The change in geology explains some of the change in activity, as well. Coastal plain soils are mostly sandy, resulting from the sedimentary rocks formed on the ancient seabed. This makes a droughty, well-draining soil, which tobacco and cotton love. The Piedmont, which we were entering, is more of a weather-in-place soil generated from igneous or metamorphic rock like granite; it doesn't drain as well, and cotton and tobacco aren't as happy there. Groups of rocks now dotted meadows—as did cattle, which do fine on the grasses farmers can get to grow on the clayey Piedmont soil.

Speaking of that flat rock. "Growing upon it in some Places," Lawson finds "a small red Berry, like a Salmon-Spawn, there boiling out of the main Rock curious Springs of as delicious Water, as ever I drank in any Parts I ever travell'd in." I found no such mysterious berries or springs at the quarry, but when I got in my car to head home I made a detour and only a couple of miles away visited Forty Acre Rock Heritage Preserve, an outcropping of the same granite. There the rock—it's actually only fourteen acres, but who's counting—spreads out and shows its face, collecting water in low places and creating pool ecosystems that support plants like elf orpine, a tiny plant "strictly limited to vernal pools on hard, crystalline rock." It has red berrylike structures, but you don't need me to tell you that, since Lawson just did himself. Not sure I'd drink of these pools, but the orpine is all over Forty Acre Rock, and I found those vernal pools some of the loveliest microclimates I've ever seen. Take away the graffiti and this is very much like what Lawson would have seen.

Yes, the rock face is sadly covered in many places with graffiti, and Brent Burgin, the archivist at the Native American Studies Center of USC-Lancaster, who sometime later revisited with me and guided me around what he called one of his favorite places, wished aloud he could chase down some of the cretins who defaced the rock with their initials, just to see if they really did last 4-ever with whichever girlfriend those initials were. (He didn't call them cretins, by the way—that was me.)

Brent judged me worthy and took me off the beaten track to what he called the rock house, a place he promised I would never find on the Forty Acre Rock territory if left to my own devices. He provided this description, which originates in the 1802 *A View of South-Carolina*, which itself quotes "a gentleman who has lately travelled there":

> We proceeded on horseback along the low lands up the creek, proposing first to visit a place called the Rock-House. After having advanced two miles, we descried it at the head of a deep valley, in which we rode; a beautiful cascade of water tumbling from the side of the hill, on which this Rock-house stands. This spot is highly romantic. The rocks rise in rude piles above the valley, to the height of about two hundred and fifty feet; crowned occasionally with red cedar and savin. About half way up the hill, is the Rock-house, resembling the roof of an house. And at the lower end of it is an aperture, from which a small stream of clear water issues forth; falling over the rocks below, into the valley. We clambered up the side of the hill to the source of the cascade, and found the Rock-house to be composed of two large flat rocks, leaning against each other at top; forming a complete shelter from the sun and rains. The area of this shelter may be about ninety feet in circumference, remarkably dark and cool: and at bottom the stream forming the cascade, brawls along over the rocks, and approaches the steep part of the hill, precipitating down its side. Upon the whole, the cascade of Juan Fernandez, celebrated by circumnavigators, may be more beautiful; as that of Niagra is more grand and sublime; but still this rock and cascade would rank high in ornamental gardening with all those, who either for pleasure or pride covet the possession of these rare and natural beauties.

I will not debase this lovely description with unequal words of my own: "brawls along over the rocks"—who could write that? Lawson, perhaps, but he never saw it, and I would not have either, had I not had a generous guide. The state of South Carolina would love to create a trail leading to the rock house, but with the constant assaults on Forty Acre Rock by vandals, one can understand their reluctance to proceed. I agree, and thus I tell you about it—but I will not tell you how to get there.

The best part about this segment of the trek leading through boulders was that most wondrous of hiking souvenirs, a piece of stone. Every hiker picks up a pretty piece of quartz or some such as a lucky stone, and the right stone hadn't yet presented itself. The rules expressly forbid taking a piece out of a park of any sort, and most natural stones are where they are because Nature wants them there, and Nature I trust and try not to defy.

But in front of Georgia Stone on Flat Rock Road were large pieces of that granite set on edge to keep people from driving onto the property (or into the quarry, I think), and around them were countless tiny shards of rock. (A broken piece of old pottery, I learned later, is a sherd, or potsherd, not a shard; I'm pretty sure I'm right on the rock, though.) Without fear that I was defrauding Georgia Stone Industries, I gathered up a few. A couple went to my wife and sons. A small one (I was scarcely looking for much extra weight) walked with me the rest of the way along the Lawson Trek.

5 : The Anthropocene and the Catawba

For the third time in a day, as I walked by a pool of water collected in a ditch by the concrete conduit beneath a driveway I heard a plop. That third time I actually heard two plops, so I sat down on someone's grass and waited. Barely a minute or two went by before two round eyes and a brown head surfaced by a rock, and a moment later a much greener frog surfaced, eyeing me suspiciously and treading water.

The green one dove when I reached for my camera, but I got a grainy image of the brown one. The point was less the frogs than that I suddenly saw this as a specific ecosystem that I walked through, the habitat defined by these two-lanes and the exurban houses along them, the little swampy areas on either side of driveways where rain collects and swamp grasses grow. I knew this habitat—I began calling it the Anthropocene Suburban—and its main denizens.

Above, vultures, feasting on the deer, possums, and raccoons killed by the cars. Various hawks circle and cry. In the evening owls feast on squirrels, mice, and chipmunks. Crows feast on the roadkill, too. Woodpeckers, blue jays, titmice, chickadees, cardinals, robins, finches, mockingbirds, and the omnipresent cooing mourning doves you would instantly recognize. The puddles in drainages that last long enough develop the same frogs, dandelions, and tiny pale-blue bluets, along with ditch gentrifiers like broomsedge and needlerush. I felt like I was hiking through my backyard.

Scientists have only recently begun calling our era the Anthropocene (they haven't even determined yet what the identifying markers will be—tiny particles of plastic in sediment? Radioactive particles from nuclear fallout?), but on my walk it was impossible not to recognize it. I walked on roads, among managed fields, surrounded by flora and fauna that in every way demonstrated the influence of humanity on our world. I suddenly recognized this one day, researching the common buttercups that populated the roadside ditches and cheered me as I strode by. Buttercups, I came to learn, are invasive—sweet yellow buttercups, of almost any variety, crossed the Atlantic with settlers. Buttercups? Hold them under

The shore is unusual, but a vernal pool is a vernal pool.

your chin and pretend you turn yellow? Everybody's first flower? Yep. And you know what else? Dandelions. And clover.

The first three flowers I expect any American child can identify. They are the first interaction with nature we have — and immigrants to North America just like we are. No colonists? No buttercups. Seeds for ancestors of the plants I viewed may have come over in the creases of Lawson's trousers. Which is, partly, what makes Lawson so interesting. Not that he necessarily brought over a lot of free riders, but part of what Lawson allows us to do is think about what the world he walked through looked like. Lawson tried to document the world as he saw it for the scientific community back in Europe.

That is, "A Journal of a Thousand Miles Travel among the Indians, from South to North Carolina" is only the first portion of his 1709 book. It is by far the most engaging, with its natural narrative flow and engaging comments, but it is still only a part. Lawson also included a thorough "description of North-Carolina" and another section on its "Present

State." Both border on descriptions an eighteenth-century chamber of commerce would have favored: "fragrant Vines and Ever-greens, whose aspiring Branches shadow and interweave themselves with the loftiest Timbers, yielding a pleasant Prospect, Shade and Smell, proper Habitations for the Sweet-singing Birds, that melodiously entertain such as travel thro' the woods of *Carolina*." Hey, sounds like a nice place, huh? Funny you should mention it, I might be able to sell you some land. One remembers that by 1709, when Lawson wrote his book and published it in England, he was a model North Carolinian and had land to develop.

He also includes in his book "An Account of the Indians of North Carolina," and as detailed as his descriptions are of the settlements and tribes he encounters in his journey narrative, the discrete section goes into even more detail. He describes hunting and fishing practices ("The Herrings in March and April run a great way up the Rivers and fresh Streams to spawn, where the Savages make great Wares, with Hedges that hinder their Passage only in the Middle, where an artificial Pound is made to take them in"), their religious practices, and their basic character ("the *Indians* ground their Wars on Enmity, not in Interest, as the *Europeans* generally do"). Not for nothing do anthropologists still refer to Lawson's book when they trace the stories of the Carolina Natives.

But Lawson reserved special effort for a "Natural History of Carolina," his scientific listing and description of the flora and fauna he encountered during his years of residency. We know from letters in the British Museum that he eventually connected with the London collector James Petiver. We have several letters from Lawson to Petiver describing the samples Lawson sent to him, "always keeping one of a sort by me giving an account of ye time & day they were gotten, when they first appearing, wt soil of ground, wn the flower seed & disapear & wt. individuall uses the Indians or English make thereof." Much of what Lawson observed is straightforward—he describes oaks and pines, turkey and deer. And if he on occasion believes he sees the occasional "tiger," we can forgive him; he was, after all, on the edge of the known world. (Apart from the tyger that was part of the crowd of animals that howled the "frightful ditty" all night near Lawson's "amazing prospect," he describes an Indian guide shooting at one and mentions that the spaniel that accompanied their party raced off after it, only to turn tail and come back when the tyger stood its ground; one only wishes for the YouTube video it would have made. It was probably a panther or a bobcat.)

In any case, Lawson loved documenting that world. The samples he sent to Petiver remain in the *Hortus Siccus* books in the Natural History Museum in London, though they retain historical rather than biological interest; Lawson identified no unknown plant species, documented no surprising habitats. In fact, in what is now the Francis Marion State Forest he walked right through territory riddled with amazing carnivorous plants—pitcher plants and the tiny, brilliant gooey sundew—and never noticed them, much less brought them to what surely would have been the enraptured attention of collectors. (*Insectivorous plants*, the first major treatise on the topic, was not written until 1875, when a fellow named Charles Darwin finally got around to it; I saw the ones in the Marion because I traveled through there with an ecologist, who makes it her business to know about things like this.)

In contrast, of all his natural observations, Lawson's observations about birds still gather citations. For one thing, he saw two birds no modern ornithologist has seen: the Carolina parakeet and the passenger pigeon. The last passenger pigeon died in September 1914; a century later people commemorated that death and in so doing brought Lawson's name into the public discussion. It turns out Lawson left one of the best early descriptions of what monstrous flocks of pigeons looked like in 1701, when he wrote these words:

"In the mean time, we went to shoot Pigeons, which were so numerous in these Parts, that you might see many Millions in a Flock; they sometimes split off the Limbs of stout Oaks, and other Trees, upon which they roost o' Nights. You may find several Indian Towns, of not above 17 Houses, that have more than 100 Gallons of Pigeons Oil, or Fat; they using it with Pulse, or Bread, as we do Butter, and making the Ground as white as a Sheet with their Dung. The Indians take a Light, and go among them in the Night, and bring away some thousands, killing them with long Poles, as they roost in the Trees. At this time of the Year, the Flocks, as they pass by, in great measure, obstruct the Light of the day."

Surely these flocks became so enormous because the Indians, their main predators, were already much reduced by smallpox, guns, alcohol, and other calamities brought by the Europeans.

These Pigeons, about Sun-Rise, when we were preparing to march on our Journey, would fly by us in such vast Flocks, that they would be near a Quarter of an Hour, before they were all pass'd by; and as soon as that Flock was gone, another would come; and so successively one after another, for great part of the Morning. It is observable, that whereever these Fowl come in such Numbers, as I saw them then, they clear all before them, scarce leaving one Acorn upon the Ground, which would, doubtless, be a great Prejudice to the Planters that should seat there, because their Swine would be thereby depriv'd of their Mast.

John James Audubon, writing much later, said of a single passenger pigeon that it "passes like a thought" through the forest. A handsome devil called by Joel Greenberg, author of *A Feathered River across the Sky*, "a mourning dove on steroids," the passenger pigeon gathered in flocks of more than a billion that took days to pass overhead. Even so they were no match for industrialized hunting and eating. Flocks dwindled in the late nineteenth century, and the last passenger pigeon died in the Cincinnati Zoo in 1914.

Lawson had a bit less to say of the "parrakeetos," though he did note that they "were of a green Colour, and Orange-Colour'd half way their Head" and that, like alligators, they preferred South to North Carolina. "They visit us first, when Mulberries are ripe, which Fruit they love extremely." Fond of apples, he says, "they are mischievous to Orchards. They are often taken alive, and will become familiar and tame in two days. They have their Nests in hollow Trees, in low, swampy Ground." The Carolina parakeet, like the passenger pigeon, went extinct in the early twentieth century, though unlike the pigeon the parakeet wasn't killed by hungry Americans—it was just collateral damage to the destruction of its forest habitat for farmland.

Though Lawson's observations of those two extinct birds have been most widely noted, scholars have annotated Lawson's entire listing and description of the birds he saw. In a publication by the Carolina Bird Club called *The Chat*, one W. L. McAtee methodically proceeds through Lawson's descriptions of birds, noting that Lawson described everything from the hummingbird, a bird unlike any known to Europeans and to him "the Miracle of all our wing'd Animals. . . . He is feather'd as a Bird, and gets his Living as the Bees, by sucking the Honey from each Flower." Lawson met a six-foot-tall tame crane among the Congarees ("they take them before they can fly, and breed 'em as tame and familiar as a Dunghill Fowl"). He also noted the prosaic red-winged blackbirds and catbirds and cardinals, which he called red-birds—as many still do. And speaking of cardinals, Lawson mentions "the Weet, so call'd because he cries always before Rain." Lawson says the weet looks like the fire-tail, which

McAtee identifies with the European redstart, though I wonder. Among rural people even now I have heard, "it's going to rain — redbird says 'wet, wet, wet.'" Lawson's lovely descriptions share his feelings about mocking-birds, too, "held to be the Choristers of *America*. . . . They sing with the greatest Diversity of Notes, that is possible for a Bird to change to." Others tame them; Lawson prefers to leave the nests "they build yearly in my Fruit-Trees, because I have their Company, as much as if tame, as to the singing Part. They often sit upon our Chimneys in Summer . . . and sing the whole Evening and most part of the Night." He follows on to the brown thrasher, which he calls the "Ground-Mocking-Bird," but I go back time and again to his sweet description of the mockingbird. I sit in my own yard and listen to mockingbirds in the evening, though since my house lacks a chimney they instead sing their little hearts out atop utility poles. It's fun to list species and play "what did he mean?" It's more fun to remind myself that Lawson, like me, liked to sit quietly of an evening and counted himself lucky when serenaded by a mockingbird.

Lawson also may have been the first observer to describe the ivory-billed woodpecker, "as big as a [passenger] Pigeon, being of a dark brown Colour, with a white Cross on his Back, his Eyes circled with white, and on his Head stands a Tuft of beautiful Scarlet Feathers." The ivory-billed is now very likely extinct — much has been made in recent years of attempts to find one or two remaining, but no evidence has ever emerged. The pileated woodpeckers whose laughing cries entertained Katie and me in the swamps of the Francis Marion State Forest are its nearest relatives.

Comparing the past with today is foundational to science, and we do it all the time. Recent years have seen scientists return to the observations of Henry David Thoreau to document the effects of climate change by comparing the dates of the blossomings and migrations he saw to our current observations; to the works of environmentalist Aldo Leopold to document what he would have heard; to the Grinnell-Storer transect of Yosemite to see how the animal populations have changed in the century since the original observations. Climatologists have for years been returning to ships' logs to gather data from centuries ago about wind, temperature, and current. Just so, writers and observers have returned to Lawson's observations since long before I decided to take a walk.

::

But again: that sciencey nature stuff for Lawson came mostly after his grand adventure; in his "Journey of a Thousand Miles," he wrote more than anything else about the terrain he passed through and the people he visited.

Which was next for me. From the rocks on which Lawson and I had lunch, I continued north of Camden up the old Catawba Trail—Flat Rock Road—past the Hanging Rock Battlefield, near which a sign reminded me that on his famous southern tour in 1791 no less a personage than George Washington passed along that same path, staying in a nearby home. Animals, then Indians, explorers, settlers, soldiers, presidents, years of cars, and me. A road goes where the people go.

Having parked my car in Lancaster, the upstate South Carolina town I'd be making my home for a few days, I struck out confidently one morning looking for a ride eleven or so miles south to the little, barely there hamlet of Heath Springs, where I had left off walking north on my previous journey. Not long after I entered the hilly exurbs I saw Elgin Feed and Garden, a gray hulk with a peaked roof, a couple of grain silos, and a long low shed filled with feed, seed, tools, and of course the obligatory spring display of recently hatched chicks, fondled by adoring children (and, honestly, pretty much everyone). When I asked for a ride, someone went and found William Hinson, a man of seventy-seven wearing a green windbreaker and a Purina feed cap. He gladly rode me down to Heath Springs in his pickup, and he educated me on the way. He told me Elgin Feed and Garden deals mostly with "companion farms"— people who have "one horse or ten chickens." He laughed. Though as the land began getting rocky, many were fields punctuated by copses of trees grown around boulders in the middle, either too big to move or shoved together to clear the rest of the field for grazing. Cattle and poultry, Mr. Hinson said, were what the land produced now, along with the timber from the pine plantations that still cropped up; soybeans too, which we'd been seeing since Lake Marion. The bright green cover crop I saw springing up in sunlit fields was hay, he said.

Heath Springs had been a big town in its day. "They had two or three cotton buyers," he told me. "They'd gin it here and they'd float it down the river." That was long before Duke Energy dammed the Catawba, of course; up by Lancaster the river had changed its name to the Catawba. It's the same river we had been following from the start, but from Santee to Wateree to Catawba, it changed its name to suit its surroundings. Anyhow, Mr. Hinson said as he dropped me off, "that was in the old horse and buggy days."

No kidding. One of the first things I found after Hinson dropped

The story of Carolina textiles in one image.

me in the little one-intersection town of Heath Springs was the empty hulk of the old U.S. Textile Corporation plant—behind chain-link fence topped with barbed wire. That fit right in with what Hinson had been telling me: "Every town had a plant," he said. Not anymore.

Though Heath Springs was doing better than most, on account of Davis Neon, a factory that drew my interest and, when informed of that interest, introduced me to assistant plant manager Scott Helms, who toured me through. Davis doesn't make much neon anymore, but it does make most of the great big signs by auto dealerships you see all over the country. I saw enormous pieces of Honda, Chevy, and Kia signs as he led me through the plant, which employs 140 people, though Helms hoped that would climb to 200 before long. It's a great business—they ship all over the world, and it's all but certain you've driven by and perhaps bought a car beneath a Davis Neon–made sign.

But as nice as that story is, it pales when you compare it with that shuttered factory I saw—and the many more I saw as I continued to walk.

"When Springs Industries went away," Helms told me, "that was probably 3,000, 3,500 jobs. My father-in-law used to say if you lived in Lancaster County and you never worked for Springs, you were the anomaly." The textile giant shuttered its plants around Lancaster in 2008, and since then textile jobs themselves are the anomaly. Jobs at textile plants once formed a second core—along with farming—of the Carolina economy. Whether through automation or relocation, those jobs too are largely gone. That empty textile plant in Heath Springs, moldering brick behind barbed wire, was like the abandoned houses we had begun passing. Artifacts of the culture whose collapse preceded our journey like that of the Indians preceded Lawson's.

:::

And I was walking into territory at this point that had tales to tell about those Indians—and about the land itself. Lancaster had a history as a textile town and had suffered the same decline, but it had bolstered its downtown with the Native American Studies Center, part of the University of South Carolina–Lancaster. Built on Main Street in 2012, the center houses an impressive collection of artifacts and records of South Carolina's various tribes, especially the Catawba. Brent Burgin, the center's archivist, and archaeologist Chris Judge, its assistant director, took me in and introduced me around.

The day I arrived there happened to be a meeting of representatives of local tribes, so my first meeting at the center involved sitting in on a group of tribal leaders discussing the nuts and bolts of modern Indian life—Chris discussed the complexities of cell phone towers, for which many tribes rented out land to companies and wanted to make sure the companies knew how to build them without running afoul of various laws and regulations meant to protect Indian artifacts. "What if it's a sacred site that we don't want disturbed?" one leader asked. Another chimed in: "Five years ago Duke [Energy] dug up graves and used the bones in the roadbed." The answer to everything was, as usual, it depends. If you're nationally recognized, like the Catawba, you have more options. If you don't, like, for example, the Pee Dee Indians (who worked for twenty-nine years before they were finally recognized by the state of South Carolina), or the Santees I had met near the coast, you have a lot more work to do. "It's been frustrating for seventy years," Chief Carolyn Chavis Bolton of the Pee Dees told me. "And we still can't prove nothing" to the satisfaction of the federal government.

After the meeting, chiefs cheerfully chatted with me. Earl Carter, of the Lumbee people whose struggles for governmental recognition are legendary, told me about his duties as a firekeeper. "We have a fire ceremony every quarter," he told me. "I tell people how to go or how to stand. I can go ahead and build a fire in the pouring down rain. I tell them about natural medicine—what's a weed and what ain't a weed."

He paused a beat.

"And ain't nothing a weed," he said, his eyes crinkling.

Out front, in the center's display room, exquisite Catawba pottery fills cases, and black-and-white photographs of cabins in which Catawba families lived in hard times hang on the walls. The displayed pottery was simple and clean, with a mottled tan, gray, black, and brown color for which the Catawbas are famous. Catawba potters build their pieces either by pinching or coiling, eventually smoothing them with river stones and sometimes impressing textures onto the surface—fabrics, shells, even bottles and cans. Archaeologists can identify different tribes and trade routes by finding artifacts with different surface patterns. Catawba potters find their clay in special places by the riverside that they share with nobody not in the tribe—a fact emphasized by almost every person with whom I discussed Catawba pottery. The pots are open-fired traditionally: warmed near the fire, then brought progressively nearer the center until finished, then moved back out. The Catawbas do not glaze their pottery, so without the smoothing glaze their objects retain that variegated surface, showing each pot's individual journey from clay pit, through hands and fire. Catawba pots are famous now, both a handcraft lovingly preserved through the centuries and a simple living for many a remaining tribe member when most other opportunities have been lost.

:::

But I'm ahead of my story. In the Native American Studies Center I had lost myself among the pots, while various other conversations occurred, when I realized that in a separate gallery someone was speaking publicly. The voice of a woman was sharing her experiences with the Catawbas, discussing her feelings about their relationship with the earth, with their crops. To be honest she seemed to be laying it on a little thick, as non-Indians sometimes do in their descriptions of indigenous people. I hung around the edge of the crowd and was getting ready to drift away when a response stopped me. The speaker had been talking about the Catawba heart, and the land, and she had said that their spiritual relationship to something or other was the heartbeat of the country. A fellow near the back said, "No, that's Chevrolet."

The woman stopped a moment, nonplussed. I looked at the man who had spoken. Wearing a denim shirt, tight black jeans, and turquoise earrings, he had his thick, shiny black hair done into twin tight braids, one cascading over each shoulder, framing the necklace of turquoise beads that hung on his chest. If I'm being honest, he could not have looked more like the white person's stereotype of an Indian if he had been gazing at roadside litter with a single tear coursing down his cheek. The woman looked at him, and he smiled. "Chevrolet is the heartbeat of America," he said. "Haven't you seen the commercial?"

The woman gave a wan smile and returned to her presentation. As for me, I had a new favorite person. His name was Jered Canty, and he was at that moment engaged in a campaign to be elected assistant chief of the Catawbas. He shook my hand and happily agreed to meet me at the tribe's reservation the next day.

:::

We met me at the Catawba longhouse, a wide octagonal meeting place with stacked stone walls supporting a low, sloping roof. The meeting room holds 350 or so, he told me, and the rest of the building contains tribal administration. In black dress pants, a burnt-orange button-down shirt, and those same braids from the day before, with his tribe identification hanging around his neck on a lanyard strung with turquoise beads, Jered wore much of what he had the previous day. But on closer investigation the symbol at the end of his turquoise-studded lanyard turned out to be the Carolina Panthers NFL logo.

Lawson stopped among the Catawbas (and the surrounding peoples who were then or eventually part of the Catawba tribe), and he provides the best description of the Indians of the Carolina Piedmont that we have for this period. In this territory Lawson seems to truly fall in love with his Indian hosts. Near here, Lawson says, "We took off our Beards with a Razor, the Indians looking on with a great deal of Admiration. They told us, they had never seen the like before, and that our Knives cut far better than those that came amongst the Indians. They would fain have borrow'd our Razors, as they had our Knives, Scissors, and Tobacco-Tongs, the day before, being as ingenious at picking of Pockets, as any, I believe, the World affords; for they will steal with their Feet."

To me this passage tells as much about the Indians—and Lawson's experience among them—as any other in the book. Surely his early passages describing funeral traditions and dancing displays give wonderful information, but here he shares details about the actual interaction between Lawson, his company, and his hosts. They're fooling around, they're getting into mix-ups, they're laughing it up. Lawson forever describes the Indians as a laughing people—they laugh even in tragedy like fire, so long as nobody has been killed. In a rare counterexample Lawson shares how many chiefs—or kings, as he calls them—offer "trading girls" for the comfort of his party. When they refused this kindness from the Catawba king, Lawson says "his Majesty flew into a violent Passion, to be thus slighted, telling the *Englishmen*, they were good for nothing." A previous night went more according to custom, when one of Lawson's party bartered with such a young woman, only to wake up in the middle of the night relieved of everything he had been carrying, including his shoes. Here, laughing with him at the loss of all the material the company had planned to use for barter of food and lodging, the Indians nonetheless find another pair of moccasins for the humiliated trader and cheerfully send them on their way. This gives a sense of the camaraderie of Lawson's trip, possibly best exemplified by Lawson's description of a simple and common show of respect. In a house Lawson mentions meeting a war captain, at which point "the Man of the House scratch'd this War-Captain on the shoulder, which is look'd upon as a very great Compliment among them." Among Cherokee we know of rituals involving scratching as body art, and Lawson may mean this, though perhaps not. He later likens it to handshaking as one of few niceties among Indians: "They are free from all manner of Compliments, except Shaking of Hands, and Scratching on the Shoulder, which two are the greatest Marks of Sincerity and Friendship, that can be shew'd one to another." I posit this as the exact cognate of the modern manly man hug, characterized by handshake, quick embrace, and two sharp pats on the back. It's a way of greeting, embracing, and honoring, all quick, all over in a second.

:::

The story of the Catawba reservation—the story of the Catawbas—is in many ways a distillation of the opposite, of all the things that could go badly for the Indians, all the different ways European contact could spell disaster for tribes. When I met up with Jered at the Long House on the Catawba reservation, I was looking at one result of a $50 million settlement the U.S. government paid to the Catawba people in 1993. It's a long story, and the first thing my notes tell me Jered said was, "It's not official until you have it on ink and paper."

So true. Okay, in brief: As Lawson makes his way north from the flat rock, he runs into tribe after tribe of Indians that all share some version of the Catawba Siouan language and end up, before much longer, being part of the Catawba tribe. According to various censuses either taken or calculated before Lawson's time, the Catawbas were the biggest tribe in the Piedmont, numbering 6,000 or so members in the century before Lawson came. Nearby tribes—the Sugerees, Waterees, Congarees, Waxhaws, all mentioned by Lawson as he moves through—probably numbered another couple of thousand, though all would have been depleted by the time Lawson showed up, victims of the four riders of the Settler Apocalypse: slavery, disease, dispossession, and alcohol. By Lawson's time their number may have dropped to below 2,000, according to a chart in the Native American Study Center. By the time of King Hagler, whose story we had learned in Camden, the number of Catawbas had probably diminished to less than a thousand. So when in 1760 Hagler managed to get the Crown to cede title to 144,000 acres of land, fully supported by survey and deed, that seemed like a godsend to the remnants of the tribes that were by then fully banded together as Catawbas. (The original name of the group was *yeh is'wah h'reh*, meaning people of the river; Lawson mentions the Esaws, which were probably a part of the people, though he talks of the Catawbas, too; it was a complicated time.)

That may seem like a raw deal for a tribal confederation that had held much of the central Carolinas, but signing a treaty actually gave the ragged end of the Catawbas—devastated by repeated smallpox outbreaks and fights with other tribes—a weapon to use against settlers very hard to persuade to stop farming Catawba land: "They say they will continue to do so," Hagler said, "unless we show them a paper to restrain them." As historian James Merrell said, the arrival of a surveyor "with sextant and chain—and paper—marked a victory for the Nation, not a defeat." Of course, since the lingering Catawbas could never defend their land against Europeans who wanted to settle on it, they began trusting that power of ink on paper and leasing portions of it to settlers, in the hope they could coexist in that way.

Yeah, right. As more settlers leased more land and the time of Indian Removal came in the early 1800s, Catawbas had less and less control of their land and less and less likelihood of regaining it. In 1840 what was left of the tribe agreed to a treaty with the state of South Carolina, yielding all claim to their territory for $5,000. "They are, in effect, dissolved," said then-governor David Johnson. As it would turn out, the federal government never bothered to ratify the treaty. In 1934, with the Indian Reorganization Act, the United States began trying to develop a more reasonable Indian policy, though by the mid-1940s the country had reverted to old habits and adopted the aptly if horrifically named policy of termination. Indians were encouraged to leave reservations, tribes were declared dissolved, and their land was absorbed by the federal government. In 1959 the United States officially ceased to recognize the Catawba tribe. In 1973 organized Catawbas began to fight back—emerging from hiding, from diaspora, and from poverty much like the Santees Peggy Scott described to us and filing for recognition. Because the federal government never signed that 1840 treaty, all kinds of legal wrangling led in 1993 to the Catawbas once again attaining not just federal recognition but a settlement of $50 million for the government's failure to protect the tribe. The current reservation, across the Catawba River and northwest of Lancaster, contains less than five square miles.

:::

So how's that for backstory, helping you to understand the path Jered Canty, candidate for assistant chief of the Catawba tribe, chose to walk when he welcomed me and Brent Burgin of the Native American Study Center to the Catawba reservation to share part of an afternoon. He showed me his Catawba Tribal enrollment card, making the point nearly every Indian person I met made about the indignity of Indians having to prove their identities. Then he added a surprising twist: The card actually felt good sometimes. "Man—to get a card" in 1993, when the tribe finally received federal recognition? "I didn't know what to think. It was mindblowing. It's like a culture shock. Somebody was finally recognizing your culture, your people. When you witness that, finally getting acceptance when you've only been talked about on Thanksgiving." He hesitated a moment. A people all but eradicated has come back and reestablished itself. "History tells a tale of itself, you know?"

He showed me around the longhouse—the octagonal room, the one that defines the building from the outside, can hold 350 people, and he describes when the powwows finally left Winthrop University and moved there the way Peggy Scott described the first Santee dance on their own land. "Having your *own*," he murmured. "Having your own." Still, he disabused me of any notion that the land, and the longhouse, and the settlement had turned his poor, struggling people to sudden prosperity. "The settlement never reached any of us because of greed and corruption and power," he said. Same as everywhere.

We spoke as we walked, heading away from the longhouse and down a trail to the Catawba River. The Catawbas are called the people of the river, and yet Canty didn't talk to me of old Catawba paths; he told me the trail we were walking had once been an old wagon trail. I learned later that the Catawbas who had lived on that riverside land for centuries had in the twentieth century managed a ferry across the river from one road to another, making a living with what the river afforded. The mud for the famous Catawba pottery comes from the riverbanks here, though exactly where each potter has their own spot, no potter will tell you; it's a secret sometimes passed on through generations, all the way back to Catawba potters Lawson might have met.

It was a cloudy day and not hot, so the walk down to the river was fine, first along a wide path that made a nice view of the river from the longhouse (they call it the Avenue of the Nations), and then that wagon road along the river. The river was low and very wide; it chattered amiably over rocks as Canty, Burgin, and I walked past weathered barns, pastures full of horses, and long stretches of forest. The reservation features several walking trails, both along the river and around a loop by the cultural center, where it winds past a re-creation of one of the round cabins favored by southeastern Indians. "Wigwams," Lawson describes them, "or Cabins built of Bark, which are made round like an Oven, to prevent any Damage by hard Gales of Wind. They make the Fire in the middle of the House, and have a Hole at the Top of the Roof right above the Fire, to let out the Smoke." Lawson describes the structural poles as the "Thickness of the Small of a Man's Leg," which is about exactly the size of the poles bent over on the reservation. Lawson talks about the heat of the wigwams, and as we walked by the wigwam frame Canty told me that the tribe still uses them for sweats, which normally take four rounds and should not be undertaken by people who don't know what they're doing. He spoke of retreats involving sweats and what he called "morning songs, canoe songs—songs that give back to the river."

He also spoke of giving back to his tribe. Before running for assistant chief, he had been away to college, traveled to the Southwest, married a Diné (Navajo) woman. As his Indian identity strengthened, he felt the call to come back. "I guess what brought me back was so many of my elders kept passing away." There are around 3,400 Catawba now, and he wants to help a new generation of leaders emerge. "I just want whoever wins to step up"—himself or someone else. "If you don't keep that enthusiasm your tribe is lost."

"People think tribes are gone from here," he said. "They think we were wiped out." Proving them wrong takes a lot of work, so he and Burgin left me at the river, both returning to jobs helping create that proof. I sat by the river for a long time on the path, sitting on a Catawba dock, on a Catawba trail, on Catawba land, from a tribe that had come back from nothing. Lawson had met them as they dwindled. I hoped I was meeting them as they were renewed.

:::

The land the Catawbas now had was the tiniest fragment of land they had once had, and in the Native American Study Center in Lancaster hung, in a frame, one of the leases by which it had been taken from them—from 1811, a lease between one Andrew King and "Indian Chiefs." It's old and yellow and bears the weight of history—it's wrinkled like the Declaration of Independence—but it's got beautiful penmanship and takes you right back to that moment, when some settler convinced some beleaguered chief or chiefs into making a mark on paper ("make Paper speak, which they call our Way of Writing," Lawson says later) and poof, there goes another 1,000 acres, or 10,000, gone.

Which helped connect me not just to Catawba history, on their new reservation, but to the history of the land they no longer hold. You want to know how things have changed since Lawson's time? Look at the land; if I learned anything on the Lawson Trek it's that it all comes down to the land.

Walking north out of Camden left no doubt we were in the midlands, the Piedmont of South Carolina. In Camden we had noticed that the walk into town from the south had been almost completely flat but that the walk out of town to the north had enough rolling hills that you might not notice them as you walked but you would notice morning fog settling in the low places. We saw the land shift from pure loam and clay to rock. We noticed we had begun regularly passing enormous boulders, which just like the lay of the land help determine the land's use.

But for the clearest indication of how a culture has changed look at what's come next, and the place to do that is the Ivy Place, a few miles up the Catawba River from Lancaster. A fellow named Adam Ivy bought that land in the 1840s, after the Treaty of Nations Ford stripped the

Catawbas of any remaining rights to it. In 1850 Ivy built the enormous clapboard home that still stands there, supposedly using as capital gold dust from western Carolina mines. In 1888 he sold it to James Nisbet, a New York physician with local roots who bought Ivy Place as a homestead, then retired to it in the 1920s, turning it into a dairy farm. It remained a farm until the 1950s; descendants of Nisbet still own it, renting it as an event venue. But the Ivy Place is more than just that beautiful 1850 house, barns, pick-your-own strawberry patches, and a great facility you can rent for weddings.

The Ivy Place is surrounded by land—empty land, and that emptiness is its future as well as its present. Because its owners have placed a conservation easement on it through the Katawba Valley Land Trust, the Ivy Place will never be developed. It will continue to be a working venue, and the family will own it, use it for its own purposes, farm strawberries and pine trees and beef cattle, host events—but the land will never be developed. If you want to know what that means, you can pull up an image on Google Maps, centering the image on the Ivy Place. On the lower left of the image is the Catawba reservation; across the river is Ivy Place and other land owned by the Nisbet family. North of that is what happens to land without conservation easements.

Sun City Carolina Lakes is a development for adults fifty-five and older, and it could not be more different from the landscape it replaced. A map of it looks like a pile of dropped spaghetti, and a drive through it is the famous Malvina Reynolds song "Little Boxes" come to life, only the boxes are big. It's a golf course community, so there's green there, but otherwise think mostly beige and gray. It's every modern, clear-cut, lot-maximizing development you've ever seen, and only the fact that it caters solely to older adults spares it from the irony of sending its children to Indian Lands High School, which borders it. A very brief visit makes you yearn to see territory that still feels like it's wearing clothes the earth itself might put on it to feel comfortable. It makes you want to see the land of the Ivy Place.

To see that land, we spent a morning walking with Jimmy White (a member of the Nisbet family), Barry Beasley of the Land Trust, and Chris Judge of the Native American Studies Center. We walked along the Catawba River, at least a quarter mile wide and rarely more than knee deep; we saw bluffs of Piedmont granite overlooking the river. We saw eagles nesting in snags, the sites of old Catawba and Waxhaw towns (excavated by archaeologists from the University of North Carolina), the remains of an old mill, and piles and piles of empty plastic bottles and other flotsam that comes down the Sugar Creek, which drains Charlotte and enters the Catawba just upstream. Barry told us that one dedicated and public-spirited paddler has pulled more than 17,000 basketballs out of the Catawba in recent years, evidence of its urban character—especially the Sugar.

"It's the typical story," Barry told us of the land. "People move into the panhandle [the rural portion of Lancaster County also called Indian Land] for a better quality of life." As more people come, the sprawl they fled follows them. "Now it's Charlotte," Chris says of the way northern Lancaster County has connected to the Charlotte amoeba.

Which was why Jimmy was so pleased as he walked us through the territory his family owns (and even some his family sold, though with easements on it protecting the river). Until the late 1950s the Catawbas operated a one-car ferry where Route 5 now crosses the river, but the new bridge ended that. The more than three miles of riverside the Nisbets own at least give open land a fighting chance. Jimmy walked us to a site that had once been a Catawba town, and doing nothing more energetic than idly kicking around dirt he unearthed eighteenth-century pottery fragments that he gave to me—a connection with centuries past. We walked along old double-track that was part of the old Catawba Trail. "Old Town was on this high spot," Jimmy White said. "It was Waxhaws," a group also known as Flatheads from their practice of binding their infants to boards, their heads pressed in front and behind with bags of sand: "It makes the Eyes stand a prodigious Way asunder," Lawson says, "and the Hair hang over the Forehead like the Eves of a House, which seems very frightful: They being ask'd the Reason why they practis'd this Method, reply'd, the Indian's Sight was much strengthened and quicker, thereby, to discern the Game in hunting." Jim White told me Catawba potters still travel to the protected riverside to gather clay for their pots— and because of his easement, they'll never have to stop. They'll always have access to that land.

Not that the land I saw, with lovely second-growth forest and old mills and town sites and such, would have been as it is now when Lawson passed. "The coastal plain would've been magnificent longleaf pine forests," Barry reminded us, as we followed old Waxhaw paths and double-tracks as old as horse and buggies along the conserved land. And the land along the river would have been corn—plenty of it, and healthy, according to Lawson: "Here were Corn-Stalks in their Fields as thick as the Small of a Man's Leg," he says of this area. "And they are ordinarily to be seen."

Not that it's wrong to develop housing subdivisions, mind you, or that it's wrong to sell your land when your land is your only resource. But what the Land Trust does, with families like the Nisbets, is preserve an earth that can retain its memories of the Lawsons and Waxhaws and Catawbas (and Nisbets) of this world.

:::

Before I left Lancaster I again visited the Native American Studies Center. I spoke with Beckee Garris, a smiling Catawba woman with long, full white hair and a radiant energy who pointed out that one of the large black-and-white photos on the gallery wall showed her grandmother's house. "I still wait for her to step out onto the porch," she told me. She works at the center, she works on the reservation at the Catawba Cultural Center, and she teaches reservation kids the Catawba language. "Natchedeha," she said to me in greeting ("I am happy to see you") and described the thrill of teaching Catawba children she described as multicultural, given the intermarrying among tribes and among the various marginalized peoples who survived together through centuries on the fringes. "Hearing them count to ten in Catawba," she said, smiling and shaking her head. "They know about thirty animal names. And the very first one they learned was the *dipindatlaksouksouk*," the Catawba word for chipmunk. Her obvious joy in teaching reminded me of something Jered Canty had said: "Once you lose your language, your culture is gone."

The Catawbas — and the Sewees, the Santees, the Waterees, the Congarees, the Sugerees, the Waxhaws — aren't gone. I felt that like Lawson I had been running an accommodating, welcoming gauntlet of the once-dispossessed. And of course it's not just the Indians whose traditional lifestyles have been altered. I spent my last hours in Lancaster walking the streets, which despite the improvements the Studies Center has brought to downtown still seemed stark and empty. A little wandering away from center had me glumly mulling the complexity of our world when I crunched into the gravel parking lot of a whitewashed cinderblock roadhouse, with an iron signpost from which hung only an empty frame. Signs adjured me not to block the driveway or loiter but urged me to consider a cold beer. The sun was hot, and that did seem like a good idea.

Inside I made the acquaintance of Larry Tidwell and James Ballard, one behind the bar and one at the bar, though my notes don't make clear which was which. A dollar got me a can of Bud out of a cooler. Ice chips slid down the side as I sipped, and I am not sure I have ever enjoyed a beer more. "In the days that we was coming up there were more people that cared about stuff than there is now," Ballard told me. "All around you was mills . . . jobs everywhere, when I was coming up." He was born and raised near Heath Springs, and he said he still preferred that country life. "I like it like that, myself," he said. "It's no aggravation." Lancaster had become a bedroom community for Charlotte, he said—his two sons worked in Charlotte. "Most of the business is on the bypass now," he said.

The three of us sat amiably for a while, and then Tidwell—I think— left to go to work. Ballard and I remained in companionable silence, drinking out of cans and watching a ceiling fan rotate against the heat of a late spring day. The open front door was a bright rectangle against the dim wall at the front of the bar, the black-and-white linoleum floor visible at the doorway and then fading into the darkness of the interior. In the quiet I bought another beer. After a while it was time for me to go, and I did.

6 : The Paths and the Rivers

sat at a picnic table across from Dale Loberger, a specialist in geographical information systems or GIS, who is also a living history practitioner—that is, he dresses in period garb and reenacts seventeenth- and eighteenth-century techniques of surveying and mapmaking. That day, Dale wore a tricornered hat and wool period clothing, having woken up in a mid-eighteenth century tent. He planned to spend the rest of the day teaching me to use period surveying tools. I had met Dale when I attended a lecture he gave on the practice of finding old roads. Then when I was just beginning my journey I shared on social media a picture of the absurd pile of twenty-first-century outdoors accoutrements I planned to haul in the canoe on my first venture out; tents, backpack, compasses, knives, water bottles, and on and on. It took up most of my living room. In response Dale tweeted a photograph of what he expected would have been Lawson's kit, and it all fit on a three-by-three table: gun and powder, shoulder bag, knife, notebook, hatchet, sewing kit, water bag, spoon. That was about it. From our correspondence I had gathered I would have much to learn from Dale, and when I asked he packed up his equipment and came camping.

But some days historical accuracy doesn't cut it. That wet and humid morning by the picnic table Dale tried manfully to get a fire going with flint and steel and char cloth. No luck. For that matter we couldn't even make fire with my lighter, though when we finally used Dale's candle we got things going. Dale cooked sausage and onions and potatoes, which he prepared, served, and ate using no other utensil than his knife. I made coffee on my gas campstove.

Dale practices living history, but he's not a fool. In between starting fire and eating with his knife like a proper explorer, Dale took calls for work on his cell phone and at one point pulled out his laptop to send someone a spreadsheet. Meanwhile I documented everything with my phone and then sat and typed with my keyboard and tablet. This felt far from inauthentic—it felt perfectly true and valid. We were living people in the early twenty-first century, and even if Dale wore period dress, I focused not on reenacting Lawson's project but on doing what Lawson

Lawson was right: Carolina country is delicious country.

did: walking, talking to people, looking around and seeing what's out there. The food Dale cooked that morning tasted like the fire. My coffee tasted like plastic. "If Lawson had only had mobile hotspots," Dale said. He could have live-tweeted his trip.

The next leg of my travels took me from Lancaster into Pineville, North Carolina, about thirty-two miles, and it wasn't always pleasant walking. Along two lanes north of Lancaster I found farms with little donkeys anxious for an ear scratch rubbing against fences; sometimes even a pasture of goats or a few head of cattle. Enormous purple bull thistle buds sported halos of dew in the morning, and the irregular petals of hairy skullcap threw more purple among the green leaves. There were yellow sneezeweeds, with multiple daisy-like heads at waist-height when I wandered through hunting territory, and great carpets of yellow cinquefoils and buttercups and thistles and sunflowers and dandelions when I walked the roads. It was like a convention for yellow. I crossed several little creeks and walked along rusted metal fencing held up by old wooden posts, and there's not much lovelier and more peaceful than that. I walked through a hunting preserve and left my name in a bound log protected by a little hut, where hunters announced their presence in nearby stands. I wished them luck.

The tiny towns remained the same: abandoned houses of varying ages—some too young to be so empty. Wooden clapboard with paint chipping off and sorrowful swings hanging on empty porches; tin roofs long gone to rust. Empty cinderblock buildings, their stores or diners or garages long emptied of customers; two-story brick strips of storefronts or apartments, empty windows staring blindly; enormous lots and warehouses with signs advertising auctions long past, and that saddest of all signs, in the middle of a weed-choked parking lot that hasn't held cars for decades: "Available."

Worse, I walked for a long time on U.S. Route 521, a four-lane divided highway with no sidewalks that was among the most dispiriting routes I had to fight my way along, hoping to stay alive against cars racing by utterly unprepared to see a lone figure trudging along a roadway designed for them and not for me. Still—when I found little vernal pools, I sat and watched tadpoles. I crossed into and out of North Carolina a couple of times as the route wiggled along the big right angle of southern North Carolina, where the boundary, heading west, suddenly strikes due north for a while. I looked forward to understanding why that was.

:::

Enter Dale. I met him at the Andrew Jackson State Park, on the exact borderline between the two states, which is still, as it happens, occasionally debated and disputed in court. "It's a long story," Dale told me, and no kidding. The Carolina province split in two because its southern portion focused on the port of Charleston; the Virginia settlers, often growing tobacco, who had spread south from the Tidewater and began settling on the Albermarle Sound had goals and needs far closer to those of Virginia than to those of their fellow Carolinians. Over time it became clear that something had to give. The Lords Proprietor tried to solve the problem in 1691, giving the north a deputy governor, but he only nominally reported to Charleston and separate legislatures and court systems continued to grow. Separation among the settlers was asserting itself even in Lawson's time—Lawson himself describes his journey as going from Charleston to North Carolina, an entity that at that point did not exist on paper. (Lawson's book is considered its first public mention; the

Lords Proprietor began officially treating the governors of North and South Carolina as equals in 1712.)

When nobody agrees on who's in charge, land and boundaries remain very much in flux. The boundary between the two Carolinas was not settled until centuries later. Even now occasional reconsiderations abruptly move people from one state to the other. (The boundary's sudden jerk northward near Charlotte, by the way, came because the Catawbas had in 1763 signed that treaty, so the boundary kept all the Catawba land in South Carolina. In fact, at one point during our days camping together Dale, a surveyor in his very soul, led me to a stone marking that corner set down in 1813 in one of the many herky-jerky attempts by the two states to get things right.)

That's the kind of thing you get from Dale. The first time we met, in Raleigh, months earlier, he dressed in his nineteenth-century surveyor's garb, which included a top hat. There he described his interest in uncovering the old roads in the Charlotte area where he lives: the Great Wagon Road, the Trading Path, and other ancient trails that led through the area. As someone skilled in GIS, Dale knew how to take the old maps he was familiar with and link them to modern maps, but he still wondered how he could find his way to the actual spots where the original roads lay.

In the seventeenth and eighteenth centuries, Dale said, something like the Great Wagon Road "was less a name than a description." The road referred to various ways leading, in general, from Philadelphia in the Northeast down into Georgia, generally following the eastern edge of the Appalachians—and, not coincidentally, also following the Trading Path, which had existed before the Wagon Road, and the animal paths that existed before that. Roads were mobile things in those days before significant paving—they moved to accommodate new towns, to avoid swamps or ditches, to solve the needs of new kinds of wagons.

The maps were meant to be nothing like we think of maps now, he said, and returning to old maps to try to get specific pathways is a game of "teasing information from maps never designed to give that information." "The map is not the territory," Alfred Korzybski famously said in 1931, but that wasn't news to Lawson or people of his time.

To understand those maps, Dale learned to survey. Most educated men of the eighteenth century, he said, would have learned surveying— less as a job skill than as a way to truly learn math and computation. And Lawson, who in 1709 became surveyor general of the Carolina colony, surely knew surveying. Surveying in those days, Dale has learned, often

Dale Loberger demonstrates the surveying methods of Lawson's time.

focused to a level of detail no greater than a single link in a surveyor's chain (7.92 inches) or even a single surveyor's pole (16.5 feet). I found this a wonderful relief. Once you realize that the original surveyors of the territory figured that three person-lengths was close enough, you're going to feel a little foolish trying to apply your phone's calculation of your position in degrees to fourteen decimal points.

But Dale didn't give up. "These are not documents of truth," he says of old maps. "They're documents full of secrets." He reasoned that the roads drawn on early maps were closer to legend images, like picnic tables for parks or big question marks for information centers, than actual representations of specific paths: all they did was say, "Charlotte and Salisbury are connected by road," not "the road from Charlotte to Salisbury looks like this." Just the same, the paths had to exist—and if they did, they'd do what roads always did. They'd go the easiest way possible from significant point to significant point—village, watering hole, mountain pass—following the most sensible path: choosing rocky places where you can easily ford a creek, following dry ridges where you can avoid insects and moisture without constantly climbing and descending, traversing open land where you didn't have to wrestle through underbrush.

So Dale turned to modern maps. The Natural Resources Conservation Service, he saw, rates soils for various purposes — including limitations on utility for paths and trails. He realized that hydric soils — those formed under conditions of wetness — would make for bad roads, given that the wet conditions may remain. Soils indicative of thick undergrowth during formation would give the same hint: why would people — or animals — wrestle through the brush if they could easily avoid it? Same with hilly terrain — horses and wagons are just as dangerous on slopes as an eighteen-wheeler, so Dale included slope, soil type, proximity to landmarks, and other elements as he began to develop a sort of diagnostic tool for terrain. It ranks places on a 0–10 scale for road suitability. And as he's begun to apply it to old maps and old descriptions — he hasn't published his results yet — he's found, at least anecdotally, that his method works. He's followed likely clues and had them lead directly to centuries-old granite way-markers, both by the side of forgotten roads and built into fences. That level of investigative acumen has helped Dale (and others like him) know exactly where the Trading Path went.

Because I was so interested in the path, the gear Lawson would have carried, and the methods Lawson would have used to survey the territory, I convinced Dale to join me on the trail, which is how we found ourselves sharing breakfast at a campground on that damp morning. Having, mind you, a breakfast that was by far the best I enjoyed on the entire trail. (And the trail began many mornings with bacon-egg-and-cheese biscuits from tiny local grills, so that's saying something.) The potatoes-au-hunting-knife were made better by what followed it: A lesson into surveying as Lawson would have done it. "You're going to buy land, you've got to know whether you're getting what you're paying for," Dale said of the gentlemanly art of surveying. "It was a practical skill that taught you all these concepts."

:::

The first thing I learned about surveying was, counterintuitively, what backbreaking work it was. Surveying, especially of the newly divided land early colonial surveyors like Lawson would have surveyed, addressed land that was usually covered with scrub, so just hacking your way through the brush took enormous effort. Then place yourself in Carolina, where it was nice and hot most of the year, to say nothing of the bugs. Take a big honking knife, start whacking away, and there you are: surveying.

Next, amazingly, was how much surveying was done by people who didn't know the math. The surveyor would use complex equipment like the circumferentor, a surveyor's compass that enabled the surveyor to sight a distant object through slots called an alidade. But the hacking away and the holding of distant poles would have been done by his assistant, who would stand where the surveyor told him and perhaps blaze a tree, stone, or other object while the surveyor noted on the circumferentor the exact angle to the object from his starting point. Then the surveyor would carry his equipment—a tripod and his circumferentor—to the spot, send his assistant to the next spot he wanted to sight, then begin again.

Meanwhile, the chain gang—they were actually called that—would take a surveyor's chain and measure the distance from point to point. A surveyor's chain was sixty-six feet long and consisted of 100 links, and the chain gang measured to the nearest link. With the surveyor measuring angles to the nearest degree and the chain gang measuring distance to the nearest link, there was plenty of wiggle room, but when your landmarks are inherently nonpermanent things like trees, close enough will do. Dale demonstrated all this to me in a clearing by a picnic shelter at the state park, bending over his equipment and taking sights in his wool jacket and tricornered hat. I held the pole and measured the chain. Dale also demonstrated the use of a plane table, with which surveyors could take sightings from two chosen positions and end up with a perfect map of a vast area without leaving those two spots.

The point is this: using technology available in 1700 and mathematics he would surely have known, Lawson was able to determine his position and, later, when he became surveyor general, parcel out land and design the towns of Bath and New Bern. As a developer, he became part of the land-grubbing tide of Europeans dispossessing the Indians of their land, but for the moment let's look past that. Let's focus on Lawson, a man of his time, who had the tools and understanding to stride out into the countryside and figure it out.

An even more fundamental point Dale taught me was the essential do-ability of all this stuff. It wasn't magic—it didn't require modern total stations and thousands of dollars of computing equipment. It didn't require a portable computer and a series of satellites ringing the Earth. It required only the mathematics a young gentleman would know, a few pieces of equipment, and a little bit of want-to. You and I could do all of it with a pocket compass, a pencil, a pad, and a tape measure and come up with maps and measures that weren't ridiculous. The world is amazing; the world is understandable. When Lawson wandered the world, people hadn't yet forgotten that you could understand it so well by using mostly your brain, your hands, your feet, and your back. Apart from meeting interesting people and seeing beautiful terrain and wildlife, Lawson's trail reminded me of all that. People like Dale stay reminded of that and try to remind the rest of us. You can still get the lay of the land.

:::

Leaving Dale behind, I continued north, finally crossing into North Carolina for good, walking from Pineville into Charlotte. What I want to say about Charlotte and the way into it is that I understood, from the feet up, what my friends had been talking about at Ivy Place—how the nearby land was being consumed by the amoeba of Charlotte. I spent time with Dale learning how to survey—to mark and divide the land. As I walked into Charlotte I was surrounded by the dispiriting result of 300 years of that division development.

Heading north toward Pineville in a daylong drizzle I walked along mostly two-lanes, occasionally cut deep into the orange Piedmont clay; the country was very hilly now, and I was constantly reminded of that fact. But I noticed more that I was leaving exurbs behind and finding my way along more developed roads and streets and, especially, housing subdivisions. I have heard it said that subdivisions are named for the last species turned out of its territory and the last geographical feature leveled for the houses—Deer Hills, say, or Magnolia Creek. I began tracking these names when I passed Fox Trail and Almond Glen, though the closer I got to Pineville—itself a Charlotte suburb, at the end of the transit line to downtown—names lost even that and began sounding a bit more pretentious: The Haven; Farrington; and even The Cottages in The Village at Carolina Place. But once you've got to Parkway Crossing (real place!) you have to understand that they're just building them faster than they can name them. What's next: Don't Walk Acres? The Blight at Traffic Circle?

You want to know nameless? I was stopped by the driver of a truck from Covington, Georgia, with a load of cotton to deliver and lost beyond his capacity to judge. Where did his load need to go? "I don't know," he told me. So: Faceless Carolina suburbia. Lost truck. Load of cotton. I now think it's possible he was looking for Keer America (I had passed a large industrial building in Indian Lands, jotting down its name). I have since learned Keer is a new attempt at textiles in the Carolinas—a subsidiary of a company based in China. It's like a make-your-own metaphor kit for the post-agroindustrial South.

I stood and pulled out my various maps to try to direct the driver. Lawson probably had a single map of the entire Carolina territory, assuming he had a map at all. This driver relied on his phone, but he couldn't get a signal, and I unfolded my DeLorme photocopies and sheets printed from Google Maps, but I was no use to him. Meanwhile, cars drove by in bursts, which I learned to recognize as another sign of nearing urban civilization: traffic lights nearby cause those little bursts of cars. Then I started walking by soccer fields and sportsplexes. I saw a pine harvest and then realized it wasn't—the tractors were clearing land for a business park—however many generations from Lawson to then: surveying and developing. And then it was an elementary school and then a strip mall and then I was in Pineville and I sat down for a late lunch to get out of the rain.

:::

In my journal I at one point wrote down the series of transitions I was making as I followed Lawson's path. Lawson left Charleston and went from ocean to marshland to river to swamp to forest, and as far as that goes so did I. Then it was towns. I had cake and coffee in the tiny crossroads hamlet of Jamestown and slept in the church, visiting little Randolph's Landing, the spot at the end of the road where the government plonked Lake Marion. From there I walked on to the revolutionary town of Camden, and from there to Lancaster, where I met not only the delightful people at usc-Lancaster but the Catawba Indians themselves, who treated me as well as they had treated Lawson three centuries ago, and then on up to Pineville, the last little stop before Charlotte.

And then I walked into Charlotte. So I had gone ocean, marsh, river, swamp, hills, town, city, and then big city. It felt like the apex of an arc, and it was—Charlotte was the biggest city I visited along Lawson's path, and from there the path would follow the same sequence in reverse: a couple of smaller cities, then small towns, then rural areas and farms, ending up back in the marshes and creeks and finally the Pamlico Sound and the ocean. I knew I was about halfway along as I approached Charlotte. And the best surprise I had was the sidewalks.

Throughout my walk I complained, pretty much constantly, about the lack of sidewalks and capacity for pedestrians to share the roads. Some of that came simply from walking through very rural territory. But the approach to every city meant running for my life, and approaching Charlotte from Pineville was no different. Pineville is a comfortable little suburb, with streets and sidewalks and shops, and then you run out of sidewalk and you cross an enormous bridge over I-485 and you just pray that you stay lucky. And then you walk along a strip of soul-sucking highway with about 16,741 car dealerships (that's an estimate; I might have missed a couple).

I had followed Lawson along fully half his route, and despite the changes along the way I couldn't help but feel his passage before me, feel the paths his feet had trod, whether on the "roadness" of the sand track through the state park or the welcome offered by the descendants of his own hosts. And then I got to Charlotte, and the trail went cold. Not that I had any doubt about where I was going—the road I followed through Charlotte follows the old Trading Path, all the experts agree. But in a big, sprawling pavement farm like Charlotte, it's just hard to feel the presence of those moccasined feet, that line of walkers moving along a narrow path.

And yet, just as I began to feel something like despondence, an astonishing thing happened. I found myself on South Boulevard and … there's sidewalk. And I'm here to tell you, that for the ten-or-so miles it takes you to get into Charlotte, you have sidewalk the whole way, and for that I could have just wept with gratitude. I'm not kidding: To be walking on sidewalk, protected from or at least acknowledged by road traffic felt like a gift. It felt like a place that at least acknowledged people. It helped me to get back to a taste of the hospitality Lawson seemed to enjoy so much on his journey.

Which brings us to Charlotte, whose origin story states that Trade and Tryon, the main downtown intersection, has been a crossroads from time out of mind. Tryon, running north-south(ish) is pretty much the Trading Path, which I'd been following (and Lawson followed) since about Camden, South Carolina. Trade was another path, running between the coast and the Cherokee settlements to the west. At the crossroads was a Catawba settlement, and that made a great place to hang out, trade, smoke tobacco, and wait for whatever was next.

In fact, at that point Lawson met someone he didn't expect. Lawson, like me, knew he was coming into the city: "This day, we pass'd through a great many Towns, and Settlements," he says. "About three in the After-noon, we reach'd the Kadapau King's House, where we met with one John Stewart, a Scot, then an inhabitant of James-River in Virginia." Stewart was one of the Indian traders from the Chesapeake who made their way up and down the Trading Path, bringing European goods and returning with deerskins and furs. Stewart was waiting around with the Catawbas because a Seneca raiding party was in the area and he didn't care to travel alone. Lawson mentions that Stewart had heard of the approach of Lawson's group nearly three weeks before and had waited for him, giving a little sense of how effectively Indians communicated without any help from the Internet. Stewart joined Lawson's gang and they agreed to journey forward together.

They hung around a couple of days, baking bread and otherwise preparing for their journey, which at this point though still northward began to turn east, back toward the coast.

:::

Charlotte honors its history as a place where people meet to do business—it's an enormous banking capital now, and it has a few astonishing steel-and-glass skyscrapers to show it, along with the explosive redevelopment that tends to go with prosperous Sun Belt cities. It even has a light-rail transit line, which made my life extremely easy. I left my car at the southernmost end of the line, so when I finished making my way into town all I had to do to get back to my car was jump on the trolley.

Walking into Charlotte up South Boulevard you pass about a million self-storage places, which along with the limitless car lots cannot fail to lead a visitor to the conclusion that people in Charlotte—and I suppose all modern people—have cars only so they can fill them with stuff, which they then drive to warehouses for storage. I passed through neighborhoods easily identifiable through signs on restaurants and roadside stores, through language and accent when I stopped for a soda or restroom: Latino, then Asian, then African American. Then as I closed in toward town, manufacturing plants stopped being empty and started turning into upscale-living-and-shopping developments, and by the time I could get glimpses of downtown I was in neighborhoods that took serious coin to inhabit—if you walked a block off the main drag, you could see that one or two of the old millhouses remained, but almost everything else was a teardown, replaced by a three-story Gentrifying Postmodern occupying every square inch of land it was legal to occupy. Plenty of nice stores and bars accompany these neighborhoods, often, as I said, in one-time industrial buildings. Atherton Mill, for example, housed the Big Ben British Restaurant and Pub, expensive shops for spices and coffee, and a Warby Parker.

Once I got into downtown it was like the Peterson's Guide to the Ecosystems of the Big Cities. Big steel-and-glass skyscrapers? Check: seven! Sports stadium? Check (three! minor league baseball, pro football, and pro basketball!). Adorable minipark? Check: One with a literary theme and, for some reason, spitting fish. Then there was Trade and Tryon, and though no Catawba king greeted me, I had been well treated by the Catawbas already. Regarding Seneca raiding parties, I had no worries. Cars, however, kept me busy.

∷

As I made my way into Charlotte, according to notes in the little journal I kept handy, I crossed a little unnamed tributary of the Sugar Creek, and I was moved: "Green and lovely," I wrote, after sitting on the grassy bank for only a few minutes, watching the current burble over rocks. Scrubby trees leaned out over the narrow creek, brown from recent rain but still a place of peace and beauty, even near a roaring city road. "I will never get enough of this." It was a powerful moment—a moment repeated over and over along the trek. I was outside. I sat by creeks, I felt the hot sun, I got wet in the rain. My muscles grew tired when I walked a long time, and I got hungry, too. This is not common for us in our time, but in Lawson's it would have been constant.

I spend at least 90 percent of my time now inside: my house, my car, my work, a store; I walk largely from one of those to another, or I choose to walk outdoors as recreation. Lawson would have spent virtually all of his waking hours outdoors. Not just on his journey but also as a surveyor, a developer, a man who met with Indians, a man who traveled around. As much as I enjoyed following Lawson, as much as I enjoyed learning history and meeting people like Peggy Scott, Dale Loberger, Val Green, the family Guerry, my canoe guides on the coast, Jered Canty. As much I loved all that, I may have appreciated nothing as much as I appreciated simply being outside all the time, moving through space, walking the trails of the country, and sitting by the creeks and beneath the trees. It's worth remembering that.

Funny I should have noticed the creek then, because Lawson too noticed the creeks around Charlotte: "Many pleasant and delightsome

Rivulets"; later he calls them "curious bold Creeks, (navigable for small Craft) disgorging themselves into the main Rivers, that vent themselves into the Ocean. These Creeks are well stor'd with sundry sorts of Fish, and Fowl." He elsewhere mentions seeing "a pleasant Rivulet, with a fine gravelly Bottom." What makes that especially noteworthy is that Lawson was probably one of the last people to have seen the bottoms of Carolina creeks. We have discussed elsewhere the sad history of damming that affected the Santee. But the Catawba or Wateree, which Lawson — and I — followed north with the Trading Path, has now been dammed to within an inch of its life, supporting no fewer than fourteen large dams and many smaller ones, turning the watershed into less a flowing river than a series of connected lakes. Though the current dams were built in the last century for flood control, power generation, and recreation, dams have been reality, especially on the creeks, since European settlers showed up.

I once watched a researcher poke a shovel into the steep bank of a Carolina creek. The water trickled its cloudy way along its usual path, about ten feet below the flat surrounding land. He used his shovel to dig into the lower bank, exposing the gray original river gravel and the sand below it. The ten feet of yellow sandy ground above it, he explained, was not natural floodplain—it was the sediment trapped by the dams built there by settlers in the eighteenth and nineteenth centuries. Virtually every dammable creek was dammed; water, after all, was power. The first thing the mills did was saw timber as settlers cleared the land; then they ground the grain from the wheat and corn they grew. But without its natural trees, the land eroded hundreds of times faster than normal; the Piedmont soil, never particularly good in the first place, soon eroded to uselessness. Farmers left and dams eventually collapsed, with creeks and rivers quickly carving their way down through the sediment. The creeks now run through these silty deposits left behind, which will continue crumbling into the creeks for, I have heard, as much as 6,000 years before the silt is gone and the rivers can once again have clear waters and fine gravelly bottoms. That silt feeds into the major rivers too, of course; even the Catawba, were it left to run free, would have to wait a long time before it again ran clear.

But it's not left to run free, and far more than old silt assaults the clear-running streams Lawson once saw. As I walked through Charlotte I got to spend some time with Mary Newsom, of the University of North Carolina–Charlotte Urban Institute, which applies its time and study to the social, economic, and environmental challenges facing communities.

She had just been involved in a project called Up the Creeks, whose website documented the troubled treatment of the creeks that drain Charlotte.

To Lawson's descriptions I mentioned above I add that he also encountered the Haw, which he calls "most pleasant," and later a river he calls the Rocky, which he also describes as "very pretty." Newsom picked me up as I picked my way through road construction north of Charlotte and hauled me only a few blocks away, to a section of the Little Sugar Creek that might have been the saddest stretch of waterway I'd ever seen in my entire life. The green space surrounding the creek, which emerged from a pipe in a grocery store parking lot, couldn't have been fifty feet total; scrub woods and little else grew there. When it rained, the trash and oil and brake dust and pet waste and everything else in that parking lot poured directly into the Little Sugar, which before much longer ducked, perhaps in embarrassment, into another culvert. "Very pretty" were not the words that came to mind.

And this has been the case with Piedmont creeks and streams for decades and even centuries. Looked at as little more than sluices for runoff and garbage, Piedmont waterways, like those throughout the United States, were unprotected and pretty much ruined. These creeks had, you might say, industrial disease. Until the Clean Water Act of 1972, that's just how things went. And even then, the CWA initially focused mostly on point sources like factories or wastewater treatment plants.

But in recent years, the worst sources of pollution have been non-point sources: farms and storm-water runoff and, especially in rapidly urbanizing places like Charlotte, the silty runoff from construction sites and parking. So to address the flow of silt, pollutants, and nutrients that cause algae blooms and fish kills, many jurisdictions—including the state of North Carolina—adopted the common-sense technique of riparian buffers. That is, they leave a strip of land along creeks and streams undisturbed, allowing the natural plants to flourish. Those plants clean water flowing through, absorbing pollutants, with the added benefits of providing wildlife habitat, sequestering carbon, and offering recreational space for kids, hikers, explorers. In North Carolina, starting in 1997, the buffer was fifty feet. Wetlands have flourished, as have rain and water gardens that collect water from buildings and parking lots and let it hang around long enough to drop most of its pollutants and sediment, supporting ponds and native plants. Waters have improved. Riparian buffers have been a success story throughout the country—and significantly in North Carolina—protecting streams and giving them a fighting chance. The first thirty feet on each side of the stream is left natural; the next twenty can be maintained as yard and used for pretty much anything the landowner likes, as long as it isn't paved.

So everybody wins: planet, streams, citizens, animals—and walkers retracing the paths of explorers from hundreds of years before.

Except, as Newsom noted, the very week I walked through Charlotte, the North Carolina legislators passed a bill allowing developers to dig right up to the waterside, as long as they eventually planted something back on the thirty feet closest to the river. So think this through. Silt and fertilizer are the two scourges of modern waterways, and this change allows developers to silt up the creek while they build and then plant new stuff and fertilize it afterward. "And that's planting stuff," said Newsom, noting that the plantings would come long after invasive plants had established footholds in the scarred creekside. Add in what any gardener worth her or his soil knows—half of what you plant will probably die no matter what you do; establishing a garden takes years—and you've got an assault on the state's waterways. Given the enormous amount of development taking place in North Carolina, no one could claim that developers are having a tough time there due to stringent environmental regulations. The new law looked like something between pure greed and vandalism. Just about any creek east of the mountains in the Carolinas now has a bottom covered in mucky brown silt. In 2008, the Catawba had suffered enough that it was actually named the nation's most endangered river by the waterway advocacy group American Rivers. By 2013 it had emerged from that classification, though other Carolina rivers remained regulars.

Newsom treated me to an expensive coffee as we sat in the air-conditioning of a little French cafe, and the news isn't all bad. Charlotte—like Raleigh and other wealthy Piedmont cities—has learned that its green spaces are valuable amenities as well as vital ecosystems and ecological service providers. Greenways are built, and local laws protect waterways—when the legislature allows.

But the little creek I had sat by south of town was the last peaceful creek I crossed on my path through Charlotte. The Little Sugar—and the Sugar, which it feeds—drains much of Charlotte. ("Sugar" comes from *sugaw*, a Catawba word meaning "group of huts." Lawson's Sugeree Indians, it turns out, may have just been some Catawbas who told him,

"We live in those wigwams over yonder.") Modern development destroys creeks, and the state of the Little Sugar by that supermarket (and the overwhelming information provided by Up the Creeks) was sobering.

Newsom dropped me back in the middle of the road construction, and once again I began picking my way forward, through what could not fail to feel like the wreckage of the wilderness Lawson had traversed.

:::

Before I left Charlotte, though, I had one more stop to make. I had to get some barbecue.

You've heard plenty about Carolina barbecue; you know that in North Carolina there's a fault line running through something like the middle of the state—in the east people favor vinegar-based barbecue sauce; in the west it's tomato-based. South Carolina too has its own varieties, preferring a mustardy sauce midstate and a tomato-based one in the west. On the coast, like their neighbors to the north, the people tend to prefer the vinegar sauce. In both states people toward the coast tend to barbecue the whole hog, whereas in the west they stick with a shoulder or butt.

Any Carolinian, north or south, can talk to you about barbecue— and pig pickings, where the whole hog is slow-cooked and shredded for 'cue—for hours. I am not kidding. Absolutely any Carolinian will have barbecue opinions, opinions of a strength that make college basketball rivalries seem petty by comparison. If you take my advice, you'll ask and listen—and eat. But do not develop an opinion. They all taste good. So when I could no longer ignore the fact that Lawson mentions barbecue, I went looking for the story of barbecue, that favored food of the South— and, it turns out, the Indians.

As early as his visit with the Santee Indians, only a couple of weeks into his trek, Lawson describes how they Santee "made us very welcome with fat barbacu'd Venison, which the Woman of the Cabin took and tore in Pieces with her Teeth, so put it into a Mortar, beating it to Rags, afterwards stew[ing] it with Water, and other Ingredients, which makes a very savoury Dish." You want my opinion? That sounds so exactly like the pulled-apart pig eastern Carolinians eat today that you could put it in a cookbook.

Dan the Pig Man could not agree more. A retired journalist and long-time lover of barbecue (and old friend), he now runs a food truck and catering company and met with me in front of his headquarters off a gravel road near York, South Carolina, built in what you might call the

Rural-Palatial style: tree trunks holding up the porch roof, license plates and signs nailed to the mill-hewn boards on the front, no shortage of just stuff piled here and there.

Dan quickly dismissed any of the crazier claims for how the word *barbecue* came into the language. It came with European interaction with Caribbean and Central American Native populations, who used the word *barbacoa* to describe a way of cooking that involved placing meat on a lattice of poles above a fire that kept it from cooking too quickly, enabling the heat and smoke to cure as well as cook it. Lawson spells it "barbacue" and "barbakue," but he's talking about meat smoked on a grill.

Dan has done enormous research on barbecue, and he sees its history as follows: In the 1500s, either pigs brought by Spanish expeditions found their way to the island off the coast of Georgia now known as Ossabaw or they were left there purposely to remain as a food source when the men returned. The men never did, but the hogs remain. De Soto was thus responsible for the introduction of old-world hogs into the new world, which Dan sees as significant. "Old world pigs have fatback two inches thick," he says. This meant you could take the entire pig, lay it on its back on a pit of coals, and cook it. Its own hide and fat would serve as skillet and grease, enabling the entire animal to be prepared, not just the prime cuts—the ham, the loin, the butt, and so forth—that the Europeans would have been used to preparing.

"The whole deal about *barbacoa* is they would gut them and use the whole animal, as opposed to the Europeans," Dan told me. Most important, says Dan, you could cook the animal without any kind of grill or other iron implement—making this pit method of cooking perfect for pre-Iron Age cultures like those of the American Indians. "I talk about barbecue coming up with the pirates along the East Coast," Dan says. "The tradition wafted inland like hickory smoke."

Speaking of smoke, of course, that's the point: the smoke contains elements that kill bacteria and, along with the fire drying out the meat, meant an animal could be eaten for months, rather than days. Turns out the smoke makes it taste good, too—whether you're plucking pieces off a pit-smoked pig during a nice all-day Carolina pig-picking or eating venison in February that you killed in November. Nowadays many people use professional-grade smokers like the one Dan has in what he calls the Pig Palace, but you'll be invited to plenty of parties with a pig coming out of a pit—or on a grill. One of Raleigh's barbecue restaurants is still called The Pit.

And as much as Dan loves Carolina barbecue and its many approaches, he knows that in reality it's that simplest of things: meat + fire + smoke + time = good eating. "The great food cultures of the world start with poor people getting the poor cuts of meat," he says. "How do you tenderize it? What do poor people have a lot of? Time, wood, smoke.

"When I grew up in Charlotte in the fifties and sixties, barbecue was not an urban white thing at all," he says. It was something you went out to the poorer quarters for and bought there. What's more, if you get right down to it, "it's meat and fire. It's animals and lightning. Barbecue started when the first wooly mammoth fell in the campfire."

Still, he sees Lawson as playing an important role with barbecue like he does with so much of Carolina and southeastern culture. "The significance of Lawson is he didn't hang around the coast. He went into the backwoods." He witnessed all the ways Indian cultures barbecued their meat, and "I would argue that it was Lawson who first took that tradition back over the Atlantic." Lawson did return to England in 1709 and stay for a year. I expect he ate with some tastemakers, and if he didn't carry the message, surely his book did when it came out that year.

The Indians offered Lawson other foods that met with less favor. Though Lawson had venison, we have our modern barbecue mostly with pork. "Which is a gross Food," Lawson says, "and a great Propagator of such Juices as it often meets withal in human Bodies, once tainted with this Malady; which may differently (in some Respects) act its Tragedy." He is speaking of syphilis, which he recognizes is indigenous with the Indians, though he's off base on whether pork makes it any worse. He talks of eating "a Dish, in great Fashion amongst the Indians, which was Two young Fawns, taken out of the Doe's Bellies, and boil'd in the same slimy Bags Nature had plac'd them in, and one of the Country-Hares, stew'd with the Guts in her Belly, and her Skin with the Hair on." Not an enormous hit with the more timid European palate: "This new-fashion'd Cookery wrought Abstinence in our Fellow-Travellers, which I somewhat wonder'd at, because one of them made nothing of eating Allegators, as heartily as if it had been Pork and Turneps. The Indians dress most things after the Wood-cock Fashion, never taking the Guts out. At the House we lay at, there was very good Entertainment of Venison, Turkies, and Bears; and which is customary amongst the Indians."

When walking, the men sent their Indian guides to shoot turkey and deer, which they never failed to do; in settlements they took what they got, usually liking it far better than the fetal deer. Lawson talks of the

Indians drying chinquapin nuts to eat all winter long and of grinding "Hickerie-Nuts" to use as a thickener for venison broth; they used acorns similarly, even grinding them to paste and making little patties they ate like bread, spreading them with oil made from the enormous stocks of passenger pigeons, to say nothing of "hot Bread and Bear's-Oil," which he notes "is wholsome Food for Travelers." They ate so much turkey and venison that he got sick of them; he appreciated later being served "the Tail of a Bever, which is a choice Food," and feasting on fish near the coast and crawfish near creeks. "Stewed Peaches and green Corn, that is preserv'd in their Cabins before it is ripe, and sodden and boil'd when they use it," he calls "a pretty sort of Food, and a great Increaser of the Blood."

Not for me—I'm just not a grits guy. My food highlights in Lawson's footsteps mostly came from the almost innumerable local convenience stores, providing everything from breakfast sandwiches to bait for morning fishermen. I started my trip out of Lancaster at the Korner Kupboard, but possibly the best breakfast sandwich I've had in my life came from the multi-everything Batten's of Wedgewood, not far from the Manchester State Forest in South Carolina. Batten's has two green fabric awnings: one says "Restaurant" and one says "Fishing-Hunting Supplies." While I waited for my bologna and cheese on a biscuit I wandered among hunting trophies, including a bobcat, the only one I saw alive or dead on the journey, though they range throughout both North and South Carolina. It looked somewhat the worse for being dead, though attractively posed in a niche in the paneled wall. I felt bad for the bobcat, but I loved that biscuit so much I Instagrammed a picture of it. It got six likes. Maybe the picture didn't do it justice; I shared a picture of my eggs-and-bacon-and-waffle-and-toast from Waffle House later on, and that one got ten. No accounting for taste.

If Instagram seems a little Jetsonian for the Lawson Trek, recall that Lawson and his party went north with Stewart, the trader they'd met with the Catawbas in what today we'd call Charlotte. Stewart "had lost a day of the week, of which we inform'd him," Lawson reports. The trader's life, and I suppose the traveler's. I had a watch with the date on it.

7 : The Hanging Tree

'm taking a picture of a house north of Charlotte along the Old Concord Road, which is pretty much what I do as I follow Lawson. I walk along the road, and I see a house or a field or a sign or a person that seems interesting or to have a story to tell and I take a picture of it or talk to the person or stop and jot down a note. I imagine I often look like something between a private eye in a supermarket thriller and the way in high school you thought a poet would look—floating down the street, pen in hand, scrawling deathless lines as I stroll.

And sometimes someone comes over. I'm snooping or I have out a notebook or I'm pointing a camera, so somebody strides or drives over—in this case drove, pulling smoothly but quickly into the driveway directly in front of me. "You okay?" he asks me, very polite and it's worth noting without a hint of threat or defensiveness. But it was his neighborhood—he'd been hanging around with the guy across the street, at the car lot/produce market/cattle farm. I'd seen them talking as I walked past and felt like they'd noticed me. I usually would cross the street to speak with people like that, but they were deep in an asphalt parking lot by a big aluminum barn, and I just couldn't bear to walk a quarter mile with them wondering who the hell I was the whole time.

But he drove up, so I told him who I was and gave him my elevator explanation about Lawson and his journey and so forth and then we were friends. He said he had been an investigative reporter at the *Salisbury Independent Tribune*, so we enjoyed talking about writing. He told me most of the people on these roads—in these communities—are retired now, and the farms that run are either keep-busy farms or rented out, with only a few of the latter. We talked about the stories we have to tell, and then history came up, and then he mentioned that of course nowadays we're rewriting history, and then of course here came the Confederate flag.

I don't have to share the specifics. Some facts, as far as I can tell wrong, some commonly heard themes about historical revisionism and states' rights. Even a claim, new to me, that the Civil War was fought over taxes. But anyway, a simple interaction. I stopped along the road, a fellow told me how the locals lived, shared what they thought. It was a perfect interaction for a writer like me, on Lawson's trail to see what's out there.

Not much grass in the parking areas of
Charlotte Motor Speedway, but I found some.

We parted cheerfully, wished each other well without reservation. And for about thirty seconds I congratulated myself on simply reporting, letting the story come to me, instead of challenging. But it was July 2015. Freddie Gray had been killed in police custody in Baltimore in April; in June, white Dylann Roof had murdered nine black people in a church in Charleston, and the Confederate flag that inspired him was again a subject of debate; Sandra Bland, a black woman pulled over for a minor traffic violation, had been arrested and subsequently found hanged in her cell in Texas barely a week before I met this man. Though it's fine to listen to everybody I come across, I thought I had better take care to hear other voices than the ones from the people whose houses were on the main streets I walked down.

Not that this was a new goal. Lawson mentioned the Huguenots by the river, and Huguenot descendants I found. Lawson talked extensively about Indians, and I made every effort to talk with and about every tribe I encountered as well. I was doing like Lawson did—trying to get how things are here, how they've been. So I decided that since the murders of African Americans—in the streets or in churches, at the hands of police or private citizens—were so much in our world, I'd better make a special effort to ensure I got some African American voices in my chorus.

I eventually had a great opportunity.

:::

I got to Salisbury by walking north from Charlotte, along what I called the NASCAR portion of my journey. I spent one night at the Charlotte Motor Speedway, at a natural crest about thirteen miles north of uptown, my little tent almost alone in a postage stamp of green surrounded by the speedway's vast empty parking lots.

But what you get above all walking along the old Trading Path (it eventually turns into Route 29, satisfyingly known as the Old Salisbury-Concord Road) is more car stuff. The way into Charlotte from the south was new car dealerships; heading out to the north was cheap car lots, car repair, car parts, car tires, car rentals, car inspection, and "credit doctors" who will help you into a car you probably can't pay for. There is so much buying, selling, and maintaining of cars along these major roads that I consistently found it hard to believe the auto industry accounts for only 3.5 percent of the U.S. gross domestic product.

But in Charlotte, cars mean NASCAR. Nobody needs to tell you Americans love cars, and the story of the growth of stock car racing is a remarkable tale of postwar American prosperity. The speedway was started in 1959 to cash in on the growing popularity of stock car racing. The region needed a speedway for the simple reason that stock car racing lives in central Carolina. You can find a million sources explaining how farmers growing corn learned it was a lot cheaper to distill it and distribute it as whiskey than it was to transport and sell it as food, and how during Prohibition that meant delivering an illegal product. Which meant your car had to be faster than a police car but still look perfectly normal. Add in that you needed cars that could rocket along straight stretches of highway but handle in both curving mountain roads during pickup and city streets during delivery and you've covered about every element of the racecars that now fill speedways.

The day I walked through, the speedway wasn't running some enormous top-level Cup race, with 150,000 people clogging grandstand and infield. It did have small cars running on a quarter-mile oval along the front stretch, with maybe a thousand fans paying eight bucks for a ducat and enjoying the wreckfest. I had a hot dog and popcorn and an enormous soda. Racing is always fun, but my point here wasn't racing, it was Lawson. Sitting in the speedway and looking out over the hills stretching away I was reminded of Lawson's description of reaching "the Top of one of these Mountains, which yielded us a fine Prospect of a very level Country, holding so, on all sides." My guides believe this to describe the very hill on which the speedway sits, and looking out over the ranges I thought of Lawson, looking out over those receding hills and recognizing himself to be, quite literally, at the western boundary of what he would have called civilization. William Byrd, a Virginia settler and Indian trader, had written home from the colony barely ten years before Lawson's trip: "We are here," he said to his uncle, "att the end of the world." I walked along asphalt and sat in speedway seats; Lawson himself focused on his Indian hosts and tour guides. Lawson rarely mentions any sense of danger in his life so far from the England of his birth. But at moments like this I occasionally remembered: he was here, at the end of the world. That thought filled me with admiration for Lawson—and took whatever tiny privation I was enduring (hot feet, blisters, too long a walk between one icy convenience store fountain drink and the next) and offered welcome context.

When I went back to my little tent, almost alone in the sea of asphalt, a killdeer in a nearby gravel parking lot did everything she could to lure me away, pretending she had a broken wing to entice me to chase her. She must have had a nest nearby. I wasn't about to move my tent, and eventually she either figured out I presented no danger or just decided to stop shrieking and bed down for a nervous night. Everybody lived to tell the tale.

The night was hot enough that I barely slept, and when I awoke at 5 a.m. I downed a couple of Pop Tarts, policed the campsite, and headed north at six. I'm usually on the trail around 9:15 a.m. under any circumstances: if I wake at seven, I dither, and if I wake at 8:30 I rush. Lawson's guides felt the same, "Indians never setting forward 'till the Sun is an Hour or two high, and hath exhall'd the Dew from the Earth." But this day it was scheduled to be in the high nineties, and the urban heat island effect was something Lawson and his guides never had to deal with. According to the Environmental Protection Agency, asphalt can be 50–90 degrees Fahrenheit hotter than surrounding temperature. The day I walked through Charlotte the Raleigh National Weather Service station tweeted that the asphalt temperature was 151 degrees Fahrenheit. My feet would agree.

I was walking not just in terrain changed from Lawson's day—I was walking in a climate that simply did not exist in his day. He complained of freezing cold, and when I awoke one day months ago and saw the thermometer at 10 degrees I felt we shared something. What an environment of asphalt, concrete, and clear-cutting would yield would have been beyond his imagination. Having lived it, I can tell you the answer is simple: it's hot. Biologist and writer Rob Dunn writes about heat-mapping his walk to work and describes the simplest improvement imaginable: plant more trees. I'm here to tell you: walking along a bare asphalt berm can be miserable, and even in the hottest weather simply ducking under a tree makes an enormous difference. The planet hates these strip malls and parking lots. Plant trees.

:::

Along I went, north from the speedway toward Concord and its cousin Kannapolis. For a long time in the heat that even at 7 a.m. was brutal I passed racing-related shops—restoration parts, cams, engine shops. Then came a long stretch of the Anthropocene Suburban—long stretches of road between small fields raising cattle or pines, the roadside ditches swaying with Queen Anne's lace, daisies, and black-eyed Susans, primrose, *Scutellaria* (any of various purple-flowered mints), and dandelions. The land of five-digit addresses and round red reflectors on driveway posts.

Nearing Concord, however, I started running into empty textile mills advertising for tenants. Downtown Concord shows a combination of new red brick Charlotte-suburban growth mixed with small-town empty-storefront blues. I ate a delicious sandwich at Ellie's, where my wait-person knew that the Trading Path worked its way through Concord. On I went, north of Concord along, as I mentioned, the delightfully named Old Salisbury-Concord Road, where I encountered an enormous granite outcropping, right along the road, described by Lawson: "We went about

25 Miles, travelling through a pleasant, dry Country, and took up our Lodgings by a Hill-side, that was one entire Rock, out of which gush'd out pleasant Fountains of well-tasted Water." No gushing fountains now, though the rock face remains, running along the west of the road, sometimes covered in hanging foliage. I did not take up lodgings there.

:::

I diverged briefly because I wanted to go to Kannapolis, though Lawson did not. In Kannapolis—once home of Cannon Mills and known as Towel City, another Carolina textile town trying to figure out what's next—they're building a research campus and working to imitate the success of North Carolina's Research Triangle Park between Raleigh and Durham. Most important to me, though, after starting this segment of my trip in downtown Charlotte, was the Dale Earnhardt statue.

One has surely heard of Earnhardt, the Kannapolis native son who became a legendary stock car racer, perhaps the best of all time. He died in a wreck at Daytona in 2001, but long before that the taciturn, stubborn competitor had become a symbol for the rural, southern fans of NASCAR's early explosive growth. When he died, though not everyone in mainstream culture understood this, in the South and across NASCAR America it was like Elvis had died again. Earnhardt's father, Ralph, was a racer—racing was his way out of the Kannapolis textile mills he worked in. Earnhardt too was headed for the mills, but his racing gave him a way out. His success on the track became a touchstone for generations of Carolinians, and his death broke hearts.

If you go to downtown Kannapolis, you won't find much—on the redevelopment scale it's behind Concord and nowhere near Charlotte—but you will find a statue of Dale Earnhardt, in a little plaza built for that purpose. It's part of the Dale Trail, a collection of Earnhardt touchstones you can visit. You can visit Ralph's grave, the family's old neighborhood, roads named after Earnhardt, "Idiot Circle" (the cruising area of Kannapolis), and of course the plaza, which has not just the nine-foot bronze statue but a granite monument and a circle of benches. You can also drive to race shops and stores and such, but you get the idea. Lawson walked through here, describing the place to the world for the first time; no statue. George Washington also came through on his tour of the South, solidifying the nation in the aftermath of the adoption of the Constitution. No statue.

Earnhardt drove race cars, and he gets a statue. I say this as not criticism but description. You want to understand the South? Look at who the people raise up. In Camden, South Carolina, you see an awful lot of the Indian chief King Hagler, and you know why: he was a local. Earnhardt was a local in this part of North Carolina, and it's Earnhardt that Carolina loves. Let's hope they come to love Lawson as much.

:::

I walked into Salisbury from the little not-even-crossroads of Mt. Gilead, just north of Concord. Same with Lawson: from his enjoyment of the "Hills and Vallies" near present-day Charlotte, Lawson continued up the Trading Path with John Stewart (the new Indian trader who had joined his party at the Catawba town). Lawson describes reaching "the fertile and pleasant Banks of *Sapona* River [the Yadkin], whereon stands the *Indian* Town and Fort." That would be the Trading Ford, which stands just north of the current Salisbury. (Lawson thought it flowed into the Cape Fear, though in truth it feeds the Pee Dee, further south.) We have written records of the Trading Ford on the Yadkin from as early as Spaniard Juan Pardo's forays in the late 1560s, and every subsequent explorer and settler describes the same thing: a lovely settlement clearly of long standing, where Indians met, crossed the river at a safe rocky place, rested, and traded. "Nor could all *Europe* afford a pleasanter Stream," Lawson says, "were it inhabited by *Christians*, and cultivated by ingenious Hands."

Lawson lodged in the cabin of the Sapona king, who had lost an eye in the service of the English, fighting other tribes further west. The Saponas had recently taken prisoner five of the feared Senecas, and while Lawson visited the tribe planned to have a celebration and torture them to death: "The Fire of Pitch-Pine being got ready, and a Feast appointed, which is solemnly kept at the time of their acting this Tragedy, the Sufferer has his Body stuck thick with Light-Wood-Splinters, which are lighted like so many Candles, the tortur'd Person dancing round a great Fire, till his Strength fails." But a band of Tutelo Indians, a nearby Siouan tribe, pleaded for the captives; some Tutelos had been captured and released by Senecas, and the Tutelos wished to return the favor. Since the Tutelos, the Saponas, and the Keyauwees were then working on a treaty to band their declining tribes together, the king turned the prisoners over.

Lawson and his friends stayed a couple of days. The area even then was something of a multimodal hub. Stewart had a string of horses; Lawson and his gang were traveling on foot; and at the Trading Ford, traders met by canoe and exchanged goods. The Great Wagon Road had grown from the Trading Path, and where it crossed other Indian paths in 1753 Salisbury was founded. Major paths, good river crossing, easy transit: it was like an eighteenth-century highway interchange. Location, location, location—even Daniel Boone set out in 1769 for his adventures from Salisbury. George Washington slept in Salisbury. It ultimately became a rail hub with the Spencer Shops (now a transportation museum) right next door. Nowadays Salisbury has a lovely and thriving little turn-of-the-century downtown, and of course the nearby Trading Ford and High Rock Lake, a result of the dammed Yadkin.

But what it really has is lovely territory. When Lawson and two of his companions took advantage of iffy weather to visit the Sapona town by the river, Lawson kvelled about the rolling land covered with long leaf pines: "pleasant Savanna Ground, high and dry, having very few Trees upon it, and those standing at a great distance. . . . A Man near Sapona may more easily clear 10 Acres of Ground, than in some places he can one."

My old pal Val Green bid me contact in Salisbury Dr. Robert Crawford III, a seventh-(or so)-generation native son, whose family has owned River Ranch Farm, on a spit of land between Crane Creek and the Yadkin, since not long after Lawson came through, though at this point both creek and river make up arms of the dammed High Rock Lake. Crawford drove me down Crawford Road (he helped create the road driving his father's 1942 Chevy around fields when he was too young to drive on paved roads, he chortled) and offered me the use of his 200-year-old cabin (it has notches in the logs that once enabled settlers to shoot at Indians). He and his wife, Ann, and his associate, historian Susan Sides, kept me lodged, fed, and entertained during my stay.

Crawford doesn't have the slightest doubt about the Sapona town being on a vast cleared area of his farm—decades ago one day while fishing he lay back his head and found an arrowhead. Thus began a lifetime of picking things up, which led to a collection of some 20,000 items—simply picked up after plowing—that he in 2014 sold to the Laurens County Museum. A small sampling hangs in his downtown Salisbury ophthalmology office.

Lawson talks of this area in a tone he uses for no place else. "These Indians live in a clear Field, about a Mile square, which they would have sold me," he says, "because I talked sometimes of coming into those Parts to live." He describes the river's "continual pleasant warbling Noise," says the arriving spring "welcomed us with her innumerable Train of small Choristers ... redoubling, and adding Sweetness to their melodious Tunes by their shrill Echoes." The river, he says, is "hemm'd in with mountainy Ground" on one side, the other side "providing as rich a Soil to the Eye of a knowing Person with us, as any this Western World can afford."

That is, Lawson kind of liked it here.

Me too. Crawford's River Ranch Farm has an open spot very much like the one Lawson describes the Saponas living in, and from a spot in that area you can see, across the lake—that would have been a river— High Rock Mountain (it's only 1,160 feet high but is still by far the highest point Lawson had yet seen in the New World). On your other side, in a slough that is wet only because the lake is dammed now, would surely have been thick soil, enriched by occasional floods. The land is high and dry. Crawford pointed the spot out to me. His daddy told him Lawson had walked their land, and when Val Green showed up in his office one day asking for permission to visit the land it only made sense.

:::

Leaving Salisbury I walked through town to the northeast, following the Trading Path down Long Street, quickly leaving the prosperous downtown and entering the town of East Spencer, which I will describe with these words, directly from my notebook: "Long st a parade of the burned, the collapsed, and abandoned." I have a half-dozen photographs of burned-out buildings and houses.

A town of 1,500 or so souls that has been losing population for forty years, East Spencer is a place with problems: half its children in poverty, and a quarter of its elderly. Fewer than 700 families, 85 percent of which are African American, with a commonly cited number of more than 100 empty houses. A broken town. And across Long Street, on a back porch, two guys having a chat. I walked over and met Mike and Tony, though Tony later told me his name was actually Curtis, and when I called the business card Mike gave me and asked for Mike, it was a wrong number, so Mike may have used a pseudonym too.

No matter. I introduced myself, shared my Lawson story—and the story of my roadside conversation the day before about Confederate history. And off we went, cheerfully. In a town with the problems of East Spencer, Mike and Curtis, African American, did not think the Confederate flag was a big issue—they were a lot more worried about employment, violence, and poverty and its attendant miseries. "As long as you keep a bunch of winos and run-down property in town," Tony said, you're not going to improve. They discussed water bills and troubled youth, irresponsible code enforcement and the failure to invest in the community. We never quite got to institutionalized racism and that sort of thing, but they said the makeup of the town was simple. Over in Spencer and Salisbury is where the white people and slave owners had lived, and East Spencer was where the black people went—literally on the other side of the tracks; enormous freights trundled through as we spoke. And they said it was within living memory that you were back across those tracks by nightfall if you knew what was good for you; Salisbury was a sundown town. As far as the flag went, Mike did say he actually approved of it: "I'd rather someone hung up the flag, then I know not to go there; I'll go somewhere else. Go there and I might get hung."

Mike had to leave—he had started a nail salon, whose card he gave me—but he expanded on that whole getting hung thing. He and Curtis had mentioned a boundary between East Spencer and Salisbury they called "the unemployment tree," and I was looking for a clarification on that, but I never got there because Mike brought up another tree. "Don't forget to see the hanging tree," he said, before he left.

A beat of silence.

Mike instructed me to Google "lynching" and "Salisbury," and I would find an image of five men hanging from a tree, and the tree still stood on Seventeenth Street where it crossed the railroad tracks. I followed instructions; the true details differ only slightly. The photograph contains not five but three men hanging from a tree—in 1906—and Seventeenth doesn't cross the tracks. Eleventh Street does, though. And according to several accounts (and maps) of the events I found, Eleventh Street was where I wanted to be. So I went there.

I had no reason to be certain the tree I took a picture of and stood by is the one from which these three men—one only fifteen years old—were lynched by a mob in August 1906. In fact, I was eventually told that there's considerable doubt whether the tree stands anymore at all. But that's not the point. Neither are the details of this particular lynching (it had to do with an ax murder; of course there was no evidence linking the three lynched black men to the crime; as it happens, this was already Salisbury's second lynching of the new century). The point—the terrible point—is that of all the historians and writers and people throughout the Salisbury area who showed me enormous kindness, pointing me in the direction of old buildings and monuments, cemeteries and trails, the Trading Path and the Trading Ford, nobody outside the black community thought to say to me, "Don't miss the hanging tree." In the black community? I spoke to two random guys for twenty minutes and it came up and came up but good.

I spoke with Curtis for a while after Mike left, and then I went to see the tree. Around Eleventh Street there are warehouses and train tracks and such, but standing by itself was a tree, plainly old enough to have been large in 1906, and I watched it for a few minutes. No wreath, no flowers, no nothing—just a tree, surrounded by a fence. It's not a symbol for Salisbury—but it's a symbol for its black residents.

::::

Naturally that turned out to be the day I saw a million Confederate flags, too. I took pictures and walked along, thinking my thoughts, until I passed the Pandemonium Performance motorcycle shop on Flat Swamp Road into Denton. There a large Confederate flag flew, and a small one, and a large American flag, and a sign saying, "You want to start something?"

I most certainly did not. I got a curt nod from the guy out front and I didn't even take a picture. Except then I walked into Denton where my car was and thought, "If I don't want to talk to the guy flying those flags, what am I out here for?" So I drove back, pulled over across the street, and shot a couple of snaps. As I sat there the same guy walked out and asked, "You okay?" With overtones only of helpfulness. "I'm fine," I said, and asked if it was okay if I took some pictures. It was, and he urged me to park in his lot. "When I saw you stop, I worried you had broken down," he said. He was genuinely checking to see if I needed help.

So I told him my story. And we talked. "The reason is, to me that flag does not represent color," Kary, the shop owner, told me. His some-number-of-greats-grandfather fought in the war, which was fought because "the North was trying to take what the South had, tell us we couldn't do what we wanted." Like, I pointed out, own slaves, a point he yielded. But "to me, that flag represents me rebelling versus the government telling me what to do." He pointed to the American flag and said, "That's another thing about that flag—you have the right to have an opinion."

Want to start something?

To be sure; and to fly any flag you like, regardless of how others perceive it. The conversation continued and never, I need to be sure I am making clear, approached disrespect, threat, or even anger. We were discussing one of the matters of the day, and Kary laughed when I told him the "You want to start something?" sign had cowed me. Turned out it came from a rack of motorcycle batteries in the shop. Kary and I spoke respectfully, decently, and cheerfully. When Kary tells me he's not racist I want to believe him. And when I told him the flag is perceived as racist by everybody else, I think he believed me. He didn't change his actions, but he believed me.

In fact, when I tried to explain that whatever his personal beliefs, there was no doubt that millions of people took the flag as a symbol that he was a racist, he said he hated that. So I made a gesture, raising my middle finger, though pointing it at the wall, not at him. "What if I put that on a flag and waved it in your face?" I asked. He admitted that might offend him. I said, "What if I told you that though that middle finger is universally understood to mean disrespect and hostility, when I use it I just mean you should remember to have a digital exam to make sure you don't have prostate cancer? Because I'm worried about you?" He smiled and even laughed, nodding. He got the point.

He still didn't take down his flag. He still claims it's not racist. I could think of nothing more to say. We parted in a friendly way and I walked on.

:::

I look at the conversations of that day as among the most important I had on the trek. Like Lawson I was out trying to see what's out there, who's out there, what's going on, and at the moment we were talking about this flag I was walking through its home territory. Lawson walked through North and South Carolina. And it was South Carolina still flying the Confederate flag on its state capitol grounds until the Charleston church murders convinced their legislature to take it down. And it was North Carolina KKK members, don't forget, who came down to make sure nobody thought all Carolinians were civilizing.

I was so glad for these conversations. Because I want it to be easy—I want the house with the flag to be symbolic of a Bad Person with Racist Views, and I want anybody who still flies that flag to be Bad and Wrong and Mean. I want it to be easy. But there were Mike and Curtis telling me that they were a lot more concerned about jobs and education and civic investment than in some flag, and they pointed me at the hanging tree. And there was Kary—and so many like him whom I've met so often—who genuinely seem to believe that the flag is not a symbol of racism, and who genuinely seem to believe that the Civil War was fought over something other than slavery, despite all the enormous, vast, incontrovertible evidence that the Southern states seceded to protect slavery and white supremacy.

In fact, as a small aside, let me remind you that unlike Lawson, I did not have on this trek my first experience in this territory. I have lived in the South for more than two decades, and I can remind you: people in the South? If nothing else, they are stubborn. Stubborn. With all the positive and negative things that word can carry. If you're wondering why people refuse to accept the unequivocal evidence that the war was about slavery and the flag was adopted as a symbol of white resistance to civil rights, try to remember that you may be dealing with a streak of pure, gut stubbornness. That stubbornness is not unadmirable. Though I will say, in this case it's horribly misguided.

I crossed the Yadkin in a narrow spot in High Rock Lake, using to my enormous satisfaction a little rubber dinghy I had bought in the hopes of using it in the swamps and sloughs of the Francis Marion National Forest in South Carolina. It had proven useless there, but it allowed me to cross the Yadkin under my own steam; the ford itself was under water now, of course. A little brick and stone historical marker for the Trading Ford sits on a tiny, forgotten road near where I-85 crosses the lake, and you can find depressions in the ground there that still might be the old Trading Path, but it took an hour of driving and the attention of a fierce local historian, and I don't recommend it. I much preferred my own inflatable passage across the waters.

From there I kept walking northeast, along small two-lanes that aped the direction of the Trading Path. The usual abandoned houses popped up. Some had the look of a place where someone just didn't come home from work one day thirty years ago—or didn't wake up and then just turned to dust. As though if you pulled upon the front screen door and walked into the still, dusty house there would be dishes neatly stacked in the cupboards, musty napkins folded in the drawers. Others were more chaotic, showing the misuse of years of weather and transients and vandals, but you could not shake the sense of a catastrophe that wiped out a population.

When I approached a bridge across a tributary of the Yadkin, I passed a tiny store and campground, the store recently painted a bright blue, with inner tubes and kites and flags tied to the porch; a campground across the road belonged to the same group: Sutphin's Camp Ground, a hand-lettered banner announced; "under new ownership," said a similar banner on the bright blue store. There I had a pleasant if dispiriting conversation with Larry Jackson, sixty, who came from Thomasville and ended up camping in the woods near Sutphin's "when the economy collapsed," he said. "I became homeless." He was living in the woods near the creek, but "at that time the owner of the store and the campsite, the sheriff department run me off of there," he said. The new owner was more neighborly—Jackson helped clear the campground and got in return a site for himself. When that was all done, "wintertime was coming up," he told me. "They offered me to live in the basement." The particulars weren't important, he said. "House foreclosure. It's typical for this area.

"We have another guy staying with us now." He works in construction and walks to building sites during the week. During the weekends he helps around Sutphin's. As for a place of his own? "His bring-home is not enough," Jackson told me. The few of them banding together—the owners of Sutphin's, Jackson, the other man—couldn't fail to bring to mind the Tutelos, Saponas, and Keyauwees trying to band together to make a safe life for themselves. For the Indians it was smallpox and rum and organized dispossession; for these guys it was the somewhat more faceless dispossession of late-stage capitalism, but the results were the same. Like Lawson I walked through a landscape peppered with empty dwelling places and the wandering remnants of a once-thriving culture.

8 : A Delicious Country

I am standing on, as God is my witness, Golden Meadow Road. As I look northeast, puffy cumulous clouds sail luminous white against a pale blue sky. Rows of trees and deeper forest line the hills that march away, and a single higher mountain pokes above. By the roadside runs a wire fence nailed to weathered wooden posts, and the slanting late-afternoon sun illuminates the meadow in a haze of . . .

Well. The ground rolls in the most serious up-and-down hills I encountered along this walk, and though that created a little stress on feet and knees, every hill I crested afforded a view over bright green fields, a road curving charmingly off to disappear into trees to the left or right; dirt or gravel double-tracks occasionally led off to the side, as though added by an artist seeking variation. Tidy farms began appearing—dairy as well as beef cattle, and the first appearance of corn crops, tall in the fields, tassels drooping in the hot midday stillness. Crape myrtles too, with pink or white blossoms. Vast rich fields of low, deep green soy demonstrated that, though coming north I was hitting the largest hills of my journey, the hills themselves were flattening out as I continued east from the mountains. Much further west and it's hard to farm much more than pines and spruce; here I saw chicken farms and other large-scale agriculture. More, I passed clusters of radio towers—always a sign that you're coming to a change in elevation.

As the Piedmont's higher hills (in the thousand-foot range) diminished to rolling, Lawson said of this portion of the trail, "We pass'd through a delicate rich Soil this day: no great Hills, but pretty Risings, and Levels, which made a beautiful Country." Hear, hear, Mr. Lawson. I never stopped marveling at the rolling landscape—hills to gently climb, then gracefully descend, covered with green meadows, omnipresent white-and-silver barns, and those neat farms. It was walking through country like this that caused Lawson to say, "we pass'd through a delicious Country, (none that I ever saw exceeds it.)." Of the beautiful, hilly country he traverses a little further along, Lawson says simply, "The Savages do, indeed, still possess the Flower of *Carolina*, the *English* enjoying only the Fag-end of that fine Country." In my journals I see I complained of the heat, but it was July in North Carolina. To do so was simply to

*Late summer sunflowers line the road and
you can almost feel good about the world.*

accommodate reality. My camera recorded only, and constantly, breath-taking rural beauty. It was like walking through a Thomas Cole gallery.

:::

Yet the beauty came almost tangentially to my next purpose. I had one thing in mind when I left Denton, just east of Salisbury and the Yad-kin River: archaeology. I was interested in archaeology because I knew I was going to pass by Keyauwee Town, the site on the Caraway Creek of not only the Keyauwee Indians Lawson visited (though uncertainty re-mains about the exact location of that town) but of the dawn of scientific archaeology in North Carolina. In 1933, one Joffre Lanning Coe, born and educated in the state, attended the first meeting of the Archaeologi-cal Society of North Carolina, whose president, Douglas Rights, was the dean of the nascent North Carolina study of archaeology. It was Rights, in fact, who in 1931 published the article "The Trading Path to the Indi-ans," which included the first serious attempt to sketch out Lawson's

A DELICIOUS COUNTRY

path. In 1947 his book *The American Indian in North Carolina* contained "Lawson's Long Trail," a chapter that detailed the trail in far greater depth, as far as Rights could trace it; until I met Val Green, I thought Rights was as close as I was going to get.

I had made arrangements with Delk's Army-Navy Surplus Store to set up camp at the end of the day on their front lawn, which I had seen only on Google Earth. It was within a quarter mile of the Keyauwee site, plus it was a good day's walk from Denton. From my ecologist friend Katie Winsett I got help dropping off my camping stuff there and left my car in Julian, North Carolina, where I expected to finish another day later, and I bought Katie a fried bologna sandwich lunch at the Village Restaurant in Denton. If you learn nothing else from my pursuit of John Lawson, please learn that you should go to lunch someday at the Village Restaurant in Denton.

Lawson speaks of visiting the Keyauwees a day after leaving the Saponas, and finding a town of which he says that "Nature hath so fortify'd ... with Mountains, that were it a Seat of War, it might easily be made impregnable; having large Corn-Fields joining to their Cabins, and a Savanna near the Town, at the Foot of these Mountains. ... And all this environ'd round with very high Mountains, so that no hard Wind ever troubles these Inhabitants." Surrounded by a palisade, he says, it's five miles northwest of the Uwharrie River (he calls it the Heighwarrie), though that turns out to be a misprint: almost exactly five miles north*east* of the Uwharrie, it turns out, flows the Caraway Creek.

There on the Caraway the archaeological society believed it had in 1936 found part of the Keyauwee village mentioned by Lawson, after members had begun digging there a year before. (Much of this story as I relate it comes from discussions with Professor Stephen Davis at the University of North Carolina, or from the book he coauthored, *Time before History: The Archaeology of North Carolina*.) The spot sits on the river, with plenty of farmland spreading as Lawson describes, and the Caraway runs right through the Caraway Mountains, the northern branch of the Uwharrie Mountains, supporting Lawson's description of the spot's protected environs. Here also is where the Keyauwees provided to Lawson's party the fawns "boil'd in the same slimy Bags Nature had placed them in." I was glad I'd enjoyed the fried bologna at the Village.

As I was walking along the hot road, a white pickup slowed down next to me and the driver asked if I wanted a ride. This is a nice thing that happened fairly often, and as I commonly did I said I preferred to walk, and I briefly explained about Lawson and the whole point of this undertaking being to walk along the ground, not to bicycle or drive or take helicopters or something. Walking put me right on the earth, where Lawson had been, and you just see better at that height and that pace. David Harris, the driver, broke into an enormous smile and we began to talk. He talked about his family—he's a Harris, his wife is a Johnson, and there used to be a mill called the Harris Johnson Mill down on Toms Creek, a tributary of the Uwharrie River just off the road where we chatted, near his property. He runs a logging and chipping company, but he loves history and has looked back into the stories on his property.

His family eventually acquired a piece of that mill property: "Mr. Johnson lived back there—he had a two-story house," he told me. "They got a picture of it in the Randolph County archives." He's built himself a cabin where that old house stood: "It's by the same oak trees. They're huge!" The mill was a few hundred yards away, but most traces of it are gone, though searching around he's found parts of an old safe, the back cover of a pocket watch, and an old millstone, which he's pulled out and used as ornament; many such stones grace the gardens of the houses in this area. With every dammable creek used for colonial-era power, there were many mills.

It seems that piece of land that used to be Johnson's house is land-locked—surrounded by other properties with no road in. "I have to go over three separate landowners to get to it," David Harris says of his property now, and one unfriendly neighbor refuses an easement, so Harris has spent hours, thousands of dollars, and countless miles driving back and forth to Raleigh looking up property records to demonstrate his claim for an easement. "I walk through the woods and follow the old road beds," he says. "I pass two, three old house places," abandoned but still standing—one even still has power. But lost roads are the way of things, especially since the mills closed. "That was a big thing in these areas," he says. "Everyone went to the watermill to get their wheat and corn ground. Then the power come, and they all shut down and everyone went into town." His aunt, born in 1918 but still sharp, tells him stories. "She was born back in there, and she told me of all the people that lived down in there."

That is, just as Coe and Davis were doing archaeology at the Keyauwee site, so was David Harris at his old mill. Finding the evidence—road depressions, millstones, the safe, the pocket watch back. Checking the stories—his aunt, his wife, the library, state archives in Raleigh. The

Somewhat less wild than others, but still one of
the coolest places I have ever camped.

story lives in those roadbeds, those deeds and plats, those millstones and pocket watch backs and aunts. Those empty house places, like the ones I constantly pass on the road, tell a story of how the land was once, just like the Keyauwee site; and the new cabin he's built tells a new story. And someday, one presumes, a new deed and entry in the plat book will show how a piece of land has a road easement, and the ghost road the state abandoned will reassert itself, a century later.

In reading about the Caraway site of Keyauwee Town I have learned that the site Coe excavated was likely not the exact site of Lawson's visit. The graves they found at the site show virtually no signs of the trade goods that demonstrate contact with Europeans: beads, ax heads, iron goods, and so forth. "But they had one pit they excavated that had glass beads in it," said Stephen Davis of UNC. "So it's the best candidate. We have nothing else to rival it, and the material evidence from the site, you could argue that it has artifacts that date to that site."

My campsite at Delk's at the end of that day was possibly the all-time championship weirdest and coolest campsite of my entire life. Delk's is your chaotic type of surplus store, with bins and containers overflowing not only inside the dim, sprawling warehouse but in the yard, a bit like a junkyard (including open fifty-five-gallon drums serving for convenience in mosquito breeding), with file cabinets and fan housings and bent shed roofs and so forth covering the acres of the lot. The sign, lit at night, has a torpedo on top. I set up out front amid the mayhem and loved camping there, even when someone who didn't get the memo came roaring up to my campsite in a pickup at about 9 p.m., assuring me that oh no, I *wasn't* camping on Delk's front lawn. A quick phone call of course resolved that, and no harm done, and he roared off again, furious. Still, when I dropped off my stuff early in the day, there had been a truck with a helicopter chassis loaded on it parked there, and I was going to camp between it and the rest of the yard, lightly sheltered from the all-night Route 64 traffic. Delighted by the chopper, I spent my day's walk thinking up "Apocalypse Now" captions to accompany the photos with which I planned to bombard Instagram. Imagine my heartbreak when I came to Delk's at end of day and found the truck gone: no helicopter. The best I could do was guess my pickup antagonist was trying to terminate my Lawson Trek with extreme prejudice, but without the helicopter, to be honest the joke just fell flat.

Carrying on the next morning I plodded through the Asheboro Country Club, and I noticed that rather than walking on the hot asphalt, whenever I could I followed the little double-tracks the mail Jeeps wore into the grass by the side of the road; cooler and safer. I saw orange trumpet creeper and seemingly every purple and white morning glory in creation. By lunch I was hot and sweaty enough that I apologized for my state when I found a tiny lunch counter to sit at. In the afternoon as I sat by the side of the road in the shade of a pine, the sound of thunder and a thrilling breath of breeze coaxed me back out into the welcome overcast. When the storm broke I took off my hat, and allowed it to soak me as I walked.

:::

My Delk's antagonist was an outlier; Davis had set the theme of cheerful people unexpectedly helping as I walked through this delicious hilly country. I often noted on my website that I could always use rides from one site to another as I began every two-or-three-day segment of the Trek, and people never stopped popping up to help. To get to the start of one day's hike I rode with Michael Johnston, a pharmacist in Pleasant Hill, not far from Julian, where I was starting the day's walk. Johnston gladly met me where I deposited my car in Hillsborough to grab me up, then took me to Julian before going to work that day.

The universe being the trickster that it is, Johnston turned out to be a Lawsonian, which he became when he and Cristin, his wife (then his girlfriend), visited New Bern and learned about its history—and its founding in 1710 by Lawson and von Graffenried. Entranced with New Bern's history, the couple considered moving there—and a relative of Cristin's told her that she was the eighth-great-granddaughter of Christoph von Graffenried. "He sent her a whole packet of family tree stuff," Johnston said.

I loved hearing how Johnston fell for Lawson after stumbling onto his book: "I just struck a liking for Lawson because of his attention to detail, natural history, his relationship to the natives. What I wouldn't give to be able to go back and do what he did in an untainted new world," he said. I couldn't have agreed more. Johnston had grown up in nearby Asheboro: "Grandma and them worked that land since she was an infant," he told me. "Always finding arrowheads. There were buttercups down by the creek—she said those buttercups were planted by the Indians." More likely the invasive flowers came with Lawson and his ilk, but the story is the point.

The next Hero of the Lawson Trek I met was Ann Tilley, a seamstress and textile artist who was getting her oil changed at Shoffner's, the crossroads service station/restaurant/store about halfway between Julian and Cedarock Park, the Alamance County park where I planned to spend the night. She sat on a curb in the shade reading and waiting for her car. I sat near her and had that experience where you open a bag of chips in the heat and the air inside is cold from being in the air-conditioned store. That started a delightful conversation not only about Lawson but about the farm where she lived: "It's my boyfriend's stepdad's sister's husband's childhood home." Which, in a sticky region where everybody seemed to have relatives stretching back to Lawson's time, was about par for the course. What's more, she told me that like so many, the farm doesn't work anymore—or actually, it does: "It's a solar farm," she said, now harvesting sunlight for utility companies instead of tobacco. She told me about another one I'd pass along my way. I found it and took a picture of it—a vast meadow filled with slanted rows of cells, angled up toward the sun, though you had to know to look for it; roadside scrub trees hid it almost entirely from view. Barns tend to come down when solar arrays go up, Tilley told me. Signs of the times. Then since she and her boyfriend were going to Cedarock to play disc golf that evening, she picked me up later and drove me there, obviating the need for me to walk miles off Lawson's path to get to the park. She brought watermelon. I was the lone tent in the long riverside campground, and lying in my tent at dusk I heard barred owls and herons call. When I awoke in the morning, dew and the remnants of overnight rain glittered on the Queen Anne's lace.

Still more cool people that segment. The Trading Path has big mojo—people have been walking along it for centuries, since long before Lawson. When you have a place that people tend to go, stuff tends to happen there. Civil War troop movements, for example—and the Battle of Alamance. Years before the Revolution, in 1771, the Regulators, a group of Piedmont farmers, wanted protection from government officials taking advantage of their positions. Skirmishes led to an actual battle in 1771, where the Regulators got their butts kicked but laid down the early groundwork for resistance against the government. I visited the battleground, then wandered into the visitors center to escape the heat. There I met Lisa Cox, who had learned, once she started working there, that the Trading Path, Lawson's path, ran right through the battlefield. She also learned that she was a direct descendant of not one but two of the Regulators—Simon Dixon and Brinsley Barnes, if you're wondering.

And as I neared my stopping point for the night—the Hampton Inn near Mebane, where after a night camping in the rain I enjoyed the AC and the dry bed—I ran into a group of four people out for a nice walk. Janet Eckleberger had driven out to visit Lee and Betty Vernon and Betty's brother, Kemp Kimrey. We were less than a block from Kimrey Road, because roads named for your family is how it is around here. We talked of course about Lawson, and Eckleberger described her experience writing down the directions she followed to the Vernons' home. With the various Old Hillsborough Roads and Salem Church Roads and Saxapahaw–Bethlehem Church Roads, "I felt like I was walking through a historical short story just to get to her house." I knew just how she felt.

∷

In the well-watered Piedmont I passed stream after stream: the Chocolate, and then the Big Alamance, which had a current though it was very slow. I watched its progress by throwing in leaves as I crossed it on a concrete highway bridge south of Burlington. I had wandered into the subdivisions looking to cut a mile out of my walk by fording the Big Alamance, but its big brown waters resisted me. Lawson and his companions I suppose splashed right through it: "We likewise passed over three Rivers this day," he says, "the first about the bigness of *Rocky* River, the other not much differing in Size." The Rocky is a creek Lawson had crossed around where Charlotte Motor Speedway is now; the campers outside the racetrack splash around in it on race weekends. That Lawson says it's the same size as the Big Alamance reminded me: the Big Alamance flows into the Haw, and the Haw is now dammed six miles downstream at Saxapahaw. No wonder the river was big and I couldn't get across it. The dam at Saxapahaw of course once supported a river mill, which powered textile factories, which powered a town. The mill closed decades ago, and things fell apart. Now Saxapahaw is the model for a certain species of rural gentrification: loft condos in the mill building, a general store, kayaking on the lake, the Haw River Ballroom that packs in the locals for music shows. There's something even bigger— huge—planned not far off, and the locals (including the new ones in the lofts) are terrified of the loss of rural character. Lawson called this land so "extraordinary Rich, no Man that will be content within the Bounds of Reason, can have any grounds to dislike it." Evidently. In the rural places the houses stand empty and so do the old mills and the towns they once supported. Meanwhile the urbanizing centers gobble up land like a game of Hungry Hungry Hippos, then begin exporting weary urbanites yearning for open land, which they buy up and, eventually, develop. Saxapahaw is barely fifteen miles from Chapel Hill in North Carolina's explosively urbanizing Research Triangle; it's less than forty from downtown Raleigh. Enormous new developments regularly threaten open space, and citizens' groups regularly organize to resist; I saw signs for these throughout the Piedmont. Stop me if you've heard this before; it seems we're just that kind of species.

In any case, the next big river for Lawson was the Haw, which had a reputation.

"Much taken with the Fertility and Pleasantness," Lawson allowed himself to become "pleas'd, that we had pass'd the River, which us'd to frighten Passengers from fording it." Psych! Determining to rest on the other side of a hill he's climbing, Lawson crests the hill and is then, quite literally, crestfallen: "there appear'd to us such another delicious, rapid Stream, as that of Sapona, having large Stones, about the bigness of an ordinary House, lying up and down the River. As the Wind blew very cold at N.W. and we were very weary, and hungry, the Swiftness of the Current gave us some cause to fear; but, at last, we concluded to venture over that Night. Accordingly, we stripp'd, and with great Difficulty, (by God's Assistance) got safe to the North-side of the famous Hau-River." (Named for its resident Sissipahaw Indians, whose name now graces the loft development. Lawson mentions that some call it the Reatkin.)

:::

Oh yeah, the Haw. Geography has consequences, as the Big Alamance had reminded me. Going northeast was fine, and the Trading Path provided easy enough going, but Lawson still had to worry about the big rivers. I crossed the Haw on the Swepsonville-Saxapahaw Road, and just like Lawson I climbed a hill and then, on the other side of it, there suddenly was the river. Still full of boulders and granite ledges, like a somewhat smaller version of the Catawba at which I had gazed from the dock on the reservation. A Piedmont river. The current was quick, but the water was low and wide—I could have found a likely spot and hopped rock to rock across it. I would have had to be careful, and it would have taken fifteen minutes, and I'd have gotten my feet wet and maybe even fallen, but I'd have been able to do it. On a hot summer day that didn't seem like a bad bet. But finding a way to scramble down the bank from the bridge didn't seem nearly so attractive. I took a video.

Also I noticed that for some reason since Charlotte I had been running across a constant wave of grasshoppers; every vacant lot with weeds or grasses swarmed with grasshoppers. I loved it—when I was little we lived next to an enormous field, and chasing grasshoppers was a summerlong pastime. Not anymore—even in my semisuburban neighborhood at home I rarely see a grasshopper, and studies worldwide show insect populations declining precipitously. It's not just bees and monarch butterflies; it's everything. Monoculture agriculture, pesticides, and habitat loss are the most commonly cited causes, but scientists estimate that our insect population has declined by 45 percent since the 1970s. That's shocking and deeply disturbing; it also means I can scarcely imagine what Lawson would have encountered. He complained about "Musketoes, and other troublesome Insects," but he otherwise seems to find little of interest regarding insects. In the section on insects in his "Natural History of Carolina," he includes for some reason frogs, snakes, alligators, lizards, and other reptiles—but no actual insects. (If his classification seems odd, remember please that the Linnaean system of scientific classification we all take for granted was first published only in 1735; Carl Linnaeus himself, at the time of the publication of Lawson's book about his journey, was two years old.) As a writer most interested in animals for human use, he may have simply found insects not worth mentioning. In any case, I don't know if the scenery changed or the season, but grasshoppers came. And grasshoppers, even as I trudged day after day beneath stinging sun along blistering asphalt two-lanes, lift the spirit wonderfully.

:::

The other thing I began seeing with regularity was the interstate. The combined I-40 and I-85, to be specific. And I-85 follows the railroads, which follow the Old Hillsborough Road, which follows our old friend the Trading Path. I heard the whine of tires for many miles, my path paralleling the interstate closer and closer as I made my way toward Hillsborough, where Lawson met with the Occaneechi tribe. In the rolling hills I passed goat farms and heard roosters, mourning doves lining the overhead wires, cooing, with the hiss of the interstate for background. I saw a lot of baby snakes and frogs who had failed to cross the road; morning glories trained around mailboxes, and I occasionally passed one of those long rows of mailboxes near the entrance to a neighborhood or trailer park where the mail carriers just don't go—reminding me of how many people, how many houses, how many lives, how many stories there are. Cornflowers and goldenrod dominated the ditches, and I saw box turtles, who evidently have developed better road instincts than baby snakes and frogs. Near a little town called Efland my path crossed beneath the freeway, and once again I marveled at the interstate as a physical artifact—a monstrous culvert, almost a tunnel, beneath eight lanes of highway that hissed and boomed so loudly that I took a video. The roaring and shuddering of the trucks and cars overhead was terrifying even to me; the environment felt alien and hideous. A place to pass through, not to be—a place for cars, not people.

From there I followed a road with a person's name—a rural commonplace—into Hillsborough itself, crossing the Eno River, on which Hillsborough has created a paved riverwalk. Before heading into "*Achonechy-Town*," Lawson runs into a group of English Indian traders, who share with Lawson "Two Wheaten Biskets, and a little Ammunition"; this group of a half-dozen traders with thirty or so heavily loaded horses is a hint that Lawson is getting closer to the coast again, and to European settlers, who with that volume of goods are just entering the territory of the Indians with whom they plan to trade. Their leader warns Lawson of dangers further north along the Trading Path. "He advised us, by all means, to strike down the Country for *Ronoack*, and not think of *Virginia*, because of the *Sinnagers*, of whom they were afraid, tho' so well arm'd, and numerous." Significantly, the traders also advise Lawson "to call upon one *Enoe Will*, . . . for that he would conduct us safe among the *English*, giving him the Character of a very faithful *Indian*, which we afterwards found true by Experience." The men all agreed that the land between the Haw River and the Eno (as it's spelled today) was the richest they had ever seen. The groups parted ways and Lawson and his companions entered the Occaneechi town that afternoon, receiving "good fat Bear, and Venison" for welcome. The Occaneechi village turned out to be Lawson's last great good Indian village. "Their Cabins were hung with a good sort of Tapestry, as fat Bear, and barbakued or dried Venison; no *Indians* having greater Plenty of Provisions than these." After they've eaten and rested Enoe Will comes in, and in response to their offer to hire him to lead them to the English settlement on the Pamlico, "he answer'd, he would go along with us, and for what he was to have, he left that to our Discretion."

The friendship between Will and Lawson was clearly strong from the first. After their cheerful meeting, Will begins leading Lawson's group to the east, toward a settlement Lawson calls Adshusheer, which the Enoes shared with the Shakoris. "It was a sad stony way," Lawson says, and tenderfoot Lawson falls "an Hour or two behind the rest; but honest Will would not leave me, but bid me welcome when we came to his House, feasting us with hot Bread, and Bears-Oil; which is wholsome Food for Travellers." Will feeds Lawson chicken, too, and has some of his tribesmen come into Lawson's sleeping quarters: "2 of them having a Drum, and a Rattle, sung by us, as we lay in Bed, and struck up their Music to serenade and welcome us to their Town. And tho' at last, we fell asleep, yet they continu'd their Consort till Morning." Lawson describes Will as "of the best and most agreeable Temper that ever I met with in an Indian, being always ready to serve the *English*, not out of Gain, but real Affection." So close was he to the settlers that Will feared poisoning by other Indians and begged Lawson "to revenge his Death, if it should so happen."

Will walks with Lawson to the end of his journey, and the two became sufficiently close that he tells Lawson "if I would take his son Jack, who was then about 14 Years of Age, and teach him to talk in that Book, and make Paper speak, which they call our Way of Writing, he would wholly resign him to my Tuition: telling me, he was of Opinion, I was very well affected to the *Indians*." Will asks Lawson about his Bible; Lawson seeing Will's interest in a picture of King David encourages him to become a Christian. "He made me a very sharp Reply, assuring me, That he lov'd the English extraordinary well, and did believe their Ways to be very good for those that had already practis'd them, and had been brought up therein: But as for himself, he was too much in Years to think of a Change."

The mutual, honest friendship fairly radiates from the page; Lawson's laconic observations glow as he describes Will. And though we have no records of whether young Jack ever did study with Lawson, we have "New World Testament," the breathtaking short story by Marjorie Hudson, which tells the story of Lawson and Will's friendship from Will's perspective, as transcribed by young Jack. "John Lawson asked me would I come with him and show him the way to the English who live across three rivers and I said Of course. He asked me if I would show him the ways of my people and the beasts of the forest and the birds of the air and the sacred plants and spirit trees and I said Yes. He asked me if I would accept gifts for traveling with him and I said Who knows? For I was embarrassed that he would mention a gift to a friend."

:::

That beautiful evocation of open meeting between new friends felt to me as though Hudson had written it about my meetings with Indian peoples all along my way, so it did not surprise me that in Hillsborough I met a descendant of those Occaneechi people, John Blackfeather Jeffries, a man who has played an enormous role in resurrecting the Occaneechi presence there. Hillsborough has a marker set up to the trading path—an iron plaque set in a stone post, saying, "Here passed the Trading Path— 1700," with a profile of an Indian in full headdress, so Hillsborough felt right from the moment I walked in at the end of a long hot day. When I wandered into the offices of one of the city leaders who had provided me with history and helped me organize my walk into town, he led me immediately to Kelsey's, a catering shop and backroom restaurant in Hillsborough's charming, brick, colonial downtown. There he introduced me to Jeffries, who was preparing to eat something far removed from the fetal fawns in placenta Lawson's party ate in these parts. "Lemme have a rib-eye sandwich," he said to our server. Jeffries wore a bear-claw necklace, a green T-shirt with "Native American Veteran" emblazoned on the front, and a vast and welcoming grin.

"You from O-hee-o?" he asked when he learned of my background, using an Indian pronunciation that, an Ohio native, I had never before heard, and began telling me stories. "My father was the lone Indian in Hillsborough for a time," he told me, looking back to when Indian identity had far from its current level of acceptance. But Blackfeather was interested in his heritage from the start—hunting, learning to use traditional tools and weapons, planting and harvesting crops like tobacco in traditional ways. "This is the way the Indian people did it," he recalls his grandmother telling him; though back then his isolated, segregated community did not know even what tribe it descended from. "That woman was something," he said. "She was the matriarch of the Occaneechi. She was my driving force in all this." An Eagle Scout and a Marine, he grew up knowing but not quite knowing his heritage. His focus clicked up a notch in 1984, when archaeological work done by the University of North Carolina identified areas where the Occaneechis had lived, and Jeffries and his people came to understand their own background. The Occaneechis had before Lawson met them lived just over the state line in Virginia, around the Roanoke River at what is now Clarksville. But during Bacon's Rebellion in 1676, settlers turned on the Indians and drove the Occaneechis south to the Eno River, where they settled and lived when Lawson came through. As modern knowledge and tribal identity began to grow, Jeffries was—literally—pulled into the circle: "I went on through the gate," he told me of an early powwow. "And I been in there ever since." The tribe began lobbying for recognition from the state, which finally came in 2002; federal recognition, as usual, remains another story entirely.

Archaeology is a mixed bag for the tribe—they learn a great deal, and the uncovered history has helped them win state recognition. At the same time, they must watch their ancestors' remains dug up and pawed over, and laws and regulations govern the disposition of an arrowhead or pot found at an archaeological site. Jeffries focuses on the value beneath the conflicting perspectives. He once told an interviewer, "We can make arrowheads. Owning an arrowhead doesn't mean anything to me. *Making* an arrowhead—that means something to us." And he has spent years perfecting those techniques. He invited me back to a shed on his land near the edge of town, where he started by showing me scrapbooks full of photographs of the recreated Occaneechi village he helped build in the mid-1990s. He created the poles for everything from the encircling palisade to the bent saplings for wigwams, described by Lawson as "the Thickness of the Small of a Man's Leg, at the thickest end, which they generally strip of the Bark, and warm them well in the Fire, which makes them tough and fit to bend; afterward, they stick the thickest ends of them in the Ground, about two Yards asunder, in a Circular Form." Jeffries described to me using a stone ax to cut the poles, which didn't work well, so he instead held them over a fire and burned them to size. "Steve Davis [the UNC archaeologist] told me that's right—they found charcoal in the holes." He enjoyed relearning the old techniques, though he used modern methods when required. "I had a chainsaw and a tomahawk," he told me with his enormous smile. He used poplar and cedar and recreated the village, though as complications arose between various stewards of the site the recreated village was eventually allowed to molder.

His own shed became the holding place of Occaneechi heritage, and when he opened the doors I gasped aloud. The walls are covered with skins and quivers, arrows and bows and spears and animal skulls. Everywhere natural resources: quivers of leather, arrowheads of stone, arrows of river cane or sourwood with heads tied on by sinew, flights made of wild turkey feathers, with their distinctive brown and white stripes. (I was glad to know the Occaneechis made use of turkey feathers; when a few days previously I had found one by the side of the road it had seemed auspicious, and I wore it for a while in my hat.) He told me stories of particular spears, bows made for particular friends. He had grindstones and bowls, tools for making arrowheads and cracking nuts. It was like being in a museum—and some of his arrowheads and other crafts are displayed in Hillsborough galleries. In some boxes he notes that some are historical and some are his, but he sees little distinction. They're arrowheads made by Occaneechis. In 1952, Joffre Lanning Coe, the groundbreaking Carolina archaeologist, wrote "The Cultural Sequence of the Carolina Piedmont," in which he said of the vanished tribes of the Piedmont, "There is no record of the last Saponian or of the last Occaneechian," and Jeffries gives the lie to that word, "last." He recounted a conversation he had with a western-states Indian who wanted to look at the Occaneechis as somehow less-Indian for being less aware of their bloodlines over the years. Jeffries scoffed. "If you were full-blood, you would be a doomed race," he said to him. "You're just like us. We followed our culture. What little we could find, we followed. What I'm doing, it may not be Occaneechi cul-

ture back then, but it's Occaneechi culture now. Because I'm doing it."
As for being full-blooded, he laughed. "You go on and think about that.
Full blood. I am full blood. I got sixteen pints!"

Since our visit he's led the community in a second recreation of the
Occaneechi village, and it now brings tourists to Hillsborough. When
I left him after that day in his shed, the rebuilt village was just an idea.
Jeffries gave me one of his own arrows, which to this day hangs in my
home. Even more powerfully, when I moved to leave, he extended not
his right hand but his left. "The left hand," he said, grabbing my hand
and smiling at me, his right hand on my arm. "Close to the heart." My
hair practically stood on end. Lawson describes special greetings among
the Indians, which he says are rare: "They are free from all manner of
Compliments, except Shaking of Hands, and Scratching on the Shoulder," which had impressed him previously. This left-handed shake with
Jeffries felt close to that shoulder-scratching show of respect that Lawson
likened to a handshake. I will not forget it.

: : :

Not long after he left the Occaneechi village Lawson tells of a strange
custom his Indian guides demonstrate.

"The next day, we went over several Tracts of rich Land, but mix'd with
Pines and other indifferent Soil. In our way, there stood a great Stone
about the Size of a large Oven, and hollow; this the Indians took great
Notice of, putting some Tobacco into the Concavity, and spitting after it.
I ask'd them the reason of their so doing, but they made me no Answer."
Something similar to the practice of adding stones to cairns marking
fallen warriors? Respect for the locals? A bad taste in their mouths? We
don't know. As for the hollow rock, it simply came and went.

Given which, when at exactly the right time you find that your path
takes you by the Hollow Rock Racquet and Swim Club in western Durham, you have to take a look, and to get exact directions I reached out to
the club. Within a day or two I had heard from activities and camp director Christopher Jacques, who told me that the query inspired a nameless board member to go on a quest he'd meant to make for five years:
"Namely, where is the actual Hollow Rock?" the member said. Well, not
far off, as it happens. Just down Erwin Road from the club you follow
a private drive up to the New Hope Creek, which runs along a seam of
Triassic sandstone on its south side, the creek a good ten feet or more
below the gravel road above. In the side of that outcropping that is almost

a cliff, beneath the lichens and the mosses, are many large rock protrusions, and in some of them you find little potholes—rendering the stone hollow, just as Lawson said.

Potholes are easy to understand—rain collects in low places, begins to erode the porous rock, whether because of acids in the water or the action of freezing and cooling. That makes the depression deeper and soon you have a pothole; in rivers or areas that supply the flow of water, swirling around sediment that scours the hole makes the pothole even deeper. I found at least a half-dozen rocks with appropriate hollows, and if the rocks were not oven-sized by modern standards, they ranged anywhere from the size of refrigerators to the size of cars. Grayish rocks with green moss, and hollows the size of a fist—or a forearm.

Anyhow, it was nice for a moment to once again know I was exactly where Lawson went, because the hollow rocks were about the last place before the end of the trek that I did. Along the way from Hillsborough to western Durham, Lawson followed what local Tom Magnuson, old-roads enthusiast and founder of the Trading Path Association, called "the old central coast road—it goes all the way from the mountains to the sea." Magnuson doubts that Lawson ever actually made it to Hillsborough, mind you—he believes he stopped somewhat short of there and didn't cross the Eno until days later—but from that area to the Indian settlement Lawson called Adshusheer, the central coast road was the way. That road eventually turned into Old N.C. 10, which I walked along toward the Hollow Rocks.

Magnuson and Val Green disagree about Lawson's exact route here—Magnuson has him walking north of the hollows and Green has him coming up from the south. Green's route has to recommend it that it actually walks right past them, but either route takes you within a quarter mile of these potholes. I explored them and found utterly thrilling that I was where I knew Lawson had been. By what route he got there seemed somehow less important. I had no tobacco, and I didn't spit. Val tells me he's heard from somewhere that the Indian families used to tell their children that lightning would hide in those holes, so they should keep their hands out of them. Val suspects the tall tale was a scare tactic to keep children from sticking their hands in and encountering venomous snakes.

Magnuson, already generous with his time, became a true Hero of the Lawson Trek by taking me on a driving tour of the area, stopping here and there to show me spots where fragments of the old road still exist. I loved seeing them—you can usually tell because there are berms to the side, showing where road builders dug to maintain slope, which Magnuson links back to the English Highways Act of 1555, which first organized highway cost and maintenance as an obligation of the population. Magnuson has spent years of his life digging into the history of the path and loves to explain it.

About the hollow rocks I most loved two things. One was how easy it is to see these old roads—when you have Tom or Val to point them out, as I so often have. But with Tom I found, as I have with Val, that even though they might have pointed me directly at an old road bed in the morning, I am perfectly capable of walking right past it and utterly failing to notice it by noon that same day. This stuff takes work, and their hours of study enrich us all.

:::

The other thing I deeply loved about the hollow rocks was Lawson's note that the Indians just refused to answer his question. "Hey, you guys—why'd you spit in that rock, huh? What's the deal with the tobacco, too? Huh? Come on, you guys. What's the deal?" No answer. Shut up, tourist—not everything is your business. Anybody who's ever been a reporter or interviewed anybody for any reason at all recognizes this interaction. No matter how helpful people are, after a while even the nicest and most patient just get sick of you. Lawson had been following Indian guides for nearly two months, and though he went from guide to guide, one can easily imagine them tiring of his questions. It may also be that, coming closer to European settlers, he was visiting tribes suffering more from their proximity and the difficulties of losing their land, their resources, their trading partners, their health. "Most of these Indians have but one Eye," he says of a group with whom he stays. "But what Mischance or Quarrel has bereav'd them of the other I could not learn. They are not so free to us, as most of the other Indians had been; Victuals being somewhat scarce among them."

So as I stood at the hollow rocks, because of the patient, generous help of countless people answering constant questions, I took a moment of pure gratitude. Lawson never mentioned it, but I suspect that when he noted in his book that someone refused to answer his questions, he took a moment to reflect on how grateful he was that mostly they did answer him. Certainly I did.

Another thing worth noting about Lawson's description of the territory around the hollow rocks is that it's pretty sparse. "East of Orange

County," Magnuson says, regarding Lawson's journey after Hillsborough, "you really end up with a lot of surmise." In the early days of his journey Lawson devotes page after page of loving description to every Indian tribe, every funeral custom, every change in terrain or type of rock; here he simply mentions pine trees or a pocosin and carries on. Early in his journal he often spends two or three pages telling the stories of a single day, the "Tuesday" or "Wednesday" that dot the margins to help the reader hanging in space; now, nearing the end of his journey, he's clearly grown weary: the last twelve days of his trip occupy three pages total, the italic days looking in the margins like ladders.

For my own part I could not say this was difficult to understand, and I noticed it especially as I walked into the Triangle region of Raleigh, Durham, and Chapel Hill—my home territory. Perhaps it was dragging my sore feet and heavy backpack along one more damned asphalt road with no sidewalk, leaping into the bushes when some texting driver or wide utility truck left me no choice. Perhaps it was hitting more development, and seeing the dispiriting plethora of choked five-lane highways and big box stores and malls and five-story stick-built condo developments popping up in this territory like toast on Sunday morning. I stopped in one outdoors supplier to get a strap for my glasses, which slipped off my face from sweat, and inside encountered a wall of guns for sale (pink shirts reminding girls that guns were for them, too) and heard country music singing the praises of small-town life. Having been walking through collapsing and dying small towns for the better part of a year that gave the lie to that song, I got the willies from the whole place.

As I review my files from this leg of my journey, they do not bulge with museum brochures and interview transcripts and recipes; they have my maps, photocopied from the Delorme *North Carolina Atlas & Gazetteer*, and that's about it. It may have just gotten, for me as it had for Lawson, to be that part of the trip, where you just keep going because you keep going. Lawson here was similarly about done with this whole adventuring thing: crossing a river, he says, he spends a night in "the *Indian* Town, which was a Parcel of nasty smoaky Holes ... their Town having a great Swamp running directly through the Middle thereof." Hey, a big adventure! Everybody's having fun, right? Coming out of the long section of delicious country and cheerful, welcoming tribes, perhaps Lawson, like me in this stretch, had just had it.

I walked along the old Chapel Hill Road from Durham into Morrisville, following train tracks as well—train tracks and roads with place names always being a good sign that you're following a path that's been around a while. Train tracks are also a good sign you're walking along level ground, and it was true—Raleigh sits on the eastern edge of the Piedmont, and I could feel the ground evening out beneath my feet. Lawson said the same: "The Land here begins to abate of its Height, and has some few Swamps." The Research Triangle Park, the university-sponsored technological campus that has caused the region's explosive growth, exists because almost nothing wants to grow in the Triassic Basin soils that had by this point replaced the granite outcroppings further west. In flatter territory, soils weather in place, and the metamorphosed volcanic rock breeds what one geologist called "that sticky, red, stain-everything clay" for which the Piedmont is famous. North Carolina makes more bricks than any other state, but that soil isn't much for crops. Lawson noticed it himself: "the Earth is of a red Colour, and seems to me to be wholly design'd by Nature for the Production of Minerals, being of too hot a Quality, to suffer any Verdure upon its Surface." Settlers grew what they could, usually tobacco and cotton, themselves rough on soil, and then moved on, leaving behind ruined farms. That means the Triangle has a nice state park, where on land useless for agriculture second-growth forest has had a century or so to reset, and that there was plenty of space for tech companies when someone in the 1950s had the good idea for a research park. It also means greenways—as I passed through the park I walked along asphalt paths laid down so that scientists and programmers can ride their bikes on their lunch breaks. It was pleasant for a moment not to worry about getting run over.

Just the same, I was heading into Raleigh, my own city—I actually recognized a friend driving along one of the roads, and met another at a mall for lunch. Ironic, but hardly a delicious country. As I crossed over the railroad on one of the main streets in Cary, once a crossroads town but now a suburb of Raleigh, I saw a quote carved into the brick of the bridge: "Art is born of the observation and investigation of nature," supposedly said by Cicero, though I cannot find a source for this claim. I am sure Cicero said nothing of big-box stores and malls and asphalt, and Lawson had nothing to add on this topic. For once neither did I.

9 : Losing the Way

About ten miles east of the little exurban city of Clayton, itself a dozen miles or so southeast of Raleigh, Route 42 crosses the Little River, and as you cross the bridge you look down over a concrete dam; next to it stands a two-story white clapboard mill, where at the Atkinson Milling Company the Wheeler family grinds corn and packages meal all day long. The Little River has had some sort of dam since 1757, when one John Richardson built the first. The mill passed through the Richardson family for years. It was hardly their only source of income; one Richardson scion, Lunsford, bought a pharmacy in nearby Selma and developed a helpful salve for croupy babies. His sister Rozetta had married a Greensboro doctor who helped Lunsford get his business started, so in honor of Dr. Vick, Richardson named the salve Vick's. Everyone did rather well.

One sister married an Atkinson, and the mill property continued developing, at different points hosting blacksmiths, a sawmill, a cotton gin, and a general store. That stuff is mostly gone, though the Atkinson Milling Company still has a store where you can buy their many flour and cornmeal products. When I walked through the property the Wheelers welcomed me—Ray, the seventy-nine-year-old patriarch of the family that now owns and runs the mill, cheerfully walked me through and I got to watch them grind and bag, everything covered in fine white dust.

I stuck my nose in their business because I had been led to believe that this spot on the Little River was a place Lawson described: "We went about 10 Miles, and sat down at the Falls of a large Creek, where lay mighty Rocks, the Water making a strange Noise, as if a great many Water-Mills were going at once," Lawson says. "I take this to be the Falls of *Neus*-Creek, called by the *Indians, Wee quo Whom.*" The Neuse, of course, being the river that starts near Hillsborough as the Eno, now fills Falls Lake north of Raleigh, and then continues through and east of Raleigh, snaking its way out of the Piedmont and through the coastal plain until it pours into the southern elbow of the Pamlico Sound at New Bern. The Tar River pours into the Pamlico further north, at Washington, Lawson's destination. Carolinians call the city Little Washington;

*Tobacco doesn't completely cover eastern
North Carolina, but it can feel like it does.*

the Indians probably would have called it "the place that British guy lives with his daughter." But that lay some days ahead; we were talking about the Neuse.

Now, on my own path I crossed the Neuse, as Lawson would have, about ten miles previously, at Clayton. It was sluggish, brown, and low— a couple of feet deep—but it still had a current: on an average day at Clayton the Neuse runs about 300 cubic feet (more than 2,200 gallons) per second, a few feet high. So, given that Lawson tells us it had been raining for days, the Neuse could easily have been the river that Lawson describes having recently forded, thus: "This River is near as large as *Reatkin*; the South-side having curious Tracts of good Land, the Banks high, and Stone-Quarries. The *Tuskeruros* being come to us, we ventur'd over the River, which we found to be a strong Current, and the Water about Breast-high. However, we all got safe to the North-Shore." The Reatkin, mind, was another name for the Haw, which was a full-size river, no tiny stream.

LOSING THE WAY

The point of all this being that the waterfall Lawson finds here is extremely unlikely to be the Falls of the Neuse, a spot that actually exists. It is the rocky place where Raleigh eventually dammed Falls Lake for drinking water and water quality; that dam is some forty miles back, too close to Hillsborough to be likely. Tom Magnuson and Val Green, my sources for Lawson's route in this area, sometimes disagree with one another, but they agree here: Lawson went too far south to have visited the Falls of the Neuse.

Yet despite the undeniable joy of pairing Lawson's description of the falls sounding like water mills with the finding of an actual water mill in the right vicinity, the dam and falls at Atkinson Milling hardly seemed to answer. Ray Wheeler, who owns the mill and had been deep in the water behind the dam fixing things, dismissed the assertion that this was Wee Quo Whom. The dam is scarcely a dozen feet high; he had drained the reservoir at times and he just couldn't imagine this being a waterfall of any note. To be sure, the base of the dam sits on rocks on its southwest bank, as Lawson describes, though "mighty" may be overselling the rocks. And the steady rain of which Lawson writes a couple of days previous would have had any stream, going over any rocks, making quite a racket. But that starts to sound like we're trying to convince ourselves of something and reminds me of Tom Magnuson's comment that regarding placing Lawson's route on the map, after Hillsborough you have little more than surmise. Or as Vince Bellis, a professor emeritus of botany who has spent his retirement years investigating the end of Lawson's journey, told me, "Lawson disappears after Hillsborough."

:::

So I started south of Raleigh, looking up a congested highway at Raleigh's skyscrapers shimmering in the heat. I then turned south through the little town of Garner, stopping briefly in the Rather Unique Barber Shop, because with that name how could you not? The gentlemen in there knew nothing of Lawson, but when quizzed suspected that what would surprise Lawson most about our modern world was paved roads. Next door were two churches: Christ Temple of the Apostolic Faith, in a storefront, and Palmer Memorial Free Will Baptist, in a more traditional peaked-roof brick building with a small steeple. I thought about the southern truism that every adjective equals a sect split: thus one can imagine that the Free Will Baptists split from the General Baptists, though whether the Palmer Memorial Church is simply an example of that sect or whether the Memorials split, and then the Palmers split from them, I do not know. As the territory south of Raleigh turned rural, traditionally southern Christian sects once again emerged as predominant; in the cosmopolitan Triangle I had passed the Masjid An-Noor Al-Muhammadi, the Raleigh Chinese Christian Church, Korean churches, and entire neighborhoods of religious and commercial buildings dedicated to Tibetan, Hindu, Indian, and Nepali communities, to say nothing of the common Hispanic neighborhoods.

A little further away from Raleigh and I was returning to something that had been around the Carolina Piedmont a much longer time.

Again my overwhelming impression was walking along a hot road, though I was very glad, as long as Garner held out, for sidewalks and shade trees. Downtown Garner was a two-block row of stores on one side of Main Street (mostly, it seemed, hair salons) and the railroad tracks on the other side. Also a water tower and the obligatory red caboose on a little track of its own. Thereafter the usual metal shops and car repair shops and warehouses, full and empty, that one expects when approaching the fringes of a major metropolitan area, including a quarry, reminding me that we were still, just barely, in the Piedmont; you don't find enough rock to merit a quarry once you're in the coastal plain. About halfway between Garner and Clayton, among metal shops I found a little white gazebo on a wooded corner; no plaque, no indication of whose largesse provided it, just a white wooden octagonal gazebo. I do not know when I have been more grateful for such an act of kindness. I had my lunch there in the shade. The hot afternoon's walk then led me to Clayton, a town of some 20,000 doing a complicated dance between being a bedroom community for Raleigh and maintaining a sense of itself. Its low brick downtown has a public library and the usual spate of hair salons and taverns—and also a community garden and a brewery and, most important to me when I walked in at the end of a hot day, Lee's Produce and Garden Center, where I got an electric blue shaved ice. A lumber, cotton, and tobacco town, Clayton followed the usual cycle of post–Civil War growth, a stall during the Depression, and collapse with the loss of first cotton and then tobacco. Close to Raleigh, though, Clayton has diversified and is growing again: my path out of town headed due east, between the Caterpillar plant with a big yellow backhoe out front and the Bayer Environmental Science plant, where they teach things like golf course management.

Yet Clayton also suffers from the troubles endemic to even healthyish twenty-first-century small towns. The population is again on the rise, but developers outside town have bought up land across the city line, offering homes to people who will be able use the town as a resource—but pay no city taxes. So I was told by one city booster to keep my eyes open for the Flowers Plantation, a vast development just outside the city limits as I walked east.

:::

It would have been hard to miss. Not long after I crossed the Neuse I passed an attractive little lake—with a sign informing me that the lakes and trails were for members and guests only. Soon signs popped up for sub-subdivisions with names like Sweetgrass (houses starting at $350,000) and Longleaf (starting at $190,000). At the first major crossroads east of Clayton I came to the Percy Flowers Store, an enormous three-story brick gas station/restaurant/general store/liquor store. Busy for lunch, it boasted specials with fries and a couple of bright red hot dogs (a Carolina specialty; the red color is just dye, and no, I've never been able to get anybody to explain why). I dawdled over lunch in the air conditioning and read the *Flowers Plantation Treasure*, the biannual publication telling me everything I needed to know about the Plantation.

Lawson may have walked through here on an Indian trail, but the first road was eventually cut by troops commanded by General William Tryon in 1770, on their way from New Bern to go fight the Regulators in the Battle of Alamance. Flowers Plantation is a southern development that can wear its "Plantation" name unironically—John Watson, a veteran of the Revolution, bought up land east of the Neuse. His son was a doctor who served under Andrew Jackson, and the 10,000 acres the family owned and farmed (with about 350 slaves) soon became known as the Pineville Plantation; Watson ran for Congress once, and the Dr. Watson Inn on the Plantation grounds now contains the occasional piece of a house the first Watson built in the 1700s. During and after the Depression, one Joshua Percy Flowers began buying up Watson's land. (The *Treasure* mentions that when he died, Flowers owned more than 300 walker hounds. It does not mention that the Watsons owned more than 300 people; perhaps that's implied by the name.) The Flowers opened their first store around 1940, and in 1986 they rebuilt it in its current brick incarnation. Since then the place has become Flowers Crossroads, with a grocery store, a pharmacy, a pet supply store, and Italian and Chinese restaurants. A model of southern exurban parking-lot-based development. The *Treasure* contains a quiz about Clayton and a celebration of Clayton's visual arts. The Plantation website, in contrast, asks buyers, "Looking to live on a property where you will never have to pay city taxes?" So it's complicated.

Those were some dynamite hot dogs, though.

:::

Not far beyond Flowers Crossroads I came upon Atkinson Milling, and from there I continued, but with a new perspective on retracing Lawson's steps. That is, the uncertainty about the waterfall of Wee Quo Whom underscored the uncertainty of even my most trusted sources about exactly where Lawson went, especially at this point in his journey. "Even Lawson didn't know where he was," Tom Magnuson said. "How could we know?" A good point, and worth keeping in consideration as I traveled onward. When I began looking into Lawson's life, the general sketch of his route by Douglas Rights seemed perfectly satisfactory, but then because of people like Val Green and Tom Magnuson and Vince Bellis I ended up knowing far more about Lawson's exact path than I had expected. The danger was that the route would become more important than the walk, and openly admitting that we were just shrugging and hoping we were close felt like a release. After all, was the point really whether the Atkinson Milling Company dam actually was Wee Quo Whom? Or was it more important to learn that since Lawson's time just about every possible spot had been dammed (Ray Wheeler told me there had once been twenty-eight grist mills on the Eno River alone— not the Neuse, which flows to the sea, but the Eno, forty miles long); that the silt that had built up behind those dams remained, whether or not the dams did, and would present a challenge for stream health for centuries to come; that the little communities created by those innumerable mills were dying; that even the Atkinson Milling Company now looks forward and wonders whether its future lies, as Ray Wheeler told me, not as a working concern but as a museum. Or for example I noticed on my way east from Clayton that as we neared the edge of town I started seeing the abandoned houses and empty cinderblock strip buildings that I expected when leaving every little town—then saw, once I passed the town boundary, the enormous Flowers development, and the story those observations told about how people feel about taxes and what they value. I think that's what Lawson did: he saw and he tried to understand. "He was a great noticer," a friend and fellow Lawsonian told me, and on my walk my chief job was not to slavishly retrace. My job was to notice.

I noticed that we had come to tobacco country. As the terrain finally begins to lay flat, east of the fall line and into the coastal plain, the soil becomes sandy, the mineral-rich result of the weathering of sedimentary rocks laid down on ancient beaches. The resulting soil drains well and is perfect for tobacco, which needs to be dry so the leaves can yellow at the end of the season, fixing into the leaves the chemicals that satisfy those who love tobacco—and made it such a worthy investment for those slave-driving drug lords who prospered in the early colonies of the North American South. My wife's family farmed tobacco, and her mom tells stories of tobacco as a family enterprise: the older kids would top the plants (take off the blossoms so the plants put their muscle into those leaves, not into reproduction); younger kids would tie the leaves at harvest, when the adults and helpers were out picking. She—and everyone I've ever spoken to about it—talks about wearing bandannas to cover her hair because hands would become so sticky from the tarry tobacco sap. They would hang the tied leaves over rods, then hang the rods in what may be the most omnipresent piece of rural North Carolina architecture: the tobacco barn. The simplest structures in the world—framed with as few rough-sawn pine trunks as would hold them up; sided with tin or splintery planks; cracks filled with plaster, rocks, cement, or anything else that came to hand; a peaked tin roof to keep off the rain. Tobacco barns once dotted Carolina fields everywhere you looked; I noticed them in the early 1990s, when I moved to the state. Farm families would hang those long sticks covered with tied leaves until a barn, usually two stories, was full, then, mostly, flue-cure it—burning wood in a connected furnace that carried air through the barn over the better part of a week to get the yellow leaves dry and fragrant, but not brittle. Every family had its own recipe for what wood to burn, what temperature to reach, how long to go.

No more. I noticed the lack of barns as I walked through tobacco country, and when I looked up statistics I found estimates that the North Carolina tobacco barn population has in recent years dropped by 90 percent: from a half million to 50,000 as tobacco has collapsed along with the family-sized growing operation. Some of them just rot away—they're flimsy under the best of circumstances—but others show up as reuse materials in buildings now; I have been to a recording studio made from pieces of recycled tobacco barns.

Another tale of emptiness told by a lovely silent building.

But though small family tobacco operations are largely gone, large-scale tobacco farming continues in the coastal plain, and I saw every aspect of it as I walked to and through Wilson, once the capital of the to-bacco industry, filled in those days with warehouses and auctions, hotels and restaurants supporting the industry. Now a city of some 40,000 people, Wilson has a devastated downtown, though inexpensive land has made new subdivisions reasonable in price. As county seat, Wilson has a courthouse and civic Wi-Fi and a long-term vision of its future as the capital of a rural coastal plain region that needs one. There's no ignoring the blocks—neighborhoods—of empty downtown warehouses and once-thriving businesses; faded white paint on two-story brick rows of store-fronts, window sockets sometimes sporting the kind of empty-display ex-hibitions to which struggling downtowns resort: brightly colored happy silhouettes, for example. More commonly they display plywood. In the stillness window lettering informs you of expired functions ("office");

LOSING THE WAY

notices painted on brick walls advertise forgotten uses: the "Hi Dollar Warehouse," for example, is gone but not forgotten. It may be redeveloped into, what else—lofts.

Yet despite its struggles Wilson is actually one of the rare rural cities making a go of it. It has dedicated a new downtown park to its greatest cultural resource—world-famous outsider artist Vollis Simpson, who created metal whirligigs the height of three-story buildings that face into the wind and spin like propellers and rotate like Ferris wheels and crank up sheet-metal people riding bicycles and sawing logs and strumming musical instruments like the world's largest lawn motion-art, which I guess they really are. The park has opened now, but when I walked through town a good dozen whirligigs already spun in the then-unopened park; hundreds more dot yards and living rooms in the region; a museum comes next. Locals in the know will send you to Simpson's abandoned workshop in Lucama, southeast of town, where the astonishing chaos of his process remained scattered, with a few still-standing whirligigs, along Vollis Shop Road. Visit around sundown, because a ghost story goes with it. Local teens, fascinated like everyone else by the freakiness of the place, would cruise the neighborhood. Some of them got to tripping on acid, and according to the story, one night things didn't end well. Supposedly you can still see the remains of a wreck that killed teens if you know where to look, which I evidently did not. Just the same, spooking around the remains of the Simpson Repair Shop, where Vollis's imagination took flight and created his remarkable moving sculptures, was worth the side trip. If nothing else it was worth it for the sunset, which in this part of the world had begun to remind me of the almost daily sky parties I remembered from the beginning of the trek in the South Carolina coastal plain. When the land is flat you get a good look at the clouds, and come sundown look out.

But the real story of Wilson is still tobacco. Lawson describes the terrain in these parts as "poor, white, sandy Land, and bears no Timber, but small shrubby Oaks." That nice sandy soil makes for tobacco country, of course, and in tobacco Wilson once did not merely survive or even thrive but excelled—it was known as the world's greatest tobacco market in the 1800s, and it still has tobacco warehouses and distribution centers aplenty; the smell, especially south of town near many warehouses, borders on the heavenly. Along every road I saw the tobacco harvest taking place, and in Wilson I found the warehouses and distributors for that leaf.

:::

The harvest was a treat to watch. Unlike the stories my wife's family tells about picking, tying, hanging, and curing by hand, the entire process is now almost completely automated, and as I walked the roads around Kinston I saw it. First a picker about the size of a Zamboni straddles two rows of plants, slowly making its way up the field, spinning metal wires snatching leaves and running them up conveyors into a Dumpster-sized bin. Then up drives a flatbed, onto which the picker dumps its load of yellow-green. The vast majority of flatbeds in Wilson County are repurposed school buses: the cab remains but the part for the kids is gone, replaced by a flat bed and walls; as I walked those buses passed me a dozen times a day during the harvest. Once the flatbed is full they cover the harvested leaves and drive to what now pass for tobacco barns: corrugated steel outbuildings in which gas heaters and fans provide the heat to cure the leaves. No tying these days; the same crew of three or four (almost exclusively Latino and Latina) workers takes armloads of leaves and throws them in piles on a metal hanging unit that would fit in a pickup bed, a sort of frame with spikes inside to hold the leaves. They snap closed the frame and that's a load of leaf ready for curing, which they slide into the outbuilding while other workers throw armfuls of leaves onto the next frame. The two who carried the completed frame into the curing building get back almost exactly when the loading is done. Spin and start again. Larger operations used Dumpster-size bins. This all takes place under the seemingly constantly cloudless skies of the coastal plan: a green sea of tobacco vanishes in days. Then it enters these metal, mobile-home-sized gas-fired curing units; a week later it's baled for the warehouse. The whining of their fans punctuated my early September walk through tobacco country like air conditioners when you walk of an evening through suburban streets.

I passed the big metal warehouse for Universal Leaf North America US as I walked out of Wilson, and I smelled it for a half-mile before I passed it. They let me step inside to see the bales of tobacco, but even outside I could smell it. We all know tobacco is a bad thing, but . . . that cured tobacco smell. Cured tobacco—not burned, mind you, just the sweet, smoky flue-cured leaves—has a richness and a sort of organic muscle to it that belies the danger of the leaves. I stopped in the Friendly Mart across from the enormous Alliance One warehouse and distribution plant on the way south out of town, and I mentioned to the young woman behind the counter—Amethyst, she eventually told me—that I loved the smell.

"I can't tell if you're being sarcastic," she said, and once I reassured her we got to talking. "They have a building that takes care of all their flavors," she told me. "So you walk by one day and the whole place smells like cherry." You can see why Walter Raleigh and company went for it in such a big way when it suddenly showed up. They fell for tobacco grown in Virginia from seeds produced by colonies in the Caribbean and South America, by the way. The scrub tobacco the Indians used for their pleasure and economy and rituals was too rough for the European palate. The Virginia Colony, the first British colony in North America, already imported seeds for the tobacco operations that helped it eventually succeed, and Virginia tobacco farmers were spreading south into the coastal plain of what would be Carolina Colony territory by the 1650s, decades before the colony was even chartered.

As for Lawson, by his time tobacco was well established in trade and even as currency; he regularly mentions economic use by both Indians and traders of "Beads, Tobacco, and such like Commodities that are useful amongst them." He never mentions smoking himself, but the whole thing was already big business; he notes that proximity to Virginia makes Carolina attractive, not just for security and access to trade but "to sell our Provisions to the Tobacco-fleets; for the Planting of Tobacco generally in those Colonies, prevents their being supplyed with Stores, sufficient for victualling their Ships." Perhaps not the first and surely not the last example of a community focusing so powerfully on its drugs that it loses track of its basic needs.

:::

"This day, we pass'd through several swamps," Lawson says of this territory, and copy that. I walked through a swamp along a trickle called the Beaman Run that contained such a plague of gnats and mosquitoes that I found myself cursing them aloud as I walked along. "We had now lost our rapid Streams, and were come to slow, dead Waters, of a brown Colour, proceeding from the *Swamps*," he says, to which, check. Lawson's group begins encountering Tuscarora Indians around here, and one pair tells them if they hurry they can meet up with a large hunting party, but Lawson and his gang being "tired, we rested that Night, in the Woods." I suspect Lawson knew his journey neared its end, and he just wasn't ready to run into a crowd again.

I felt much the same way; I was developing prenostalgia for my time walking among the tiny towns of Carolina. Tobacco was still everywhere, of course—at the side of the roads I'd see big pale yellow-green leaves, like something from a giant overwatered cabbage. Leaves fell off cured bales on their way to the warehouse, too, and I would find little twists of cured tobacco lying by the side of the road, and they smelled wonderful, too. And of course every field doesn't grow tobacco: I took videos of a sweet potato harvest by big noisy machines and of a seed corn harvest by other big noisy machines. I had been passing corn for weeks, and that's rural corn—I would stand on the road by acres of corn, taller than me, and listen as in the breeze it surrounded me with that dry rustling sound; sometimes I stood for five minutes just listening to that. Butterflies, little yellow ones, seem to adore soy fields, and I would watch them chase each other around among the crops. Bigger butterflies love watermelon; a smashed watermelon left after a harvest seemed never to fail to be feeding at least one monarch. With the struggles monarchs currently face, I found their presence a comfort.

As the late summer was turning to fall I saw stands of goldenrod in the ditches but also summer standards like sprays of white asters everywhere and also jimsonweed, which Lawson mentions as "James-Town-Weed," recognizing its origin in the Jamestown settlement (though it's likely the settlers brought it with them; it probably originates in Mexico), and he already knew its properties. "It is excellent for curing Burns, and asswaging Inflammations," he says, "but taken inwardly brings on a sort of drunken Madness." Another marsh weed has a similar effect, he notes, "and possesses the Party with Fear and Watchings." No word on whether it causes repeated viewing of *Saturday Night Live* skits on YouTube or induces Oreo cravings. Speaking of blossoms of crazy plants, did you know that kudzu has a breathtakingly lovely blossom, a spike of irregular purple blossoms that divert your attention from the fact that it covers some 7 million acres in the Southeast and would probably cover you if you stood still long enough. Still promoted as an erosion strategy by the U.S. Soil Conservation Service as recently as the 1940s, the Asian native was declared a noxious weed by an act of Congress in 1998. Modern farmers are finding uses for the plant—it feeds goats and does indeed hold the soil down. And as bad as it looks by the roadside—and it looks like it's eating the countryside—it spreads only by vine, not by seed, so the roadside is mostly where it stays. North America has seen a lot of invaders that have not been as polite.

The walk from Wilson toward Washington distilled the feeling of the down east coastal plain: one tiny town after another—Stantonsburg, with railroad tracks, a drug store, a little bank branch, the usual antiques/resale store, a hair salon, a pizza place, and on Main Street the most beautiful and heartbreaking strip of empty whitewashed two-story brick storefronts I saw on my entire walk. Several of the windows of the ten or so storefronts were boarded with plywood, but in one hung dresses in dry cleaner bags. No sign, no indication of when or whether the store had hours for people to buy this decent used clothing. It was the only sign of life on the block—the unneeded remains of lives long past. A sidewalk roof, painted white many years ago, would have protected shoppers from the sun. The second story—offices once, or apartments—had attractive arches over the windows, brick dentils demonstrating that Stantonsburg merchants had money to spend, probably back in the 1940s. And still—a street or two of neat houses; a tile set in the concrete sidewalk: "Keep the Neuse River clean and save us," in a thought bubble by a blue fish; schoolchildren. Stantonsburg hasn't given up. There's a strip mall on Highway 55 where you can find a chain burger or Chinese food.

Past more swamps to Speights Bridge and to Castoria, places still in the Delorme *North Carolina Atlas & Gazetteer* but not on Google Maps no matter how close you zoom, though if you type in the name the program will fling you into the area. Abandoned houses, including one with a recliner on the front lawn, and the usual string of barns in the usual phases of returning to nature, being consumed by greenery. Castoria, simply a crossroads with a fire department and the remains of what once—long ago—was a roadhouse. Castoria thrilled my guide Val Green because in this area Lawson stayed with an Indian who, interested in heading toward the British settlement to get some rum, offered to guide Lawson, Enoe Will, and their gang there if they waited a couple of days, which of course they did. This is where Lawson describes eating the delicacy of beaver tail. The Linnaean genus for beaver being *castor*, of course, Val felt confident that his guidance was sure as he sketched my final days.

Yeah, maybe. Remember Vince Bellis? The emeritus botany professor (from the University of North Carolina–Greenville, less than twenty miles northeast of Castoria and an equal distance from Washington, my—and Lawson's—destination)? When I met with him, nearing the end of my walk, he dismissed that. Already interested in Lawson's botanical contributions, Bellis in his retirement got to wondering about where Lawson ended his journey—where, that is, lived this Richard Smith, at whose settlement Lawson dropped his pack. He worked with Val, searched archives and maps, and even wrote up an unpublished paper, "Searching for the Ashes of Mr. Lawson's Campfires," which he shared with me.

He invited me one evening into his delightful Greenville home and, amid maps and land records, showed me exactly where Smith's house was—rather west of Washington, much closer to where I had already walked than I had expected. Moreover, in conversation with Bellis (and checking in with Val Green) we discovered that to at least a certain extent my last twenty-five miles or so had been somewhat at variance with Val and Vince's best and latest estimates for Lawson's actual track. I must have had an early version of Val's course; Val had gone through several of those DeLorme books, and people used to believe Lawson had gone as far south as Goldsboro before heading north. So I suspect Val had been iteratively moving Lawson north, and I got route version 5.3 instead of 5.5 or 6.0. In any case, when I drove back to compare the two routes, with the exception of the river crossing in Greenville, about ten miles further west than my crossing closer to Washington, the two routes passed through almost identical territory: flat, broad farms, exurban blight, and heartbreaking old buildings and barns collapsing back into the soil. Lawson said, "The Country here is very thick of Indian Towns and Plantations," and it's still that way, though the towns have few residents and are dying. He also mentions how in this area some of his companions, invited by Indians, went to visit their town "but got nothing extraordinary, except a dozen Miles March out of their Way." I could relate.

And again, one ought not to get too worked up over that; it was Bellis, after all, who said that "Lawson disappears after Hillsborough." This is how it is when you try to get directions from a guy who last visited the area 315 years ago and didn't know where he was when he did it. Bellis knew where he ended, though, and that felt important. Plus, had I taken Vince and Val's most updated route I would have missed Amethyst and her story of the haunting of the Vollis Simpson shop and her description of smelling cherry tobacco flavoring.

:::

I don't mean to sound cavalier, and I don't want to diminish the importance of hewing as close as possible to Lawson's path, which was, after all, the point. And there's much to be gained by learning as much as possible about Lawson's route—and his moment. In fact, Val Green, like a dog with a bone, has done some original research utterly unmatched on this topic and has figured out, with a rather strong degree of likelihood, not only Lawson's path but Lawson's companions. Not Enoe Will, Santee Jack, or the various Scipios he mentions; regrettably his Native guides and companions bordered on nonpersonhood at the time, and giving them more historical detail than Lawson did is probably not possible.

But remember those "six *English*-men in Company, with three *Indian*-men, and one Woman" who set out from Charleston months before? Val Green has put names on those English (and, it turns out, French) men. It's a long story. Since Lawson wrote his book, people have idly wondered whom he traveled with. He makes various references to his companions hither and yon, but nobody has ever come close to even imagining they could find information on who accompanied Lawson on his trip.

As I say, enter Val. One day, someone in the library of the Virginia Historical Society noticed that their collection included a manuscript by one Richard Traunter, who describes traveling between Fort Henry in the Virginia colony and Charles-Town, in Carolina, by land—in 1698 and 1699, a couple of years before Lawson's famous journey. The manuscript was bequeathed to the library in 1999 with the collection of Paul Mellon and has been cited once or twice—in *Indian Slavery in Colonial America*, for example, and *The Goose Creek Bridge: Gateway to Sacred Places*. But it's unpublished: if you don't go looking for it in the Virginia Historical Society, you don't read it. Traunter's manuscript made its way to Val, and Val started looking at things.

Here's what he found. Traunter, an Indian trader in the employ of Robert Byrd at Fort Henry on the falls of the James River in Virginia (it's Petersburg now), set out in 1698 for Charles-Town, for what he describes as two motives: one, "from a Naturall propensity I always had to travel; but more especially in untroden paths, thoroly to discover thye wonderfull workes of the Almighty brought forth by Nature, as well to Enlighten the Intellect, As to gratifie the externall Senses." His other goal, he says, was to "Apply my discoveris & Travels to the common Good of my Country, soe as to make them Usefull to the Traders to those places I passed through."

Traunter describes setting out in 1698 to return a slave to one James Moore, one of the chief citizens of Goose Creek. Moore's name shows up all through South Carolina colonial records, hunting for gold and other wealth. (Called the Goose Creek Men after their community north of

Charles-Town, they were a cadre of rich guys pulling strings for their own interests: Indian slavery, trade with pirates, and other refusals to cooperate with the Lords Proprietor. As surveyor general Edward Randolph wrote to the Lords of Trade, who helped manage the colonies, in London in May 1700, "In this Province their Lordships, by misinformation, have at least made choice of very naughty men to be their deputies.")

Traunter evidently spent time with Moore, then sailed back to Virginia. He made a second journey like the first in 1699, arriving in Charles-Town in October 1699, then joining an expedition for gold with Moore and one of the greatest Indian traders of the day, Jean Couture, a French *coureur du bois*—a runner in the woods. It failed when one of the main explorers drowned. Undaunted, Moore, sure of untold riches to come, wrote to the Lords of Trade asking for backing for another journey to the mountains.

Their Lordships were not impressed. "Their Lordships do not meddle in what Capt. Moor desires of them and what Smith and Cutler think fit to do upon his request," they said in a letter of September 27, 1699. Smith was a trader named John Smith, and Cutler was Thomas Cutler, a friend of Moore's and the business partner of a Londoner named Henry Netherton, for whom he investigated Indian trading and mining opportunities in Carolina, where he had arrived in 1698.

This all took place, mind, in late 1699—and a few months later our own John Lawson in London "accidentally met with a Gentleman, who had been Abroad, and was very well acquainted with the Ways of Living in both Indies; ... he assur'd me, that Carolina was the best Country I could go to." From this and several other corroborating details Val has deduced the following.

Cutler was the guy Lawson met in London, and coming back with Cutler Lawson met virtually every connected person in Charles-Town. With their Lordships deriding foolish chases for gold in the hills, Traunter and Couture would have been looking for what was next. Traunter's stated objects, of "opening A free passage for Trade betweene South Carolina, & Virginia, that never had any Communication before by Land" and "to render the Travelling to them more Safe than before had been," would certainly seem attractive—to adventurer and to investor alike.

Add in that Londoner Netherton's wastrel son had arrived in Charles-Town, where he immediately set about asking for money, according to a letter from Moore to Cutler dated December 27, 1700, to pay his freight and "to buy a servant woman," with whom "he had kept company all voyage." Moore notes with irritation that "Mr. Netherton is by land on his way to Virginia." On December 28, 1700, our own John Lawson left Charles-Town with five other Europeans and four Indians, trying to go to Virginia by land.

What makes this work is the corroborations you find within Lawson. Lawson accounts with special glee the night among the Catawbas, one member of his group "having a great Mind for an Indian Lass, for his Bed-Fellow that Night"—the incident of the robber bride, who left the young man without even his shoes. That has to be Netherton. It sounds like every adventure of every wastrel son, sent by a frustrated father to his partner to make something of himself and instantly getting into trouble. (Netherton had already hooked up once, recall, on the boat to Carolina.) Add in that, according to the record, Netherton the younger ultimately married a Virginia heiress and you're telling a story familiar to everyone who ever went to college with a screw-up scion of some rich family who nonetheless, with privilege on his side, always seemed to have things work out just fine.

Lawson does not name his fellow travelers, though several times he describes one or another as "a person of Credit, and a great Traveler in America," or "a Traveller of Credit." That easily describes Couture and Traunter, and Val draws only slightly weaker deductions about the remaining two Europeans, identifying one as possibly Solomon LeGare, a member of one of Charleston's first families.

It's breathtaking research, and you can poke holes if you like. But with a couple of exceptions, nobody has tried to gain anything from Traunter's narrative for 300 years. Starting with that narrative, Val has drawn amazing conclusions. Given that Lawson and Traunter follow so much of the same path, it seems absurd not to conclude that Traunter traveled with Lawson. Once you've included Traunter and recognized that the group was planning an enterprise together, Couture and Netherton follow almost certainly, especially since we know Netherton left for Virginia at exactly that time. As for the remaining two, there's plenty of question. But until Val Green came along we had Lawson and five question marks. I'm pretty convinced we've now got Lawson, Traunter, Couture, and Netherton. As for the other two, we'll see.

The point isn't so much that Val Green has done this powerful research; Val's research, after all, mostly guided me. I think in fact the point is just the opposite: despite the fact that Val's great research guided me,

I nonetheless found myself off course for parts of the end of the journey. That is, there's always more research to do, and no matter how certain we are, next year we may find ourselves off course. As I found in my walking, being off course by a mile or so didn't turn out to be a bad thing, and in many ways made my trip better. The point, as ever, was the walk.

There's an enormous amount to gain from serious engagement with the historical record; I don't mean to casually dismiss the importance of trying to be historically accurate on this walk. Val's research only deepens the sense that for Lawson, at that moment in his life, this was an adventure for its own sake. Surely he had plans for himself, and this journey gave him lots of opportunities, but at bottom he joined up with a gang of guys taking a cool walk. Taking a cool walk is a good idea. And after Castoria—or wherever he was—Lawson was almost done.

So was I.

10 : A Bed in Bath, and Beyond

A day out from Washington, outside the little crossroads of Grimesland, I stopped to look over yet another swamp, this one along the tiny Chicod Creek. I saw cypresses, tupelos, and the swaying Spanish moss that I hadn't seen since Lake Marion in South Carolina. Right on time: in this territory Lawson too knows he's back in the flattest, swampiest part of the coastal plain, edging toward the coast. They "went on through many *Swamps*," he says, "finding, this day, the long ragged Moss on the Trees, which we had not seen for above 600 Miles." It was actually more like 400 than 600 miles, but Lawson exaggerates his walking; he regularly says that he went 20 or 30 miles on a given day, though it seems a lot more likely that he went between 10 and 14 miles most days. Val Green has calculated it and I've walked it and we both came to about the same conclusion. And don't forget, by the time it gets into print, Lawson has stretched that already generous 600 miles into "A Journal of a Thousand Miles, Travel'd." Even in 1709 a good subtitle might sell a book, and Lawson was never one to get in his own way when it came to telling a story.

I could tell you about the grinding poverty of places like Maury and Scuffleton, but it would just be another litany of empty warehouses and stores, collapsing buildings on the way into town, and three-block downtowns with a few stores still open among the empty plate glass. Grimesland did boast a used furniture store called Stanford and Son, of which I approved, and Maury, a few miles southeast of Greenville, had in its mostly empty crossroads downtown a little pool hall with walls covered in hand-scrawled signs telling you what you could not do: dance, listen to the radio, smoke, hang out, put anything on the pool tables. Just the same, I had very cheerful conversations with a few Mauryites who, seeing me take notes and pictures, stopped to chat. They don't have much work in Maury is about all I can tell you, but they're nice to visitors, and they haven't given up. If you visit, don't put drinks on the pool tables.

The tobacco harvest continued as I walked along, so I saw pickers and flatbeds full of leaf; I also saw big wide low crates of sweet potatoes. It seemed to be the season for a grasshopper with a sandy brown exterior that would suddenly leap into the air and spread astonishing black wings fringed with yellow. It's called the Carolina grasshopper, as it turns out. I walked by feed corn rustling in the wind, and now and again birds would burst upward from within with a whir and a flutter and a commotion. Also I had worn through two pairs of hiking shoes—I preferred nice light trail runners for walking along both paved roads and grassy berms— and breaking in a new pair so near to the end of my journey I ended up with possibly the biggest blister I've ever had.

:::

So I was not sad to come to the Tar River, just north of Grimesland. Crossing here, on Grimesland Bridge Road, or a few miles further east in what is now a park in Greenville (as those who know better than me now think Lawson did), the Tar is the last major geographical barrier to Washington. Lawson describes crossing it by a canoe stashed there by one of his Indian guides. He had spent a night with that large hunting party the Tuscaroras had told him about: "about 500 *Tuskeruros* in one Hunting-Quarter," organized enough that they had built streets and houses, though not round, wigwam style, but "Ridge-Fashion, after the manner of most other *Indians*"—and the manner, it's worth noting, of European settlers. This last visit is the first time Lawson notes that the fare among his Indian hosts is meager: "We got nothing amongst them but Corn, Flesh being not plentiful, by reason of the great Number of their People," Lawson says, perfectly describing a people being crowded and starved out of their homeland. Among the Tuscaroras he watched a doctor treat a snakebite victim by making an incision with rattlesnake teeth and sucking out venom and blood. He also notes that he sees a funeral, "which Ceremony is much the same with that of the *Santees*." Lawson's days of long, detailed descriptions are over.

Fed on only corn, he may have just been hungry: "We were forced to march, this day, for Want of Provisions," he says, describing meeting an Indian carrying shad, a fish so endemic in eastern North Carolina streams that the town of Grifton, not twenty miles from where Lawson stood, has an annual Shad Festival even now. The fish were "ready barba-ku'd. We bought 24 of them, for a dress'd Doe-Skin." Lawson spends his last night on the trail "under two or three Pieces of Bark, at the Foot of a large Oak. There fell abundance of Snow and Rain in the Night, with much Thunder and Lightning."

And then in they go: "Next Day, it clear'd up, and it being about 12 Miles to the English, about half-way we passed over a deep Creek, and came safe to Mr. *Richard Smith*'s, of *Pampticough*-River, in North-Carolina; where being well receiv'd by the Inhabitants, and pleas'd with the Goodness of the Country, we all resolv'd to continue."

:::

Lawson was home, and it was my turn to follow him. Vince Bellis had given me his unpublished paper on Lawson's final stop. Agreeing that Lawson had crossed the Tar in Greenville, he followed Lawson past "a deep Creek" that was most likely the Grindle Creek, which pours into the Tar after almost exactly the twelve miles Lawson says he walked from his stay in the Tuscarora hunting camp to the creek. (That's the old Grindle, mind you; enterprising farmers have since improved their land by channeling the Grindle to the Tar a good mile and a half west of where it used to flow in; the old Grindle still asserts itself, but more as a marsh than a flowing creek. You can see it on Google Maps.) However, if Lawson then walked six more miles, as he says he did, he'd have ended up in what is now downtown Washington, which he seems not to have done. No matter; it's not news that Lawson's estimates and explanations near the end of his trip are scattered. More important, in the North Carolina state archives Vince found a land patent granted to Richard Smith in 1706 that describes him already living on "Smith's Neck," which lay between two creeks. Vince identified these almost surely as the Grindle Creek and Tranter's Creek, which enters the Tar just on the edge of Washington. Now called Clark's Neck, the land between the Grindle and Tranter's just to the east of Washington answers perfectly. Vince had showed me on maps and printouts where Smith would likely have lived, and on that basis I planned my final day's walk, which it turned out would actually be only a few miles. Considering blisters, good news for me.

My notebook from that day describes taking pleasure in being a body in motion, out for a last day walking the paths of the country. I noticed the shriek of tires on the grooved concrete of the L. Elmore Hodges Bridge over the Tar, and I felt the backwash of asphalt breeze when trucks roared past. And then I reached Clark's Neck Road, which led down toward Washington through the thick of what would have once been called Smith's Neck, and then, east of the Grindle Creek, I began casting about. For a half mile or so close to the Tar the terrain is swamp; once it raises up a tad you start to feel a sort of firmness beneath your feet, and you perceive it: this is a place people could stay. They could make a home here, clear land, grow food, hunt. This is a good place. The rich sandy soil does everything but lay back and give you bedroom eyes, that's how eager it seems to grow crops for you.

I can't say I found for sure the Smith place, though one little double-track dirt road leading into the bush felt perfect, and when I went to the other side of the creek and found a similarly "homey" place, it turned out to be exactly across the river. And when I finished walking down Clark's Neck Road, through the land that Smith surely owned, it felt much the same. It was flat farm territory, with broad fields, already harvested this late, and irrigation rigs and barns with silver roofs. Here and there I found little graveyards: "Here lies until the resurrection, all that was mortal of Margaret Eliza Toole," dead in 1848, a white obelisk at the corner of one farm stated. At another little plot I found bleached gravestones with eroded death dates from the 1700s. This was home, under the arcing coastal skies. These may not have been Smith graves, but this was the Smith land. This is where Lawson stopped. And it was where I stopped too.

For a minute.

Because the thing was, I still had to get to Washington, where my car was. So I kept walking down Clark's Neck, but I also made a phone call, to one Russ Chesson, the educational director of the North Carolina Estuarium, a Washington aquarium dedicated to the estuary of the Pamlico Sound; when I had reached out for information, Chesson had offered a ride if I needed one while nearby. I had shrugged him off, but once I had found—as best as I was likely to—the site of Richard Smith's house, having walked some 550 miles, limping another six miles into Washington suddenly sounded like the exact last thing I wanted to do. I called Chesson, said "Mayday!" and kept hobbling on. He grabbed me up as I neared Tranter's Creek, ready to cross the bridge into Washington.

We had a happy ride into town to the riverfront, where I changed my shoes and Chesson walked me through the Estuarium, spouting astonishing facts about the estuary that comprises the Pamlico Sound, filled by the Tar (which becomes the Pamlico) River and further south the Neuse, and Albemarle Sound, filled by the Roanoke and the Chowan. Hemmed in by North Carolina's famous Outer Banks barrier islands, the Albemarle/Pamlico estuary is the second largest in the continental United States (the Chesapeake Bay is larger). If you've forgotten, an estuary is the part of a river system where the mouth meets the sea. Freshwater and saltwater commingle, underwater vegetation of every description flourishes, and the whole place acts as a feeding ground and nursery to just about every creature in the entire ocean. Ed Deal, my guide for the first day of my canoe trip from Charleston, had urged me to focus my attention on the edge of things—where forest met field, marsh met ground, river met sea: "That's where the action is," he told me, and through this entire trip his words had proven true. At their edges towns tended to show their true status; the edges of forests, my ecologist friend Katie Winsett had shown, give us access to wildlife and the plants of open field succession. And Chesson could not agree more: "Ninety percent of everything that lives in the ocean is born in, lives in, eats from, or is in some way connected to the estuaries," he told me as we drove in. Shad live in the ocean but reproduce in the rivers; eels do the opposite. Chesson's family has lived along the estuary for at least 200 years, so when he works all day to educate people about the estuary he means it. He led me through the museum, which included fish tanks and boats and watershed maps but also details the history of the peoples—Native and immigrant—who have lived along the rivers. Large quotes from Lawson hung on the wall (he tells us Carolina is "a delicious country") and John Brickell, who, in his 1737 *Natural History of North Carolina*, in one of the rare lines he did not plagiarize from Lawson, tells us that "Nature produces everything here for the Pleasure and Profit of the Inhabitants."

Chesson walked me out to a boardwalk out along the Pamlico, pointing out rain gardens that filtered runoff from Washington's streets. We saw herons. Chesson bid me farewell and I stood on the boardwalk and watched the river. The day was hot and sunny and the air was still, not unlike the quiet morning a year before when with my first guide I had paddled away across Charleston Harbor. No herons that day, but bottlenose dolphins. I wasn't sentimental, though, as I looked across the widening Pamlico. I had one more canoe trip to take.

:::

I would never say danger, because we weren't in danger. But three of us, me and my two boys, were in a wobbly canoe on big water. In conditions that are windier than is really safe, with not just wind-waves but a surprising swell on the wide Pamlico, still a river where we were, not yet the sound but with a fetch that allowed an unkind headwind full access to our every square inch. Everybody was wearing life vests and able to swim. So danger would be an exaggeration.

Things for Lawson and von Graffenried have just taken a rather negative turn.
Courtesy of the North Carolina Museum of History.

But still. Scudding clouds and that fifteen-mile-per-hour headwind that would turn the canoe sideways regardless of my wishes. A frustrated ten-year-old in the front seat working as hard as he could but still more sail than power plant. A joyful seven-year-old clutching the yoke, keeping low as he had been trained, shouting, "This is so fun!" as the swell lifted the front of the canoe, then slapped it down, sometimes wobbling widely enough that we all leaned hard counter-wobble. By which point I had stopped thinking it was fun one bit.

After about an hour of this we wrestled our craft safely to a dock, then to shore, then called for help and help came. This last Lawson Trek adventure occurred because Leigh Swain is in charge of things at Historic Bath. North Carolina's first incorporated town, Bath was planned and founded in 1705 by a group of three men, including Lawson, who also likely laid it out and surveyed it. Swain reached out as we neared Wash-

A BED IN BATH, AND BEYOND

ington and asked whether, since Lawson himself cofounded Bath, owned properties there, and lived there for a while, we'd like to give the trek a ceremonial finish by paddling into Bath and addressing the assembled townspeople.

I came to love the idea, especially because I could bring along Louie, ten, and Gus, seven, and neatly finish my undertaking by stepping out of a canoe, just as I had begun it by stepping into one the previous October. Plus Bath is probably the place most associated with Lawson in this world. They have a historical marker there for him and the Lawson Walk, a little dirt path on which grow several trees and other plants Lawson documented.

So I gathered canoe, life vests, and paddles and bunked with Seth Effron, an old friend from my days at the *News & Observer* in Raleigh. Seth and his wife, Nancy, have a house on a piece of the land Nancy grew up on, on Duck Creek, about a five-mile paddle from Bath. Nancy's brother's dock next door offered a great place to start our final paddle.

Thus did three Lawson Trekkers bed down in their delightful house, breakfasting on eggs from next door, bacon from a pig who had been known to the neighborhood when he was still using the bacon for his own purposes, and toast with blueberry-ginger jam Nancy had made herself. The day dawned cool, drizzly, and windy. The breakfast helped. We put the canoe on the dock, drove to Bath to leave my car there, and headed back so Seth and Nancy could drop us in around noon, to arrive in Bath by paddle around 2 p.m.

:::

The paddle started nicely enough—we put in on the Duck, Seth took our picture, and off we went. The Duck runs southwest toward its mouth on the Pamlico, so though a strong breeze pushed us effortlessly down, I didn't worry.

Except any breeze strong enough to push a canoe will make you very unhappy if you don't happen to be going downwind. Which, once we hit the Pamlico River, we were doing the exact opposite of. Louie instantly had to wrestle manfully with his paddle just to keep it in the water, and Gus clutched the yoke, shrieking with glee as we were blown hither and yon. On the map it looks like the spot where I finally called the coast guard (Seth and Nancy, that is) was about 1.6 miles' paddle from the dock, but I'm going to guess it was at least 50 percent farther for all the being blown backward. We got turned sideways and around enough times ("Whee! This is so fun, dad!") that I doubted our capacity to make it another mile and a half to the Bath Creek, to say nothing of another mile up the Bath.

I wrestled us over to a dock, between whose slats the water would geyser up when the swells came by. I hauled the canoe up, then Louie and I carried it to the roadside. Seth and Nancy drove to the rescue; Nancy took the kids for milkshakes while Seth and I loaded the canoe onto my car. Nancy was not having any of this "we're done" business—we were just going to put back in at Bonner's Point at the tip of the Bath peninsula and the boys and I would paddle up the half-mile to the town dock like we had said we'd do.

Which we did, but not before another half-hour of wind-enforced precision canoe drilling. We finally got pointed right and took advantage of a momentary drop in the wind to dig across the creek. I gave Louie control, reward for his hard work—"You have the bridge, Mr. Sulu"—and he proudly powered us in. A gathering on the shore cheered, and I can pledge to you that I have never been happier to step out of a canoe.

:::

Lawson of course had his own canoe misadventures—he describes near Charleston almost being blown to sea by "a tart Gale at N.W. which put us in some Danger of being cast away, the Bay being rough, and there running great Seas between the two Islands," and another time he tells that his "Canoe struck on a Sand near the Breakers, and were in great Danger of our Lives, but (by God's Blessing) got off safe to the Shore." I am inclined now to believe he in no way exaggerated. And he had five friends and four Indian guides paddling—and no children to worry about. I told the audience at Bath that I could see now why Lawson took his journey before he had any children to worry about, and I got a good laugh, but I wasn't kidding. We were never in danger. But I was scared. Those are my kids.

Lawson paddled away from Charleston with unexpected friends on December 28, 1700, was taken in and cared for by every group of settlers and Indians he met, and finished it with generous hosts near Washington on February 23, 1701 (we think—even before those sloppy final entries he gets a little cavalier about days). I started mine with vast and unexpected generosity in Charleston, met a constant parade of generosity, support, and kindness during a year on the way, and finished the outdoor portion of this project with yet another outpouring of help unlooked for and enormous assistance at Bath. I stepped into a canoe in Charleston on October 12, 2014, and stepped out of one in Bath on September 26, 2015.

So yeah, Lawson ended up in Little Washington, where, "Pleas'd with the Goodness of the Country," he remained. Pleased indeed—Lawson shacked up for the long haul with Hannah Smith, the daughter of Richard. We know this from his will, recorded in 1708 in "Bath Towne," which gives Hannah "the house & Lott I now live in, to enjoy the same during her Naturall life." Hannah also gets a third of everything else. The remainder goes to their daughter, Isabella, and the child with whom Hannah was then pregnant. We have no certainty about whether that child lived, but Val Green (who else?) has traced what he believes are descendants of Hannah down to present-day Georgia. I emailed with one. She was very nice. I emailed with someone else in California who for a while believed he was a descendant of Lawson but then decided the genealogy website had it all wrong. He was very nice, too.

What we know about Lawson's subsequent adventures in Carolina come largely from the *Colonial Records of North Carolina* (a collection of letters and papers of the colony from its earliest days), from *Von Graffenried's Account of the Founding of New Bern* (an interesting if highly self-serving version of not only the founding of the colony but also von Graffenried and Lawson's capture by the Tuscaroras), and letters from Lawson to James Petiver, the great apothecary and collector in London ("a very curious person," Petiver called him, which I think then as now was the highest imaginable compliment). And though the record is spotty—remember historian Francis Latham Harriss, who said, "Lawson appears to have flashed like a meteor across our ken, leaving behind him only this illuminating record of his presence and the tragic memory of his death"—there's enough to sketch out an understanding of Lawson's decade in Carolina and the ripples it left in its wake.

Given his will, things obviously went smoothly with young Hannah Smith. (If we still wonder about Lawson's age, does anything paint him as twenty-five rather than thirty-five more than his falling for, literally, the first girl he met when he emerged from the forest?) Though of course he didn't move in with young Hannah immediately: he evidently lived at first where New Bern now stands: "I had built a House about half a Mile from an Indian Town, on the Fork of Neus-River," he writes, "where I dwelt by my self, excepting a young Indian Fellow, and a Bull-Dog, that I had along with me." He tells us this as part of a funny story about alligators—evidently he had built his little house above an alligator nest. The beast began feeling spirited in the spring. Lawson was sitting peacefully at home "when, all of a sudden, this ill-favour'd Neighbour of mine, set up such a Roaring, that he made the House shake about my Ears, and so continued, like a Bittern, (but a hundred times louder, if possible) for four or five times. The Dog stared, as if he was frightned out of his Senses." Lawson imagined any number of implausible explanations, until "at last, my Man [Native servant] came in, to whom when I had told the Story, he laugh'd at me, and presently undeceiv'd me, by telling me what it was that made that Noise." Lawson, as he does, goes on: alligators lay eggs; the Indians tell him they make nests in marshes near springs; some people say alligator meat tastes good; it's good for rheumatism; alligator teeth "would make pretty Snuff-Boxes, if wrought by an Artist." And finally a bit of Lawsonian mansplaining absurdity: "After the Tail of the Allegator is separated from the Body, it will move very freely for four days."

That alligator tale is pure Lawson—some great observation, bolstered by information he gained by asking the locals; a delightful sense of story and willingness to laugh at himself; and an early sense that when the story is too good to fact-check, he ought to just let it be. No surprise that in the 1905 *Biographical History of North Carolina* Stephen B. Weeks describes Lawson as a "traveller and explorer, surveyor, historian and humorist."

And landowner. A young man out to make his mark, Lawson didn't stop with his square mile at the fork in the Neuse (even today, by the way, Lawson Creek still drains into the confluence of the Neuse and the Trent, just south of Tryon Palace in downtown New Bern). Given his interest in Hannah, Lawson must have made plenty of trips over the thirty miles or so between his house on the Neuse and the Richard Smith plantation; the first accurate map of North Carolina showing inland settlements, made in 1733, already shows a road connecting New Bern with a spot directly across the Pamlico from Bath.

:::

Oh yes, Bath. As settlers moving down from Virginia started to fill up the Albemarle region in the late 1600s, making the Pamlico region ("Pampti-cough" is one of many alternative spellings Lawson uses) more attractive to settlers, the Bath region (named for one of the Lords Proprietor and settled on a spit of land along what was then called the Old Town Creek) had already begun developing. By 1700 a store sat just east of where the town is now. There one Robert Quary dealt in lumber, crops, and naval stores. Lawson acquired land around here, as did several other settlers. By 1702, according to a publication of the N.C. Office of Archives and History, the half-dozen or so houses in the settlement were mostly rude wooden affairs, some with chimneys made of sticks and mud rather than brick or stone. However, "William Barrow hired brick mason William Tomson to plaster his home in 1701 or 1702." In addition, the state's first library arrived when the Society for the Propagation of the Gospel in Foreign Parts sent a thousand books to the Parish of St. Thomas. The parish at that point lacked preacher or church, but Bath had books.

In March 1706, the General Assembly established Bath as the first incorporated town in what is now North Carolina, with Lawson and two other men as the town commissioners; Lawson is believed to have surveyed the site and laid out the town. He bought two prime home sites, overlooking the creek; on our windy entry into Bath we paddled right by where his home would have stood. Sheltered on Bath Creek but with easy access to the Pamlico—and thereafter with easy passage to the Atlantic through the Ocracoke Inlet in the Outer Banks—Bath was poised to prosper (though the founding of New Bern a few years later and the eventual establishment of Washington ended up stealing much of its thunder). In 1707 Lawson and several other men started a gristmill, and Lawson was clerk of the court and public register of the county; and by 1708 Bath had a dozen houses and about fifty people. These last facts come from the *Dictionary of North Carolina Biography* entry by Charles Holloman; they seem to square, but there's a lot of assumption here. If you can do better, have at it. In 1709, Lawson left Carolina to sail back to London to see to the publication of his book. He seems to have been based in New Bern upon his return. Bath had two more moments in the sun—sometime after 1714 Blackbeard the pirate started hanging around there. And in 1925 writer Edna Ferber visited the "lovely decayed hamlet" of Bath to link up with the James Adams Floating Theater, one of the last of its kind, on which her novel *Show Boat* (and the eventual musical) was based.

:::

By the time he went to England, Lawson was surveying more than just Bath, and while he was there he was appointed surveyor general. Less certain is how Lawson spent his time before returning to England to publish his book. Certainly between his duties as a key citizen in Bath, his seeming enterprise of buying and selling land, and surveying, he'd have remained busy. From his book we also expect that he traveled considerably around the colonies.

He describes "Ronoak-Island, where the Ruins of a Fort are to be seen at this day, as well as some old English Coins which have been lately found; and a Brass-Gun, a Powder-Horn, and one small Quarter deck-Gun, made of Iron Staves, and hoop'd with the same Metal." He is speaking of course of the famous Lost Colony. And though today an entire cadre of mostly amateur historians industriously theorizes about the fate of the vanished settlers, Lawson found the matter utterly lacking in mystery. The settlers told their leaders, who left to resupply in England, that if they needed to they'd move, leaving a note carved into a tree (a Maltese cross would indicate trouble). This they did, carving "Croatoan," indicating they had joined the peoples on the island of that name, though we now call it Hatteras; the lack of a cross indicated that they were not in crisis.

"A farther Confirmation of this we have from the Hatteras Indians, who either then lived on Ronoak-Island, or much frequented it," Lawson goes on.

> These tell us, that several of their Ancestors were white People, and could talk in a Book, as we do; the Truth of which is confirm'd by gray Eyes being found frequently amongst these Indians, and no others. They value themselves extremely for their Affinity to the English, and are ready to do them all friendly Offices. It is probable, that this Settlement miscarry'd for want of timely Supplies from England; or thro' the Treachery of the Natives, for we may reasonably suppose that the English were forced to cohabit with them, for Relief and Conversation; and that in process of Time, they conform'd themselves to the Manners of their Indian Relations.

Regarding this, the only mystery about the Lost Colony is why people doubt the word of Lawson, who explained the whole thing three centuries ago.

Lawson talks also about the "Gigantick Stature, and Gray-Heads, so common amongst the Savages that dwell near the Mountains" and mentions "Timbers . . . too large for them to cut down, and too much burthen'd with Wood for their Labourers to make Plantations of" in the same mountainous areas. In fact, "when backwards, near the Mountains," he says, "you meet with the richest Soil, a sweet, thin Air, dry

Roads, pleasant small murmuring Streams, and several beneficial Productions and Species, which are unknown in the European World." This sounds like much more mountainous territory than he traversed in his walk. And given that Lawson likes to credit his sources when he hasn't seen things himself (he mentions hot springs but admits he knows of them only because "we have an account . . . from the Indians that frequent the Hill-Country"), it's hard to imagine Lawson not traveling the mountains. He sailed back to England from Hampton, Virginia, and he mentions in letters to Petiver that he can accept packages in Virginia and at "Collonl Quarme's in Philadelphia, Pensilvania." To the degree that one could get around the early British colonies in North America, Lawson did that.

:::

And he had a lot to say about it. One central aim of his trip to England was to publish his book, and that went about as well as it could go. Though it's unclear whether Lawson arrived in London with a finished manuscript or wrote while he was there, publisher James Knapton, head of a group of eight of London's most notable printers and booksellers, rushed the book to press. The consortium had created a periodical series called A New Collection of Voyages and Travels: With Historical Accounts of Discoveries and Conquests in All Parts of the World, and Lawson's book became the series' second volume. The first portion—his introduction and his journal—came out in April 1709, and subsequent parts came out over the next four months, at which point the entire book was available for binding. It was 1709 in England, and the scientific revolution was in full swing. Newton's *Opticks* and *Arithmetica Universalis* had been published only a few years before; the Royal Society had been publishing *Philosophical Transactions* for a few decades; and the expiration of the Licensing of the Press Act in 1695 had caused authors and printing presses both to multiply. Hans Sloane's *A Voyage to the Islands* had begun its successful serial publication in 1707, and Knapton himself had had success with William Dampier's *A New Voyage Round the World* in 1697. Lawson could not have come to London at a better time or with a better product. "Knapton's decision to publish a hitherto unknown author, thereby delaying the sale of a well-known book," according to a 2010 article in the *Archives of Natural History*, "reflects his judgment regarding the literary tastes of the public."

He was rewarded for his confidence in Lawson. The installments were

A
JOURNAL
OF
A thousand Miles Travel among the Indians, *from* South *to* North Carolina.

N *December* the 28th, 1700, I began my Voyage (for *North Carolina*) from *Charles*-Town, being fix *Englifh*-men in Company, with three *Indian*-men, and one Woman, Wife to our *Indian*-Guide, having five Mil— from the Town

Well, more like 550 miles, but Lawson had a book to sell.

printed in large amounts but bound only as needed, so when all the pieces had been printed, they could be bound together and sold as a single volume, which they were by the end of the year and several more times in the next decade, with titles like *The History of Carolina* or *A New Account of Carolina*. German editions came out, and the book was almost completely plagiarized in 1737 to form virtually all of *The Natural History of North Carolina* by Dr. John Brickell. American naturalist Elliott Coues compares Lawson's book to William Bartram's seminal *Travels through North & South Carolina, Georgia, East & West Florida*, produced in 1791. No less a collector than Hans Sloane himself relied on Lawson's book "as a reference for certain species . . . not only those acquired from Lawson," the *Archives of Natural History* article continues. Mark Catesby's *Natural History of Carolina, Florida and the Bahama Islands* came out in 1747, and with its luscious plates became the first great illustrated book of naturalism from the American South (before being eclipsed by Audubon). Catesby notes in his introduction that "Mr. *Lawson*, in his Account of

Carolina, . . . has given a curious Sketch of the natural Dispositions, Customs, &c. of these Savages. . . . I shall take the Liberty to select from him what is most material."

The aforementioned Weeks brings up writer and scientist Thomas Harriot and artist John White, who sailed with Sir Walter Raleigh's 1585–86 expedition to Roanoke, afterward creating the first printed record of British exploration in North America, the 1590 *A Briefe and True Report of the New Found Land of Virginia*, written by Harriot with drawings by White. It's one of the most important documents to emerge from colonial Carolina, and Weeks places Lawson's book in that august company: "What Harriot and White did at the end of the sixteenth century, Lawson did for the same region and in the same way at the beginning of the eighteenth," he says. "It is from White and Hariot and Lawson that our knowledge of the natural features of early North Carolina and its inhabitants is drawn." Holloman calls *A New Voyage to Carolina* "a classic of early American literature," and the *American Cyclopaedia* of 1873 calls it "one of the most valuable of the early histories of the Carolinas." The *Oxford English Dictionary* cites Lawson's book as one of its sources for a dozen or so words. As Weeks elegantly says elsewhere of Lawson, "He made good use of his eyes." That Lawson was made surveyor general of North Carolina the very month the first installment of his book came out seems to indicate that it only strengthened his status as one of the growing colony's first citizens. The Lords Proprietor also put Lawson on a commission meant to settle the boundary between Virginia and North Carolina.

:::

Since much of this subsequent literature depends heavily on illustration, I must briefly discuss the illustrations to Lawson's book. Lawson's descriptions border on the magnificent; Lawson is in many ways one of the first writers of what we now instantly recognize as purely observational nonfiction. (Some people mark the beginning of the modern era in journalism with Daniel DeFoe's crowd-sourced *The Storm*, about an enormous hurricane that struck England, written in 1704.) But the illustrations—a single page of his book with about a dozen creatures—look very much backward. "They have more in common with medieval bestiaries than scientific illustrations," said Jennifer Landin, a scientific illustrator and artist who spent an afternoon with me sketching beetles, trying to teach me how to see.

The illustrations in Lawson are evidence that old habits of simply accepting knowledge handed to the observer—rather than scrupulously observing—die hard. "He sometimes sees what he expects to see, not what is really there," Landin says of Lawson, and it's a fair criticism; Lawson describes snakes having the power to "charm Squirrels, Hares, Partridges, or any such thing, in such a manner, that they run directly into their Mouths." Landin notes especially that Lawson describes raccoons fishing for crabs with their tails (the illustration shows this), which though preposterous on its face turns out to be a worldwide myth attributed variously to bears (that's how they lost their tails, natch) and jaguars, monkeys, wolves, and jackals. As Sir Edward Burnett Tylor says in his book *Researches into the Early History of Mankind*, "It is one of those floating ideas which are taken up as the story-teller's stock in trade, and used where it suits him, but with no particular subordination to fact."

No kidding. It turns out these drawings were made in London, by an engraver, from Lawson's descriptions of what he saw; if Lawson ever drew an image himself, we have no evidence of it. Thus you get a picture of a bison that could be a bison I suppose if you really want it to be one, a bear that might be wearing swim flippers, and a possum that could be one of the R.O.U.S. from *The Princess Bride*. Landin, sitting in a park with me and a friend, taught us sighting and other practices of good representative drawing, and she reminded us that Darwin himself suggested the best topics of study were languages, Humboldt, and drawing. Lawson just came along too soon to get the advice. As for me, I documented my journey with photographs. You use the tools you have.

:::

Coming back to Carolina as surveyor general and a published scientific author was not enough for Lawson, of course; he had land to develop and was not shy about shaking a tail feather to get it done. At the time England was reeling under a tide of Protestant immigration from the Rhine region of what is now Germany, then known as the Palatinate. The arrival of some 13,000 of these refugees of French invasions caused a crisis. With lands in North America she wanted to develop, Queen Anne saw an easy solution. She committed a bunch of money to sending the refugees over, and Palatine settlements started popping up all over the colonies.

Enter Baron Cristoph von Graffenried, a bankrupt Swiss nobleman looking to recover his fortunes. Something of a wastrel scion, the baron had wandered England, Germany, and France, squandering his inheri-

Let's agree they're animals—and let's agree that the person
who drew them had never seen them.

tance, being introduced to the nobility, and always seeming to just barely fail to get one lucrative position or another; he spent quite a bit of time in various colleges, as well. He got married, of course, and as his family grew, "he made bad speculations, gave securities, and contracted debts until prospects of a catastrophe began to loom up before him." This, by the way, from *Von Graffenried's Account of the Founding of New Bern*, which borders on hagiography. "He determined to see in America the fortune which was denied him at home," the book goes on. He took a notion to mine for silver, as one does in such situations, connecting with Franz Louis Michel, a Swiss friend of Lawson's who had lived in Virginia several years and was working with a Swiss land company looking to profit from mining and settling the colonies. Von Graffenried joined on as one of the principals. Having read tracts singing the praises of Carolina— perhaps including Lawson's new book—the group purchased from the Lords Proprietor title to thousands of acres in North Carolina, mostly around the confluence of the Neuse and the Trent, "to be set out by the Surveyor General," according to the *Colonial Records*. Lawson, who owned land in the same area, was to travel to Carolina with the first group of settlers; von Graffenried would follow with additional Swiss colonists. This all appears to have been organized even as Lawson was finishing his book—he mentions that Michel "has been employ'd by the Canton of *Bern*, to find out a Tract of Land in the *English America*, where that Republick might settle some of their People; which Proposal, I believe, is now in a fair way towards a Conclusion."

:::

Lawson and the first group sailed in two ships in early 1710, and they had a terrible passage. The Crown paid captains per passenger, so captains wedged passengers in however they could: "Even before they got out of sight of the English coast [they] suffered from the foul odor and vermin, entirely apart from the fact that those lying below could neither get fresh air nor see the light of day," according to one letter cited in von Graffenried's book. With the boat overcrowded and undersupplied, many of the settlers died en route—many were dying even before they left, according to Lawson himself: "We have lost above 40 already," he wrote in a letter to James Petiver from Portsmouth in January, and "they are chiefly very youngest ones." As if things weren't going badly enough, within sight of Virginia one of the ships was raided by French privateers, robbed of even the clothes on the refugees' backs. About half the original number remained alive when they made their way from the Virginia port to the site of New Bern.

Lawson settled them evidently on land he owned, though even then it was still occupied by Indians: "I paid for the land or piece of ground . . . three times," von Graffenried says. "To the Lords Proprietors, to the Surveyor-General, and to the Indian King Taylor." We have only von Graffenried's self-serving account, but it's reasonable to believe that the settlers did suffer greatly at the new settlement and that things improved for them when von Graffenried arrived in September 1710 with more settlers and fresh supplies, especially when we know from Petiver's scientific records that while leading the starving refugees south Lawson found the time to collect botanical specimens. An admirable devotion to his scientific pursuits, perhaps, but under the circumstances surely not his finest hour.

::::

Nobody's finest hour, really. New Bern, once again, was just another European settlement on Indian land. To be sure, some sort of payment was made, but if you want to understand how the Tuscaroras felt in those days, consider a letter to the Tuscarora chiefs in response to an emissary they had sent to Pennsylvania and to the chiefs of the Five Nations of the Iroquois, with whom the Tuscaroras shared a history, and whom they wished to rejoin, leaving Carolina. With their ambassadors the Tuscaroras had sent eight belts of wampum, each from a constituency and each expressing an aspect of their hopes if they joined their northern relatives. "The third Belt was sent from their young men fitt to Hunt, that privilege to leave their Towns, & seek Provision for their aged, might be granted to them without fear of Death or Slavery. . . . The seventh was sent in order to intreat a Cessation from murdering & taking them, that by the allowance thereof, they may not be affraid of a mouse, or any other thing that Russles the Leaves." There may be a more heartbreaking plea from a suffering Native people on the American historical record. Maybe. Carolina Indian slaving was so bad that in 1705 the Pennsylvania legislature passed a law prohibiting "further importation of Indian slaves from Carolina."

The Pennsylvania representatives explained that the Tuscaroras would be welcome, "but that to Confirm the sincerity of their past Carriage towards the English, & to raise in us a good opinion of them, it would be very necessary to procure a Certificate from the Govmt. they leave, to this, of their Good behaviour, & then they might be assured of a favourable reception." Do you need to be told? No such certificate from the Carolina government. We won't stop killing and kidnapping and enslaving you, the government indicated to the Tuscaroras, but if you find that treatment intolerable, too bad; you can't leave. Rumors of an uprising of the Tuscaroras had flown throughout the Pamlico for years. Then in 1711 adding to the Indian resentment came the Cary Rebellion, a sort of religious/regional skirmish between various factions in North Carolina jealous of each other's positions, during which government factions were too busy fighting one another to pay close attention to their neighbors.

Considering which the next development can hardly be considered a surprise.

:::

It started with a trip up the Neuse, looking, once again, for a faster way to Virginia as well as some nice grapes (probably scuppernong or other muscadines, given the locale). Lawson had the idea and invited von Graffenried, along with two Indian guides and two African slaves; Christopher Gale, a Yorkshireman who had arrived in Carolina around the same time Lawson did (and returned from England in 1710 with Lawson) planned to go too, but his wife became ill, "which I may call a happy sickness to me," he wrote in a letter a month later.

Lawson, von Graffenried, and their various assistants headed up the Neuse, where after a few days one of the Indians scouted ahead on horseback, stumbling onto a large gathering of Tuscaroras in a town called Catechna, under the leadership of King Hancock. The Tuscaroras fiercely told the Indian that Lawson and von Graffenried should turn back; given the message, according to von Graffenried, Lawson first laughed but quickly stopped: "In a moment there came out of all the bushes and swimming through the river such a number of Indians and overpowered us that it was impossible to defend ourselves." The Tuscaroras, planning a series of raids on the settlements of the Pamlico, mistook von Graffenried for the governor and thought they had a coup: "Their barbarous pride swelled up so that we were compelled to run with them the whole night through forests, bushes, and swamps, until the next morning about three o'clock when we came to Catechna where the king, Hancock by name, was sitting in all his glory upon a raised platform."

The men were not bound and were free to walk around the village, but not to leave. That evening several villages of Tuscaroras gathered for a festival, during which the chiefs placed Lawson and von Graffenried on mats and discussed their fates. "There came into question a general complaint, that they, the Indians, had been very badly treated and detained ... a thing which was not to be longer endured." We are told that Lawson was especially accused, though "he being present excused himself the best he could." It worked, and the men were told they could return home the next day.

Regrettably, the next morning several more tribes arrived to join the fun, and they held a retrial. One of the kings, called Core Tom (chief of the tiny coastal Coree tribe) made an accusation against Lawson, and Lawson quarreled back. Even so, after the examination Lawson and von Graffenried were walking away. As they did so, von Graffenried says, "I reproached him very strongly for his unguardedness in such a critical condition." This seems to have been some kind of last straw: "Immediately thereafter there came suddenly three or four of the chiefs very angrily, seized us roughly by the arms, led us back and forcibly set us down in the old place." This time they were bound and their pockets were searched, which did not bode well. Among Lawson's things they found a straight razor, which boded even worse.

Von Graffenried says that over a very long night he somehow convinced the chiefs that he was not the governor, and as such was not a valuable prize, yet that he was a familiar with "the great and mighty Queen of England, who would avenge my blood" if he were harmed. The chiefs considered while the dancing went on, the men tied by the fire. Eventually von Graffenried learned that he was to be spared. Lawson was not. Von Graffenried heard "that he was to have his throat cut with a razor which was found in his sack," though he also had heard Lawson was hanged or burned. The slaves, by the way, went free, as did the two Indians of Lawson's party. Gale wrote in a letter that "the fate of Mr. Lawson (if our Indian information be true) was much more tragical, for we are informed that they stuck him full of fine small splinters of torchwood, like hogs' bristles, and so set them gradually on fire. This, I doubt not, had been my fate if Providence had not prevented; but I hope God Almighty has designed me for an instrument in the revenging such innocent Christian blood."

: : :

Evidently that's just what God almighty had in mind. Shortly after Lawson's execution the Tuscarora attacks began, killing hundreds of men, women, and children and driving settlers into the comparative safety of

New Bern and Bath. Gale was sent to Charleston for help, which eventually came in the form of troops comprising a few colonists but mostly Indians allied with them, led by John "Tuscarora Jack" Barnwell—following, for much of their journey north, the very path Lawson had traced in 1700-1701. The Tuscarora War remained fierce until a Tuscarora loss in 1713, and it finally petered out in 1715, won—spoiler alert—by the side with more horses and European guns and powder. Just the same, the Indians who had allied with the colonists could not fail to notice that the colonists were not very nice to the Indians they defeated.

Hence, in 1715, the Indians in South Carolina—many of them the same ones who had fought alongside the colonists in North Carolina—attacked the settlement at Port Royal, south of Charleston. The Yamasee War lasted until 1717 and had the same unsurprising result. The remnants of the Tuscaroras moved up north and joined the related Iroquoian tribes, becoming the Sixth Nation of the Iroquois; they are federally recognized now.

:::

A sullen end to the tale—and the life—of John Lawson, neatly if accidentally summarized in the biographical sketch by Francis Latham Harriss in the introduction to the 1951 version of Lawson's book: "The narrative is enlivened constantly by a hearty and vivid humor and betrays in every line Lawson's youthful zest in the adventure." True for sure, but the "joyful current," Harriss goes on, "does not conceal from his eyes the hardships and perils accompanying the daily life of the white man in the land of the Indian." This whole white-versus-Indian thing didn't really work out well for anybody (though the people who identify themselves as white ended up with the land), and if it generates cringes now in the reading, it helps explain how the colonists could treat the Indians in ways that eventually led to Lawson's death.

One can look too deeply into these matters, however. Billy Baldwin, writer, poet, guide, and personage in McClellanville, who kayaked with me on the Intracoastal Waterway during the first week of my journey, may in one story have hit closest to the mark in summarizing Lawson's life—and death. "He was a developer," Baldwin quoted a friend's description of Lawson. "And he got what they all deserve."

11 : Not to Amuse My Readers Any Longer

The British Library has a letter from Lawson to James Petiver from October 1710: "I have sent a small box of Collections," he says. "I hope they are come safe to you." He notes he has more specimens collected, "but of books being not full I omitt sending them untill compleated." In July 1711 he sent another letter, hoping that "long since you have Received ye Collection of plants & Insects in 4 vials wch I sent for you." Which is the last we hear from Lawson, being as he was killed by the Tuscaroras less than two months later.

But gathering those botanical specimens and sending them back to England to Petiver, an apothecary "at the sign of the White Cross in Aldersgate Street, London," was profoundly important. Apart from his book, those specimens are the record of Lawson's contribution. Collectors in those days were the equivalent of museum directors or scientific foundations now, sending agents all over the world to gather specimens or reaching out to travelers and asking them for any specimens they could provide. Lawson wrote to Petiver in 1701, after the completion of his long walk, responding to an ad Petiver had run in a book of specimens Petiver had published. In the ad Petiver acknowledges his debt to *Kind Friends* from divers parts of the World" and continued that he "therefore most humbly beg[s] the Communications and Assistance of all *Curious Persons* and *Lovers of Natural History*, the which shall be *justly* and *faithfully acknowledged.*" In that first letter Lawson mentions Robert Ellis and Edmund Bohun, two significant Charleston collectors working on Petiver's behalf, and evidently they encouraged him, though to what degree we do not know.

Contribution to natural history—and acknowledgement—seem to have driven Lawson all his life. "I design yr. advertismts. in order to for yr. collections of Animals Vegitables etc.," he wrote Petiver. "I shall be very industrious in that Employ I hope to yr. satisfaction & my own, thinking it more than sufficient Reward to have the Conversation of so great a Vertuosi." To another collector, further clarifying the goals of these vertuosi, Petiver wrote, "It is, Sir, to such Curious Persons as your selfe that we at this distance must owe what your parts of the late discov-

Specimens gathered by Lawson's own hand still reside in the Natural History Museum in London. Photograph used by permission of the Natural History Museum.

ered World can afford us." That is, people like Lawson—go-getters, out in the field, who gathered specimens of the plants and animals they encountered and shipped them back to England—were the eyes and ears of the Enlightenment hitting its stride. Apparently Petiver never responded to Lawson's first letter, and no matter: Lawson quickly got busy with other things. But clearly when Lawson visited England to publish his book the two finally got in touch, and that subsequent letter shows that Lawson sent back specimens.

He included "one book of plants very slovingly packt up," Lawson says, blaming "ye distracted Circumstances our Country has laboured under." The colony was then suffering under the Cary Rebellion, but we all recognize the apology as just a variety of the usual mealymouthed deadline excuses we all make. Anyhow, Petiver got the stuff, and he included the specimens in his collection. When Petiver died that collection landed in the hands of Sir Hans Sloane, the greatest collector of the age. And when Sloane died, his collection became the foundation of the British Museum, from which the Natural History Museum eventually spun off.

:::

I met Charlie Jarvis, a historical botanist who does research into the original collections of Petiver and Sloane, among others, in the lobby of the Natural History Museum, in London. Jarvis took me up an elevator to the top of the spectacular Darwin Center, the building that elegantly houses and preserves those original collections. The plants are kept in volumes of books organized by HS numbers (Jarvis says HS stands for *Hortus Siccus*). There are 265 of these volumes, of which four contained enough Lawson material to be worth bringing out, which Jarvis had done in advance of my arrival. They reclined, open, on those foam cushions archives use for books they want to treat nicely. I found the very notion that I would be able to gaze upon the actual plant specimens that Lawson collected astonishing, and I was not disappointed.

Lawson's specimens are wonderful to behold: dried, labeled, and all but perfect in their expression of humankind's desire to capture, to organize, to understand. In some cases Lawson's original notes are attached to the linen paper pages; in others only Petiver's notes remain. But in all cases the pages are themselves something like works of art: leaves, twigs, blossoms, and grasses, dry brown and dull green, fixed on with paste; strips of paper with cursive descriptions in brown ink that has soaked into the paper. The specimens represented not just Carolina flora but the very undertaking of early science itself; just being near them reminded me of the audacity of not only Lawson's journey but of the undertaking it represented. The old civilizations of Europe had discovered a new world at the very moment that emerging Enlightenment scientific sensibilities gave them the tools they needed to begin understanding the world better than ever before. John Ray's *Historia Plantarum* was between volumes 2 and 3 of its publication; it was Ray who established the "species as the ultimate unit of taxonomy." (Petiver helped in that endeavor by publishing illustrated works in the 1710s.) Sloane's collection was the greatest of its time, perhaps ever; the work of Linnaeus, establishing the naming conventions we use even today, was decades in the future, and Linnaeus used Sloane's collection when he did it. Today the *Hortus Siccus* books are lovingly preserved in a special climate-controlled room at the top of the Darwin Center; a window allows museumgoers to peer in, where among the elegant, leather-bound books a portrait of Sloane serenely overlooks the collection.

Lawson's specimens (300 or so) are just a tiny portion thereof—Sloane had collections from more than 300 people, though many contributions comprise just a specimen here or there from a traveling physician or clergyman. Petiver's collections constitute more than 100 of the volumes in Sloane's collection, and Petiver himself had dozens of correspondents. He called Lawson "a very curious person" after the two met in London in the summer of 1709, probably at Petiver's shop. Lawson's specimens in those elegantly bound *Hortus Siccus* books included dogwood and black gum, sunflower and blazing star and "the celebrated snake root," which supposedly cured snakebite (it doesn't). A recent article in the digital journal *Phytoneuron* very thoroughly describes Lawson's specimens, connecting them to their current Latin names, though some remain uncertain. All very interesting, to be sure, but most important to me was just to be near Lawson's plants—to know they were gathered by his hand, were labeled with his ink, and survived the centuries because people believe it's worth trying to understand this world around us. I especially gazed at a page on which Lawson had preserved dogwood leaves and flowers. I have dogwoods in my yard. The dogwood blossom is the state flower of North Carolina. There in London I once again felt like Lawson and I stood shoulder to shoulder.

Petiver and Sloane's collections were early herbaria—collections of dried plant types. You find them now at universities and museums, and in building their collections, herbaria trade plant specimens like baseball cards. You can go into an herbarium and see all these cool original specimens gathered over the last half millennium or so, and when you look at them you get that sense of being with a scientist as she or he gathers, prepares, dries, and presents a piece of the world for classification and understanding. You read about where the specimen was gathered, who gathered it, what they noticed. It's like you're with the scientist. For a moment, in the Natural History Museum, I was with Lawson.

::::

Lawson might also have met Petiver at the Chelsea Physic Garden, London's oldest botanical garden, founded in 1673 by the Worshipful Society of Apothecaries. Starting in 1709 Petiver was a "demonstrator" there, which meant he used the garden for his work. An apothecary, of course, was a combination of druggist, physician, natural scientist, and botanist; he gathered information about the world and its plants and animals in the hopes of using them to help people. In *Romeo and Juliet*, Shakespeare describes the apothecary where Romeo buys his poison:

> In his needy shop a tortoise hung,
> An alligator stuff'd, and other skins
> Of ill-shaped fishes; and about his shelves
> A beggarly account of empty boxes,
> Green earthen pots, bladders and musty seeds,
> Remnants of packthread and old cakes of roses,
> Were thinly scatter'd, to make up a show.

::::

Lawson's specimens would have fit right in—he writes of sending to Petiver "4 vials of Insects all plants that are in yr. own paper . . . & all ye bird skins and snake skins they are preserved wth. a liquor . . . & some few fossells." The Physic Garden, four acres or so hidden on the Thames in southeast London, is just as delightful, sections dedicated to medicinal plants, useful plants, and the oldest rock garden in Europe. Signs and guides provide explanations of the uses of such plants as hyssop (helps the ears) and goldenrod (helps pass bladder stones), and descriptions of the first herbal guides, published in the 1500s. A statue of Sloane stands at the center, but you follow paths and lawns to history beds (showing off species collected by famous head gardeners) and systematic order beds, filled with plants from all over the world, sent back by people like Lawson. Sloane, Petiver, and Lawson's paths seem to braid together in this historical garden. My kids poked around near the ponds and looked at the fish.

:::

At these sites celebrating the history of science it was impossible not to marvel, once again, at Lawson's contribution. Almost two centuries after its publication, American naturalist Elliott Coues compared Lawson's book to the masterwork produced by William Bartram on Florida birds, and Sloane himself relied on Lawson's book. But that leads to contributions even more important. The article in *Archives of Natural History* cites Sloane's note on the "Scorpion Lizard," regarding which Sloane says that it came from a Virginia source and that he identified it on page 131 of his copy of Lawson's book: "esteemed very venomous," he says (the modern broadhead skink, by the way, is locally called "scorpion" and is believed to be poisonous, though it's not).

Satisfying enough. But then you go—as how could you not?—to page 131 of Lawson's book and find the entry on Scorpion Lizard, and Lawson tells you it's "no more like a Scorpion, than a Hedge-Hog." The lizard is nimble and regarded as poisonous, and "He has the most Sets of Teeth in his Mouth and Throat, that ever I saw." After that he calls the Green Lizard "the most glorious Green, and very tame. They resort to the Walls of Houses in the Summer Season, and stand gazing on a Man, without any Concern or Fear."

Regardless of its value as science, this makes delightful reading. That is, whatever his contributions as a naturalist, Lawson has made a smashing contribution as a prose stylist. Of the Black Truncheon-Snake he says, "when any thing disturbs them, they dart into the Water . . . like an Arrow out of a Bow." Addressing the work of this "genial and enterprising young Englishman," Moses Coit Tyler, in the *History of American Literature of the Colonial Time*, calls it "an uncommonly strong and sprightly book," and that literary strength and sprightliness is worth celebrating. Lawson has a great sense of humor, telling stories to his own embarrassment about drunkenly falling into the creek near the Santee and being terrified by the alligator's roar near the Neuse. He shared those detailed and moving stories of Indian dancing, hospitality, funeral customs.

Throughout the book there is so much more. "Rattle-Snakes are accounted the peacablest in the World," he says, "for they never attack any one, or injure them, unless they are trod upon, or molested" (a reminder from which many modern Carolinians might profit), slyly noting that, though he's never been hurt himself, most in danger from rattlesnakes are "those that survey Land in *Carolina*." He goes on to note that rattlers "have the Power, or Art (I know not which to call it) to charm Squirrels, Hares, Partridges, or any such thing, in such a manner, that they run directly into their Mouths." He claims to have seen this himself. Which, once again, reminds us: it was the dawn of the scientific age; Lawson was a tenderfoot and either believed much foolishness or just liked to pass along a good story.

He shares the "pleasant story that passes for an uncontested Truth" among Hatteras Indians that "the Ship which brought the first Colonies, does often appear amongst them, under Sail, in a gallant Posture, which they call Sir *Walter Raleigh*'s Ship." He's heard the story repeated as true by his old standby, "Men of the best Credit in the Country." These nutty stories abound. He shares the story of Indian hunters so cleverly disguised as deer that they shot each other, which sounds highly dubious, and he even shares a story so preposterous that it has been documented in the literature of folklore: that raccoons fish for crabs by hanging their tails in the surf. "This the Crab takes for a Bait," Lawson tells us, "and fastens his Claws therein, which as soon as the Raccoon perceives, he, of a sudden, springs forward, a considerable way, on the Land, and brings the Crab along with him."

Similar stories make up some of Lawson's greatest hits. He describes Horn-Snakes, which "strike at their Enemy with their Tail, . . . which is arm'd at the End with a horny Substance, like a Cock's Spur." He has heard it "credibly reported" by eyewitnesses that a horn-snake struck a healthy locust tree in the morning and the tree died that afternoon. Of a snake somehow killing a tree Lawson at least raises doubt. "Be it how it will," he says of that story, the horn-snake is very venomous (though of course ultimately imaginary). He describes a whale that is sixty feet long and a few feet in diameter—in short, a sea serpent. And he tells us that "towards the Head of *Neus* River, there haunts a Creature, . . . the Colour of a Panther . . . and that there abides with him a Creature like an *Englishman's* Dog, which . . . gets his Prey for him." Well, okay—"The Certainty of this I cannot affirm by my own Knowledge," he avers, "yet they all agree in this Story." He tells us of eagles snatching piglets, "at which time the poor Pig makes such a Noise over Head, that Strangers . . . have thought there were Flying Sows and Pigs in that Country." Lawson was like your best crazy uncle, who had really gone so many places and done so many things that you just couldn't tell when he was fooling.

:::

To convince you of Lawson's gift as a writer I could go on quoting him at length, but at this point either you agree or you never will; he was my constant companion throughout this journey, and his delightful descriptions of what he saw helped me see what has come after. But whatever his contributions as a scientific adventurer, documentarian, and prose stylist, his greatest contribution came as an observer of the Indian tribes he met.

And by this I do not mean his wonderful descriptions of Indian customs and traditions. I mean that Lawson stands alone as an observer of the devastation of the Indians by the European colonists. His most famous quote bears repeating one last time: "The Small-Pox and Rum have made such a Destruction amongst them, that, on good grounds, I do believe, there is not the sixth Savage living within two hundred Miles of all our Settlements, as there were fifty Years ago. These poor Creatures have so many Enemies to destroy them, that it's a wonder one of them is left alive near us." But Lawson continues with this perspective in "An Account of the Indians of North Carolina," the most celebrated segment of his book after his journal. He thinks they're beautiful and notes that they have great vision and learn trades quickly. He loves their names for the months ("as one is the Herring-Month, another the Strawberry-Month, another the Mulberry-Month, Others name them by the Trees That blossom; especially, the Dogwood-Tree; or they say, we will return when Turkey-Cocks gobble") and the winds ("the North-West Wind is called the cold Wind; the North-East the wet Wind; the South the warm Wind; and so agreeably of the rest"). He marvels at their skill telling direction (through moss on trees and other mysterious signs).

But above all Lawson seems to have admired, simply, their way of being. He notes how little they scold one another, that they make war only out of personal enmity and insult, not for gain. He finds remarkable the Indian lack of interest in the ceaseless profit foundational to the colonists: "Their way of Living is so contrary to ours, that neither we nor they can fathom one anothers Designs and Methods. They never work as the *English* do, taking care for no farther than what is absolutely necessary to support Life," though "in Travelling and Hunting, they are very indefatigable, because that carries a Pleasure along with the Profit." He sees the value in this: "They never walk backward and forward as we do, nor contemplate on the Affairs of Loss and Gain: the things which daily perplex us." Lawson does not merely criticize colonists—he openly admires Indians by comparison. They laugh off misfortune, he notes, and when one suffers, the community comes together to, say, rebuild a dwelling destroyed by fire. They care for the widow and the orphan.

"They say, the Europeans are always rangling and uneasy, and wonder they do not go out of this World, since they are so uneasy and discontented in it." *Rangling and uneasy* . . . the phrase is glorious, in a few words summing up the feeling of dissatisfaction and need for something more that drove the colonization of an entire hemisphere, for good and ill. The questing spirit of science and the unquenchable desire of capitalism. *Rangling and uneasy.* The Indians, one cannot fail to conclude, saw colonists as they were. And Lawson heard them and gave them voice.

This is not your usual noble savage business, mind you. Lawson sees Indians keeping slaves; he sees their drunkenness, assigns to them a seemingly infinite capacity for vengeance. He sees them steal from colonists ("they are a very craving People") and treat prisoners with enormous cruelty. Still, he says, they are patient and decent, and largely kind, especially considering that "they met with Enemies when we came amongst them."

"They are really better to us, than we are to them," his conclusion bears repeating. "They always give us Victuals at their Quarters, and take care we are arm'd against Hunger and Thirst: We do not so by them (generally speaking) but let them walk by our Doors Hungry, and do not often relieve them. We look upon them with Scorn and Disdain, and think them little better than Beasts in Humane Shape, though if well examined, we shall find that, for all our Religion and Education, we possess more Moral Deformities, and Evils than these Savages do, or are acquainted withal."

We consider them—and make them—slaves, Lawson writes, but in reality "these Indians are the freest People in the World, and so far from being Intruders upon us, that we have abandon'd our own Native Soil, to drive them out, and possess theirs." Now mind you, Lawson himself abandoned his own native soil to drive Indians off of theirs; he's no more successful at living his values than the rest of us. But this kind of self-criticism is remarkable.

And he's just getting warmed up.

We trade with them, it's true, but to what End? Not to shew them the Steps of Vertue, and the Golden Rule, to do as we would be done by. No, we have furnished them with the Vice of Drunkenness, which is the open Road to all others, and daily cheat them in every thing we sell, and esteem it a Gift of Christianity, not to sell to them so cheap as we do to the Christians, as we call our selves. Pray let me know where is there to be found one Sacred Command or Precept of our Master, that counsels us to such Behaviour? Besides, I believe it will not appear, but that all the Wars, which we have had with the Savages, were occasion'd by the unjust Dealings of the Christians towards them.

Gracious.

Lawson thinks a much better model of interaction between settler and Native would be for settlers moving to North America to intermarry with the Indians. Part of the goal of this, of course, is to Christianize the Indians; Lawson was a man of his time. But he believed many other benefits would accrue from this arrangement:

> We should be let into a better Understanding of the Indian Tongue, by our new Converts; ... This seems to be a more reasonable Method of converting the Indians, than to set up our Christian Banner in a Field of Blood, as the Spaniards have done in New Spain, and baptize one hundred with the Sword for one at the Font. Whilst we make way for a Christian Colony through a Field of Blood, and defraud, and make away with those that one day may be wanted in this World, and in the next appear against us, we make way for a more potent Christian Enemy to invade us hereafter, of which we may repent, when too late.

So again — a mixed bag. Better understanding of our world and better trade, but also better Christianizing and better conquering of those darned Spanish and French — and, don't forget, of other Indian tribes that won't play ball. Lawson wasn't a saint. He wanted to convert the Indians into members of the culture that was overwhelming them. Just the same, he saw Indians as fully human, recognized and called out their horrific treatment at European hands, and genuinely wanted for them better lives than they had as things stood. Lawson was part of the problem, but he clearly loved and respected the Indians, "whom he always speaks of," says historian Tylor, "with a sort of gentle liking."

: : :

Perhaps a gentle liking is a good place to leave things regarding Lawson's impressions of the Indians, and perhaps of his entire world. Lawson took a walk and spent another decade hanging around, and the best conclusion he could come to was that North Carolina was a nice place to live and you'd be a fool to turn down a chance to go there. I took a similar walk and I'm not sure I have much to add. Yes, Lawson saw the collapse of Indian societies centuries old, and I could not fail to note that whatever European culture was based on here in North America, if the condition of the small towns and the people in them is any indication, that's collapsing now too. The racism that enabled colonists to devastate and enslave indigenous peoples and ship over more people to enslave still powerfully colors every aspect of life in the Carolinas. Impoverished tribes try to make a go of it after centuries of abuse and can barely manage recognition, much less respect; impoverished African American communities try to do the same; impoverished populations of descendants of those colonists in small towns face similar troubles after abandonment by textiles and agriculture. Meanwhile, big cities like Charlotte and Raleigh seem to be flourishing.

Drawing conclusions almost unfailingly makes you look foolish. In 1989 V. S. Naipaul wrote *A Turn in the South*, continuing a tradition started by the earliest explorers, amplified by Lawson, and carried on recently by people like Paul Theroux of wandering through the American South and making pronouncements. Naipaul's observations are sharp, but among them is a description of "civil-rights groups, their major battles and indeed their war won long ago, now squabbling and looking for causes." One looks away in horror, though of course it's worth remembering: however laughable it sounds now, in the late 1980s many people genuinely did think that the United States—and even the South—had suffered its last paroxysm of resistance to civil rights. Naipaul's comment itself becomes part of that record. Like Lawson's deeply observed love letters to the Indian tribes he visited, his frank observations about their treatment, his commitment nonetheless to developing their land, and his eventual murder at their hands, it becomes part of the tale of complexity through which we all do our best to muddle. Maybe the only point is that there's always room for another journey and more observation. In an original copy of one segment of Lawson's book in the University of North Carolina's Wilson Library is an advertisement by one of the booksellers in the collective that published his work: "Those Gentlemen that have any Original Voyages by them, and will bring them to *J. Baker* at the Black Boy in *Pater-Noster-Row*, shall have due Encouragement if they be worth Printing." Paternoster Row, next to St. Paul's, was the home of London's publishing industry. It's home to high finance now. Just the same, one hopes that Original Voyages will always have due Encouragement.

:::

One retraces the footsteps of others to draw comparisons. Lawson looked at the territory, so he draws our eyes to the territory, and we notice once again forests and creeks and hills that we have ceased noticing or had never noticed. He sees flora, fauna, inhabitants, and so we look at our own surroundings, and each other, anew. I cannot help feeling that the greatest observation on this entire enterprise came in the Rather Unique Barber Shop, whose denizens suggested that of all modernity, what Lawson would find most astonishing was paved roads. I never stopped marveling at our roads. Gigantic superhighways that roar and rumble, their overpasses set on earthen pyramids. Roads choked with cars near cities, further out processing pulses of traffic controlled by signals. Two-lanes running through farmlands with never a spot to walk. Near cities also endless construction sites; the grinding of backhoe gears and the rhythmic beeping of backing dump trucks as common as the call of cardinals or the chirp of cicadas. One day we heard quail. Lawson walked on earthen paths through green fields and found sound worthy of mention only when bobcats or alligators roared.

Also tools. Lawson advises potential colonists to bring obvious things like spades and hoes and tools of their trades, to say nothing of guns, powder, and shot. But he also reminds them they'll need linens and cutlery, hats, and "a few Wiggs, not long, and pretty thin of Hair." For the tools he sends them to an ironmonger. "Capt. *Sharp*, in *Canon-street*," can supply "Earthen-Ware, Window-Glass, . . . Ink-Powder, Saddles, Bridles, and what other things you are minded to take with you, for Pleasure or Ornament." Stores were in short supply in Carolina; blacksmiths probably meant a day's travel. In our own Carolina nowadays nothing is in short supply. It doesn't make a difference what we want—we can get it tomorrow or even today without even leaving our chairs, sometimes delivered by tiny helicopter.

Rangling and uneasy indeed.

Lawson probably had a copy of a map that represented the Carolina coast and even gave him some idea of what to expect from the mouths of the Neuse and the Pamlico but would have been all but useless—however lovely—for anything like wayfinding. The map he created, included with his book, identifies territory of the "Congerree" and "Tuskeraro" and places like Charleston and Bath, but you wouldn't use it to decide how to get anywhere. As for me I used those DeLorme *Atlas & Gazetteers* and Google Maps when I got crossed up—or needed to be able to check something on the house-by-house level. I had a compass in case I needed it—and one on my phone—but, really, make me laugh.

I could go on. Lawson, from list to description to documenting the cultures he witnessed, gives us a glimpse into what it would have looked like, what it would have felt like, to walk around in the last moments of the seventeenth century and the first decade of the eighteenth. I have tried, by walking through highway underpasses and eating at lunch counters and talking to everyone I met, to give a glimpse of the second decade of the twenty-first. That may be all one can do. That may be all there is to say. "But not to amuse my Readers any longer with the Encomium of Carolina," Lawson says in his book at the end of his introductory throat-clearing. "I refer 'em to my Journal, and other more particular Description of that Country and its Inhabitants, which they will find after the Natural History thereof, in which I have been very exact." He was as exact as he could be. We share what we have and then we stop talking.

:::

My final Lawsonian journey took me to Grifton, on the Contentnea Creek, where apart from their shad festival they host the annual John Lawson Legacy Days, a weekend of lectures and traditional crafts. They have an Indian village recreation, with a wigwam covered in bark; they have a little fire where someone works clay pots in the old way, moving them closer to the fire and then further away until, kiln or no kiln, they're fired. I saw a man in period dress making a dugout canoe—a cypress trunk on blocks, fire built along the side, embers placed on the trunk to burn it down. When the embers went out he scraped out the charcoal and then started again. He said he could make a canoe in two weeks if that was mostly all he did. I saw a man make a fire with sticks, make a blow-gun out of river cane, a bow and arrow out of bough and sinew.

And I took a little motorboat ride, up the Contentnea—believed to be the Catechna of Lawson's day—to a low spot on the creek, a good landing place, where many believe John Lawson and Cristoph von Graffenried were tried by a court of unhappy Tuscaroras, leading to an unhappy outcome for Lawson.

Maybe. Who can know? Tim Bright, a resident of Grifton, ran that small boat up and down the creek, past stands of ancient bald cypress old enough that Lawson likely saw them. Bald cypress doesn't grow terribly high, but you can estimate age by girth. As we putted along, Tim constantly said, "*Tell* me that tree's not 300 years old." I never did. The area that archaeologists think was the town of Catechna has everything you'd want in a settlement: clear access to the river, high spots that stay dry, a small creek useful for gathering water. Yet what was most powerful about the spot came later, when the entire festival hiked back out to the spot and placed a magnolia wreath there. "In Memory & Honor of All Those Who Came Before," it said. "May they rest in Peace." Standing on one side, dressed much as Lawson would have been dressed, was Wayne Hardee, who manages the Grifton Museum and has helped organize the festival for all of its years. Standing on the other side was Vince Schiffert—a descendant of the Tuscarora people, down from New York State, where much that remained of the tribe relocated after their inevitable devastation in the war that began with Lawson's death. The descendants of the settlers and the descendants of the Tuscaroras very much seem to consider themselves part of the same community, which was, after all, what Lawson himself had originally hoped for. The moment of silence all observed was a sweet end to the day.

An end to my journey I suppose too. After we all returned to the festival site I walked toward my car, the murmur of the crowd and the putting of generators receding. Another little walk along a rural road, another drive out of a small town, the low picked-over fields of tobacco and soybeans sliding by my windows. I saw flocks of mourning doves fluttering around, standing shoulder to shoulder on electric distribution lines.

I stopped to make a picture.

ACKNOWLEDGMENTS

The Knight Science Journalism Fellowships at MIT supported this enterprise through a 2014–15 project fellowship, and I can never fully express my gratitude to the program, to MIT, and to the John S. and James L. Knight Foundation and other program funders like the Alfred P. Sloan Foundation, the Mellon Foundation, and the Kavli Foundation. I send my deepest thanks to acting director Wade Roush and the 2014–15 fellows, who provided inspiration and support as I worked through the trek. Special appreciation goes to 2013–14 project fellow Maryn McKenna, who powerfully advocated for me and for this project as she has done many times and for many worthy journalists and causes.

The vast majority of North and South Carolinians are kind and generous and helpful and decent; through our states I met with an unceasing flood of support. I cannot possibly name everyone who helped me, but the people I name here were all called at various times Heroes of the Lawson Trek. They transported me, informed me, hosted me, fed me, and supported me in any number of ways that distinguished them even beyond the vast amount of help seemingly everyone I met offered. So many people helped me along this journey, both on land and among the bookstacks, that I apologize at the outset: these acknowledgments will be long, but I will certainly forget someone who pointed me toward an unknown source, someone who picked me up or dropped me off, someone who offered me help or a place to stay or a slice of watermelon. I apologize before beginning.

Jack Horan and Dan Huntley in 2001 undertook a newspaper story about Lawson and his journey, and reading that story more than a decade later led me to Val Green, without whom this project would never have found its way. Val's contribution to this work cannot be overstated; from beginning to end, on the trail and in various meetings, conversations, and correspondence hither and yon, he provided endless support, expertise, and assistance. My debt to him is incalculable. The equally kind Pelham Lyles often accompanied him. Jack Horan generously sent me his original files on Lawson, which led me to places and books I might easily otherwise have missed. Mike Smith at the North Carolina Archives originally provided the box of material in which I found Horan and Dan Huntley's story.

Tom Earnhardt of *Exploring North Carolina* was my first fellow Lawsonian, providing a copy of his television show on Lawson and enormous good will toward this enterprise. Other Piedmont Lawsonians gladly offered help as I planned my journey: Marjorie Hudson spoke to me about Eno Will, Tom Magnuson shared knowledge of the Trading Path, and Bland Simpson led me in several unexpected directions. Elizabeth Sparrow shared her time, her portrait of (plausibly) Lawson, and her home with me.

In Charleston, the fabulous Kathie Livingston of Nature Adventure Outfitters took this undertaking in hand and helped manage it until it was out of range upstate; Ed Deal and Elizabeth Anderegg provided guidance; Jimmy Small provided a place to sleep, as did Jana DuPre. Eddie Stroman and Martha Zierden of McClellanville guided, informed, and housed me. Thanks also there to Billy Baldwin, who provided information, inspiration, and guidance. Cheves Leland and Susan Bates provided an understanding of Huguenot history—and Sewee pottery sherds. Wil Christenson provided water and guidance.

Douglas Guerry and Jean Guerry fed, housed, and transported me and ecologist Katie Winsett, herself an invaluable traveling companion and friend. Michael Singer and Rob Waters also walked along in South Carolina. The denizens of Pack's Landing provided comfort, information, and transport, as did the Lenoir family of Horatio. Peggy Scott of the Santee Tribe inspired us and shared her time and history. Jenny Leonard put us in touch with Joanna Craig, who helped and housed us in Camden, as did Bill and Laurie Funderburk. In Lancaster everyone at the Native American Studies Center did all they could to help me on my way, but Chris Judge, Brent Burgin, and Beckee Garris stand above the crowd. Jered Canty of the Catawba Nation shared stories with me and toured me around his people's home. Jimmy White and Barry Beasley walked the land with me and told me its stories—and gave me more pottery fragments. A canoe made of riverbank clay by a Catawba potter and given to me by Brent is a treasured memento and demonstration of the way these threads all bind together.

Near Charlotte, Dale Loberger camped with me and taught me and gave generously of his time and expertise. Mike Graff drove and supported me, Mary Newsom did the same and taught me about creeks, and Dan Huntley fed me—and taught me about—barbecue. David Harris pulled over by the side of the road and told me stories about the delicious country in which he lives. Steve Davis at the University of North Carolina gave me background in Carolina archaeology. The people at Delk's provided me one of my favorite camping spots in history.

Dr. Robert Crawford III in Salisbury and his wife, Ann, put me up in a historic cabin, fed me, and filled me with lore. Historian Susan Sides there did the same. Ann Brownlee filled me with Trading Ford history. Ann Tilley and her boyfriend, Adam, told me stories, drove me around, and brought me watermelon. Speed Hallman and Michael Johnston helped me get from hither to yon in central North Carolina, and Michael Verville connected me up in Hillsborough where I met John "Blackfeather" Jeffries, who spent hours with me, sharing with me not only lore and his personal museum but also an arrow that I will never shoot. Roland Kays and Troi Perkins helped me with camera traps.

Christie Starnes provided leadership and transportation in Clayton and otherwise south of Raleigh, and Ray Wheeler toured me around his grist mill. Mary Fuller at MIT spoke with me about early exploration narratives. Cynthia Collins played host, chauffeur, and information source in Wilson. Jennifer Landin taught me how to draw and how to see; Angela Clemmons partnered along for that lesson. Chuck Twardy and Gail Munde housed and transported me during the trek's final days, and Vince Bellis gave of his time and enormous expertise about the end of Lawson's journey. Russ Chesson gathered me up and toured me through the Estuarium in Washington. At Historic Bath Leigh Swain reached out, made a fuss, and treated the Lawson Trek like it was big news. Seth and Nancy Effron hosted us in style and performed canoe rescues above and beyond the call of duty. Wayne Hardee in Grifton has kept the Lawson Trek connected with the John Lawson Legacy Days, where Vince Schiffert of the Tuscarora Tribe and historian Larry Tise talked Lawson. Tara Mei Smith taught me about stickiness.

Mark Simpson-Vos at UNC Press has been behind this project since before it existed, and it has been a pleasure working with him. The entire production team impressed this old production editor; thanks especially to copyeditor Alex Martin. Michelle Tessler too has supported this beyond the capacity of merely mortal agents. In the very small club of authors who love their agents I have advanced to the office of president. The awesome people at Duke Alumni Affairs and *Duke* magazine were very generous in giving me the time to write this book, and I am very grateful.

My two boys, Gus and Louie, waved me off from the dock at Charleston, put up with an awful lot of absence over the course of more than a year, and then joined me for the final paddle into Bath; I could desire no finer boon companions, and I wish for their own questing spirits lives of Lawsonian adventure, though with perhaps more satisfactory endings. My wife, June, was by far the truest hero of the Lawson Trek, managing a household alone while I continually vanished onto the waves or roads or up to Cambridge; I mean it in the truest sense when I say I could not have done this project without her, nor would I have wished to. I dedicated a previous book to her, but in truth they are all dedicated to her, as am I.

BIBLIOGRAPHY

Adair, James. *The History of the American Indians, Particularly Those Nations Adjoining to the Mississippi, East and West Florida, Georgia, South and North Carolina, and Virginia.* London: Edward and Charles Dilly, 1775. Reprint, New York: Promontory, 1930.

Adams, Percy G. "John Lawson's Alter-Ego: Dr. John Brickell." *North Carolina Historical Review* 34, no. 3 (July 1957): 313–26.

Alderfer, Jonathan, and Paul Hess. *National Geographic Backyard Guide to the Birds of North America.* Washington, D.C.: National Geographic, 2011.

Alsberg, Henry G., ed. *The American Guide: The South; the Southwest.* New York: Hastings House, 1949.

Ambrose, Stephen E. *Undaunted Courage: Meriwether Lewis, Thomas Jefferson, and the Opening of the American West.* New York: Simon & Schuster, 1996.

American Automobile Association. *Georgia, North Carolina & South Carolina Tour Book, 2011 Edition.* Heathrow, Fla.: AAA, 2011.

American Council of Learned Societies. "John Lawson." *Dictionary of American Biography.* New York: Charles Scribner's Sons, 1936.

American Philosophical Society. "John Lawson." Exhibit webpage. http://amphilsoc.org/exhibits/nature/lawson.htm. Retrieved 2018.

Angier, Natalie. *The Canon: A Whirligig Tour of the Beautiful Basics of Science.* New York: Houghton Mifflin, 2007.

Armitage, David. "John Locke, Carolina, and the 'Two Treatises of Government.'" *Political Theory* 32, no. 5 (October 2004): 602–27.

Ashe, Samuel A., Steven B. Weeks, and Charles L. Van Noppen, eds. *Biographical History of North Carolina from Colonial Times to the Present.* Greensboro, N.C.: Charles L. Van Noppen, 1906.

Audubon, John James. In *The Audubon Reader*, ed. Richard Rhodes. New York: Knopf, 2006.

Baily, Nick. *Chelsea Physic Garden: Connecting People with Plants since 1673.* London: Chelsea Physic Garden, 2015.

Bakeless, John. *America as Seen by Its First Explorers: The Eyes of Discovery.* New York: Dover, 1961.

Baldwin, William P., ed. *Sacred Places of the Lowcountry: Lost Photographs from the Historic American Buildings Survey.* Charleston, S.C.: History Press, 2007.

Bartram, William. *Travels Through North & South Carolina, Georgia, East & West*

Florida, the Cherokee Country, the Extensive Territories of the Muscogulges, or Creek Confederacy, and the Country of the Chactaws. Philadelphia: James & Johnson, 1791.

Bates, Susan Baldwin, and Harriet Cheves Leland. *French Santee: A Huguenot Settlement in Colonial South Carolina*. Baltimore: Otter Bay, 2015.

Bellis, Vince. "John Lawson's North Carolina." *Tar Heel Junior Historian* 47, no. 1 (Fall 2007).

———. "John Lawson's Plant Collections from North Carolina, 1710–1711." *Castanea: The Journal of the Southern Appalachian Botanical Society* 74, no. 4 (December 2009): 376–89.

———. "Searching for the Ashes of Mr. Lawson's Campfires." Unpublished manuscript, March 2, 2004.

Berry, Wendell. *A Continuous Harmony: Essays Cultural & Agricultural*. New York: Harcourt Brace Jovanovich, 1972.

Blackwell, A. H., P. D. McMillan, and C. W. Blackwell. "John Lawson's Plant Collections, Virginia and North Carolina, 1710–1711." *Phytoneuron* 94 (2014): 1–23.

Boissoneault, Lorraine. *The Last Voyageurs: Retracing La Salle's Journey across America — Sixteen Teenagers on the Adventure of a Lifetime*. New York: Pegasus, 2016.

Bonner, John Tyler. *The Scale of Nature: A Panoramic View of the Sciences*. New York: Pegasus, 1969.

Bortolus, A., J. T. Carlton, and E. Schwindt. "Reimagining South American Coasts: Unveiling the Hidden Invasion History of an Iconic Ecological Engineer." *Diversity and Distributions* 21, no. 11 (November 2015).

Bowers, Nora Mays, Rick Bowers, and Stan Tekiela. *Wildflowers of the Carolinas: Field Guide*. Cambridge, Minn.: Adventure, 2008.

Branch, Michal P., ed. *Reading the Roots: American Nature Writing before "Walden."* Athens: University of Georgia Press, 2004.

Brickell, John, MD. *The Natural History of North-Carolina, with an Account of the Trade, Manners, and Customs of the Christian and Indian Inhabitants*. Dublin: James Carson, 1737.

Brooks, Jerome E. *Green Leaf and Gold: Tobacco in North Carolina*. 4th ed. Raleigh: North Carolina Division of Archives and History, 1997.

Brown, Judith. "Museum Gala Honors Those Who Honor History." *Laurens County (S.C.) Advertiser*, April 24, 2015.

Byrd, William. *Histories of the Dividing Line betwixt Virginia and North Carolina*. New York: Dover, 1967.

Carpenter, Harry A., George C. Wood, and Paul E. Smith. *Our Environment: Its Relation to Us*. Boston: Allyn and Bacon, 1950.

Cassebaum, Anne Melyn. *Down Along the Haw: The History of a North Carolina River*. Jefferson, N.C.: McFarland, 2011.

Casson, Lionel. *Travel in the Ancient World*. Baltimore: Johns Hopkins University Press, 1994.

Catawba Riverkeeper Foundation. "About the Catawba-Wateree River." https://www.catawbariverkeeper.org/about-the-river/. Accessed February 15, 2015.

Catesby, Mark. *The Natural History of Carolina, Florida and the Bahama Islands*. London: Benjamin White, 1771.

Cobb, James C. *Redefining Southern Culture: Mind & Identity in the Modern South*. Athens: University of Georgia Press, 1999.

Coe, Joffre Lanning. "The Cultural Sequence of the Carolina Piedmont." In *Archaeology of the Eastern United States*, by J. B. Griffin. Chicago: University of Chicago Press, 1952.

———. *The Formative Cultures of the Carolina Piedmont*. Raleigh: Office of Archives and History, North Carolina Department of Cultural Resources, 2006.

Collections of the South Carolina Historical Society. Charleston: South Carolina Historical Society, 1858.

Coues, Elliott. *List of Faunal Publications Relating to North American Ornithology*. Miscellaneous Publication no. 11, 576–77, 577–78. Washington, D.C.: U.S. Geological and Geographical Survey of the Territories, 1878.

Counts, Kim, and Laura Lee Rose. "Life along the Salt Marsh: Protecting Tidal Creeks with Vegetative Buffers." *SC Waterways*, November 2013.

Crane, Verner W. *The Southern Frontier, 1670–1732*. New York: W. W. Norton, 1981.

———. "The Tennessee River as the Road to Carolina: The Beginnings of Exploration and Trade." *Mississippi Valley Historical Review* 3, no. 1 (June 1916): 3–18.

Cumming, William P. *Mapping the North Carolina Coast: Sixteenth-Century Cartography and the Roanoke Voyages*. Raleigh: Division of Archives and History, North Carolina Department of Cultural Resources, 1988.

———. *North Carolina in Maps*. Raleigh: State Department of Archives and History, 1966.

———. *The Southeast in Early Maps*. Chapel Hill: University of North Carolina Press, 1962.

Dampier, William. *A New Voyage round the World: The Journal of an English Buccaneer*. London: Knapton, 1697. Reprint, London: Hummingbird, 1998.

Daniels, R. B., S. W. Buol, H. J. Kleiss, and C. A. Ditzler. *Soil Systems in North Carolina*. Technical Bulletin 314. Raleigh: N.C. State University Soil Science Department, 1999.

Davidson, Donald. *The Tennessee*, vol. 1, *The Old River: Frontier to Secession*. Nashville: J. S. Sanders, 1946.

Davis, R. P. Stephen, Jr. "Great Trading Path." *NCPedia*, 2006. https://www .ncpedia.org/great-trading-path.

———. "John Lawson and the Native Peoples of Carolina." Unpublished manuscript, 2001.

DeLorme *Atlas & Gazetteer, North Carolina*, 10th ed. Yarmouth, Me.: Delorme, 2012.

DeLorme *Atlas & Gazetteer, South Carolina*, 4th ed. Yarmouth, Me.: Delorme, 2010.

DePratter, Chester B. "Hernando de Soto and Juan Pardo in Interior South Carolina: A Response to Val Green." *South Carolina Antiquities* 48 (2016): 75–80.

Desiderio, Dante, et al. "Detailed Sappony History." LearnNC. North Carolina Humanities Council and UNC American Indian Center. Online resource currently unavailable.

Drayton, John. *A View of South-Carolina, as Respects Her Natural and Civil Concerns*. Charleston, S.C.: W. P. Young, 1802.

Earley, Lawrence S. *Looking for Longleaf: The Fall and Rise of an American Forest*. Chapel Hill: University of North Carolina Press, 2004.

"Early Spanish Mining in Northern Georgia." *Historical Magazine* 10, no. 5 (May 1866): 137–39.

Ethridge, Robbie. *From Chicaza to Chickasaw: The European Invasion and the Transformation of the Mississippian World, 1540–1715*. Chapel Hill: University of North Carolina Press, 2010.

Ewen, Charles R. "John Lawson's Bath: A Subterranean Perspective." *North Carolina Historical Review* 88, no. 3 (July 2011): 265–79.

Fecher, Rebecca Taft. "The Trading Path and North Carolina." *Journal of Backcountry Studies* 3, no. 2 (2008).

Feduccia, Alan, ed. *Catesby's Birds of Colonial America*. Chapel Hill: University of North Carolina Press, 1985.

Ferguson, Leland, ed. *Historical Archaeology and the Importance of Material Things*. Special Publication Series, no. 2. Charleston, S.C.: Society for Historical Archaeology,

Flood, Alison. "Scientists Use Thoreau's Journals to Track Climate Change." *The Guardian*, March 14, 2012.

Foote, William Henry. *Sketches of North Carolina, Historical and Biographical*. New York: Robert Carter, 1846.

Forbes, Esther. *Paul Revere and the World He Lived In*. Boston: Houghton Mifflin, 1942.

Gallay, Alan. *The Indian Slave Trade: The Rise of the English Empire in the American South, 1670–1717.* New Haven, Conn.: Yale University Press, 2002.

———, ed. *Indian Slavery in Colonial America.* Lincoln: University of Nebraska Press, 2009.

Godfrey, Michael A. *Field Guide to the Piedmont: The Natural Habitats of America's Most Lived-In Region, from New York City to Montgomery, Alabama.* Chapel Hill: University of North Carolina Press, 1997.

Grandin, Greg. *The Empire of Necessity: Slavery, Freedom, and Deception in the New World.* New York: Henry Holt, 2014.

Grant, Richard. "Deep in the Swamps, Archaeologists Are Finding How Fugitive Slaves Kept Their Freedom." *Smithsonian Magazine*, September 2016.

Green, Val. "A Reply to Dr. Chester DePratter." *South Carolina Antiquities* 48 (2016): 81–84.

———. "The Routes of the Spanish in 16th-Century Carolina: A Historical Narrative." *South Carolina Antiquities* 47 (2015): 51–67.

———. "Six Englishmen in Company." Unpublished manuscript, n.d.

Greenberg, Joel. *A Feathered River across the Sky: The Passenger Pigeon's Flight to Extinction.* New York: Bloomsbury, 2014.

Greene, Jack P., ed. *Selling a New World: Two Colonial South Carolina Promotional Pamphlets.* Columbia: University of South Carolina Press, 1989.

Hairr, John. "John Lawson's Observations on the Animals of Carolina." *North Carolina Historical Review* 88, no. 3 (July 2011): 312–32.

Harriot, Thomas. *A Briefe and True Report of the New Found Land of Virginia; the Complete 1590 Theodor De Bry Edition.* New York: Dover: 1972.

Harris, Francis Latham. "Biographical Sketch of John Lawson." In *Lawson's History of North Carolina.* Richmond, Va.: Garrett and Massie, 1937.

Harris, Lynn. *Canoes and Canoe-Built Vessels in the Lowcountry.* Occasional Maritime Papers. Columbia: Maritime Research Division, South Carolina Division of Archaeology and Anthropology, University of South Carolina, January 1, 1998.

Hawke, David Freeman. *Everyday Life in Early America.* New York: Harper & Row, 1988.

Hayes, Miles O., and Jacqueline Michel. *A Coast for All Seasons: A Naturalist's Guide to the Coast of South Carolina.* Columbia, S.C.: Pandion, 2008.

Headlam, Cecil, ed. *Calendar of State Papers, Colonial Series, America and West Indies, 1699, also Addenda, 1621–1698.* London: Mackie, 1908.

Heard, Joseph Norman. *Handbook of the American Frontier: Four Centuries of Indian-White Relationships.* Metuchen, N.J.: Scarecrow, 1987.

Henderson, Caspar. "The Death and Life of the Frontier: A Voyage to the Limits of the Knowable." *Nautilus* 1 (Fall 2013): 24–36.

Hibbs, Mark. "Riggs' Exit Leaves Void on CRC Science Panel." *Coastal Review Online*, August 12, 2016.

Hicks, Brian. "Slavery in Charleston: A Chronicle of Human Bondage in the Holy City." *Post and Courier*, April 9, 2011.

Hill, Selden B. "John Lawson's Tale about the Sewee Indian Nation." *Origins: A Newsletter of the Village Museum, McClellanville, South Carolina* 3, no. 4 (August 2001).

Hitt, Jack. "Discovering the Deep South's Clichés All Over Again." *Washington Post*, October 2, 2015.

Holloman, Charles R. "John Lawson, 1674–1711." In *Dictionary of North Carolina Biography*, ed. William S. Powell. Chapel Hill: University of North Carolina Press, 1996.

Horan, Jack. "Ghost Prairie of the East." *Nature Conservancy*, July/August 1995.

Horan, Jack, and Dan Huntley. "Little-Known John Lawson Was the Lewis and Clark of This Region and Changed History with His 'New Voyage to Carolina.'" *Charlotte Observer*, August 5, 2001.

Horwitz, Tony. *A Voyage Long and Strange: Rediscovering the New World*. New York: Henry Holt, 2008.

Hudson, Marjorie. *Accidental Birds of the Carolinas*. Winston-Salem, N.C.: Press 53, 2011.

Huler, Scott. "The Foundation of Everything." *Our State*, September 2012.

———. "Where Are We? The Story of North Carolina Maps." *Our State*, April 2014.

Hutchinson, Dale L. *Foraging, Farming, and Coastal Biocultural Adaptation in Late Prehistoric North Carolina*. Gainesville: University Press of Florida, 2002.

Huxley, Robert, ed. *The Great Naturalists*. London: Thames & Hudson, 2007.

Isenbarger, Dennis L., ed. *Native Americans in Early North Carolina: A Documentary History*. Raleigh: North Carolina Office of Archives and History, 2013.

"Jean Couture: The Forgotten Coureur de Bois of South Carolina." *All Points West*, March 9, 2011. http://andysallpointswest.blogspot.com/2011/03/jean-couture-forgotten-coureur-de-bois.html.

"John Lawson." *Dictionary of American Biography*. New York: Charles Scribner's Sons, 1936. Biography in Context Web, November 11, 2014.

Jones, Houston Gwynne. "John Lawson's Journey." In *Scoundrels, Rogues, and Heroes of the Old North State*. Mount Pleasant, S.C.: History Press, 2007.

Jones, Scott. *A View to the Past: Experience and Experiment in Primitive Technology*. Booksurge.com, 2008.

Joseph, J. W., and Martha Zierden. *Another's Country: Archaeological and*

Historical Perspective on Cultural Interactions in the Southern Colonies.
Tuscaloosa: University of Alabama Press, 2002.

Kelly, Susan Stafford. "The Story of Tobacco Barns in North Carolina." *Our State*, August 2013.

Kornylak, Andrew. "Giants of the Forest." *Our State*, September 2016.

Kricher, John C., and Gordon Morrison. *Peterson Field Guides Ecology of Eastern Forests.* Boston: Houghton Mifflin, 1988.

Kwok, Roberta. "Rise of 'Shoreline Hardening' Threatens Coastal Ecosystems." *Conservation: The Source for Environmental Intelligence*, August 6, 2015.

Lane, John. *My Paddle to the Sea: Eleven Days on the River of the Carolinas.* Athens: University of Georgia Press, 2011.

Lane, John, and Gerald Thurmond, eds. *The Woods Stretched for Miles: New Nature Writing from the South.* Athens: University of Georgia Press, 1999.

Latham, Eva C., and Patricia M. Samford. "Naturalist, Explorer, and Town Father: John Lawson and Bath." *North Carolina Historical Review* 88, no. 3 (July 2011): 250–64.

Lawson, John. *A New Voyage to Carolina.* Edited by Hugh Talmage Lefler. Chapel Hill: University of North Carolina Press, 1967.

———. *A New Voyage to Carolina; Containing the Exact Description and Natural History of that Country: Together with the Present State Thereof. And a Journal of a Thousand Miles, Travel'd thro' Several Nations of Indians. Giving a Particular Account of their Customs, Manners, etc.* London: Knapton, 1709. Reprinted in Readex Microprint Great Americana Series, 1966.

La Vere, David. *The Tuscarora War: Indians, Settlers, and the Fight for the Carolina Colonies.* Chapel Hill: University of North Carolina Press, 2013.

Lee, Enoch Lawrence. *Indian Wars of North Carolina.* Raleigh, N.C.: Carolina Charter Tercentenary Commission, 1963.

Leed, Eric J. *The Mind of the Traveler: From Gilgamesh to Global Tourism.* New York: Basic Books, 1990.

Lefler, Hugh Talmadge, and Albert Ray Newsome. *North Carolina: The History of a Southern State.* Chapel Hill: University of North Carolina Press, 1963.

Leopold, Aldo. *A Sand County Almanac, and Sketches Here and There.* New York: Oxford, 1949.

Leslie, Laura. "DEQ: Water Rules May Not Be Working." February 10, 2016. http://www.wral.com/deq-water-rules-may-not-be-working-/15347674/.

Little, Elbert L. *National Audubon Society Field Guide to North American Trees, Eastern Region.* New York: Knopf, 1980.

Logan, J. H. *A History of the Upper Country of South Carolina from the Earliest Periods to the Close of the War of Independence.* Charleston, S.C.: Courtenay, 1859.

Love, John. *Geodaesia: Or, the Art of Surveying and Measuring Land Made Easy.* 8th ed. London: J. Rivington, 1768; facsimile reprinted Schenectady, N.Y.: United States Historical Research Service, 1997.

Magnuson, Tom. "Indian Trading Paths." *NCPedia*, 2006. https://www.ncpedia.org/indian-trading-paths.

Mann, Charles C. *1491: New Revelations of the Americas before Columbus.* New York: Vintage, 2006.

Mathewes, Perry. "John Lawson the Naturalist." *North Carolina Historical Review* 88, no. 3 (July 2011): 333–48.

Mathis, Mark A., and Jeffrey J. Crow, eds. *The Prehistory of North Carolina: An Archaeological Symposium.* Raleigh: Division of Archives and History, North Carolina Department of Cultural Resources, 1983.

Matthiessen, Peter. *Wildlife in America.* New York: Penguin, 1959.

McAtee, W. L. "The Birds in Lawson's *New Voyage to Carolina*, 1709." *The Chat* 19, no. 4 (December 1955): 74–77; and 20, no. 2 (June 1956): 23–28.

McCormick, Michael, et al. "Climate Change during and after the Roman Empire." *Journal of Interdisciplinary History* 43, no. 2 (Autumn 2012): 169–220.

McCrady, Edward. *The History of South Carolina under the Proprietary Government, 1670–1719.* New York: MacMillan, 1897.

McGill, Kathy O. "'The Most Industrious Sex': John Lawson's Carolina Women Domesticate the Land." *North Carolina Historical Review* 88, no. 3 (July 2011): 280–97.

McIlvenna, Noeleen. *A Very Mutinous People: The Struggle for North Carolina, 1660–1713.* Chapel Hill: University of North Carolina Press, 2009.

Merrell, James H. *The Indians' New World: Catawbas and Their Neighbors from European Contact through the Era of Removal.* New York: Norton, 1989.

Mills, Robert. *Atlas of the State of South Carolina, a New Facsimile Edition of the Original Published in 1825.* Columbia, S.C.: Lucy Hampton Bostick and Fant H. Thornley, 1938.

Mitchell, John Hanson. *Walking Towards Walden: A Pilgrimage in Search of Place.* Reading, Mass.: Addison Wesley, 1995.

Mitchell, Patricia B. *The Good Land: Native American and Early Colonial Food.* Chatham, Va.: Patricia Mitchell, 1998.

Mobley, Joe A., ed. *The Way We Lived in North Carolina.* Chapel Hill: University of North Carolina Press, 2003.

Mooney, James. *The Aboriginal Population of America North of Mexico.* Smithsonian Miscellaneous Collections 80, no. 7, publication 2955. Washington, D.C.: Smithsonian Institution, 1928.

Muir, John. *A Thousand-Mile Walk to the Gulf.* Boston: Houghton Mifflin, 1916.

Murray, Elizabeth Reid. *Wake: Capital County of North Carolina*. Raleigh, N.C.: Capital County Publishing, 1983.

Naipaul, V. S. *A Turn in the South*. New York: Vintage, 1989.

Nelson, E. Charles, and David J. Elliott. *The Curious Mister Catesby: A "Truly Ingenious" Naturalist Explores New Worlds*. Athens: University of Georgia Press, 2015.

North Carolina Birding Trail, Coastal Plain Trail Guide. Raleigh: North Carolina Birding Trail, 2007.

North Carolina Birding Trail, Piedmont Trail Guide. Raleigh: North Carolina Birding Trail, 2008.

North Carolina Historical Review 88, no. 3 (July 2011).

Noss, Reed F. *Forgotten Grasslands of the South: Natural History and Conservation*. Washington, D.C.: Island, 2013.

Oakley, Christopher Arris. *Keeping the Circle: American Indian Identity in Eastern North Carolina, 1885–2004*. Lincoln: University of Nebraska Press, 2005.

Paulett, Robert. *An Empire of Small Places: Mapping the Southeastern Anglo-Indian Trade, 1732–1795*. Athens: University of Georgia Press, 2012.

Parrish, Susan Scoee. *American Curiosity: Cultures of Natural History in the Colonial British Atlantic New World*. Williamsburg, Va.: Omohundro Institute of Early American History and Culture, 2006. Published for Omohundro Institute by University of North Carolina Press.

Pearson, Thomas Gilbert, Clement Samuel Brimley, and Herbert Hutchinson Brimley. *Birds of North Carolina*. Raleigh: North Carolina Department of Agriculture, 1942.

Perdue, Theda, and Christopher Arris Oakley. *Native Carolinians: The Indians of North Carolina*. Raleigh: North Carolina Department of Cultural Resources, Office of Archives and History, 2010.

Petrides, George A. *Peterson Field Guides: Trees and Shrubs*. New York: Houghton Mifflin, 1958.

Pettus, Louise. "Bradford Helped Catawbas, 1st to Write Their History." *Charlotte Observer*, January 13, 2001.

———. "Kings Bottoms Land Played Key Role for Catawbas." *Charlotte Observer*, November 25, 2000.

———. *Leasing Away a Nation: The Legacy of Catawba Indian Land Leases*. Spartanburg, S.C.: Palmetto Conservation Fund Press, 2005.

———. "Nearby History: Catawba Hunting Methods." *Charlotte Observer*, May 14, 2006.

Pocket Naturalist Guide. *North Carolina Trees & Wildflowers*. Dunedin, Fla.: Waterford, 2015.

———. *South Carolina Birds*. Dunedin, Fla.: Waterford, 2013.

Porter, Jane. "Don't Drink the Water: The General Assembly Could Gut River Protections at the Behest of Developers." *Indyweek*, June 24, 2015.

Powell, William S. *The North Carolina Gazetteer.* Chapel Hill: University of North Carolina Press, 1968.

———. *North Carolina through Four Centuries.* Chapel Hill: University of North Carolina Press, 1989.

———. *The Proprietors of Carolina.* Raleigh, N.C.: Carolina Charter Tercentenary Commission, 1963, reprinted by State Department of Archives and History, 1968.

———, ed. *The Encyclopedia of North Carolina.* Chapel Hill: University of North Carolina Press, 2006.

Prosser, Chad. *Beautiful Places: The Timeless Beauty of South Carolina's State Parks.* Columbia: South Carolina Department of Parks, Recreation, and Tourism, 2009.

Purvis, Kathleen. "Small Southern Flour Mills Fight to Find Their Bakers." *Charlotte Observer*, October 24, 2015.

Pusser, Todd. "The Last Giants: Searching for Champion Trees in North Carolina." *Wildlife in North Carolina*, March/April 2016.

Rabb, Theodore K. "The Historian and the Climatologist." *Journal of Interdisciplinary History* 10, no. 4 (Spring 1980): 831–37.

Ramsay, David. *Ramsay's History of South Carolina from Its First Settlement in 1670 to 1808.* Newberry, S.C.: W. J. Duffie, 1858.

Rankin, Richard, ed. *North Carolina Nature Writing: Four Centuries of Personal Narratives and Descriptions.* Winston-Salem, N.C.: John F. Blair, 1996.

Ray, Janisse. *Ecology of a Cracker Childhood.* Minneapolis: Milkweed, 1999.

Raynor, Bob. *Exploring Bull Island: Sailing and Waling Around a South Carolina Sea Island.* Charleston, S.C.: History Press, 2005.

———. *Tracing the Cape Romain Archipelago.* Charleston, S.C.: History Press, 2009.

Rey, H. A. *The Stars: A New Way to See Them.* Boston: Houghton Mifflin, 1952.

Rhett, Robert Goodwyn. *Charleston: An Epic of Carolina.* Richmond, Va.: Garrett and Massie, 1940.

Rice, Tony. *Voyages of Discovery: A Visual Celebration of Ten of the Greatest Natural History Expeditions.* London: Firefly, 2008.

Riggs, Stanley R., and Dorothea V. Ames. *Drowning the North Carolina Coast: Sea-Level Rise and Estuarine Dynamics.* Raleigh: North Carolina Sea Grant, 2003.

Rights, Douglas L. *The American Indian in North Carolina.* 2nd ed. Winston-Salem, N.C.: John F. Blair, 1957.

———. "The Trading Path to the Indians." *North Carolina Historical Review* 8 (1931): 403–26.

Ripley, George, and Charles A. Dana, eds. *The New American Cyclopaedia: A Popular Dictionary of General Knowledge*. Vol. 10. New York: D. Appleton, 1863.

Rivers, James. *A Sketch of the History of South Carolina to the Close of the Proprietary Government by the Revolution of 1719*. Charleston, S.C.: McCarter, 1856.

Roe, Charles E. *North Carolina Wildlife Viewing Guide*. Helena, Mont.: Falcon, 1992.

Roper, L. H. *Conceiving Carolina: Proprietors, Planters, and Plots, 1662–1729*. New York: Palgrave Macmillan, 2004.

Salley, Alexander S., Jr. *Narratives of Early Carolina, 1650–1708*. New York: Barnes & Noble, 1911.

Sandidge, Christina. "North Carolina Town 'Forgotten' as Residents' Jobs Fall Away." Associated Press, July 29, 2017.

Saunders, William L. *Colonial Records of North Carolina*. Raleigh: William Hale, Printer to the State, 1886. Searchable and available online as Colonial and State Records of North Carolina, http://docsouth.unc.edu/csr/.

Savage, Henry, Jr. *Lost Heritage: Wilderness America through the Eyes of Seven Pre-Audubon Naturalists*. New York: William Morrow, 1970.

———. *River of the Carolinas: The Santee*. Chapel Hill: University of North Carolina Press, 1956.

Shields, E. Thomson, Jr. *"A New Voyage to Carolina*: Publication History of a Classic of North Caroliniana." *North Carolina Historical Review* 88, no. 3 (July 2011): 298–311.

Shubin, Neil. *The Universe Within: Discovering the Common History of Rocks, Planets, and People*. New York: Pantheon, 2013.

Sibley, David Allen. *Sibley's Backyard Birds of the Southeast*. Wilton, N.H.: Steven M. Lewers, 2014.

———. *Sibley's Birds of the Southeast Atlantic Coast*. Wilton, N.H.: Steven M. Lewers, 2015.

Simmons, Geitner. "Guatari: Rowan's Beginning—Centuries-Old Documents Show That Spanish Explorers Visited Rowan County in the 1560s.'" *Salisbury (N.C.) Post*, August 15, 1999.

Simpson, Marcus B., Jr. "John Lawson's *A New Voyage to Carolina* and His *Compleat History*: The Mark Catesby Connection." In Nelson and Elliott, *The Curious Mister Catesby*.

Simpson, Marcus B., Jr., and Sallie W. Simpson. "John Lawson's *A New Voyage to Carolina*: Notes on the Publication History of the London (1709) Edition." *Archives of Natural History* 35, no. 2 (2008): 223–42.

———. "Zoological Material for John Lawson's *Compleat History* of Carolina (1710–1711): Specimens Recorded in Hans Sloane's Catalogues." *Archives of Natural History* 37, no. 2 (2010): 333–45.

Sloan, Kim. *A New World: England's First View of America*. Chapel Hill: University of North Carolina Press, 2007.

Smith, Andrew F. *Starving the South: How the North Won the Civil War*. New York: St. Martin's, 2011.

Snowden, Yates, ed. *History of South Carolina*. Chicago: Lewis, 1920.

Sprunt, Alexander, Jr., and E. Burnham Chamberlain. *South Carolina Bird Life*. Columbia: University of South Carolina Press, 1949; reprint 1970.

Sprunt, Alexander, Jr., and John Henry Dick (line drawings). *Carolina Low Country Impressions*. New York: Devin-Adair, 1964.

State Papers Online: The Government of Britain, 1509–1714. https://www.gale.com/primary-sources/state-papers-online.

Stephen, Sir Leslie, and Sir Sidney Lee. *Dictionary of National Biography*. Vol. 32. London: Smith, Elder; New York: Macmillan, 1892.

Steward, Kevin G., and Mary-Russell Roberson. *Exploring the Geology of the Carolinas: A Field Guide to Favorite Places from Chimney Rock to Charleston*. Chapel Hill: University of North Carolina Press, 2007.

Stilgoe, John R. *Common Landscape of America, 1580–1845*. New Haven, Conn.: Yale University Press, 1982.

———. *Outside Lies Magic: Regaining History and Awareness in Everyday Places*. New York: Walker, 1998.

Tainter, Joseph A. *The Collapse of Complex Societies*. Cambridge: Cambridge University Press, 1988.

Taylor, David, ed. *South Carolina Naturalists: An Anthology, 1700–1860*. Columbia: University of South Carolina Press, 1998.

Taylor, Tom. "The Ghost Town of Ferguson." *South Carolina Traveler*, January 20, 2016. http://www.scnhc.org/story/the-ghost-town-of-ferguson.

Taylor, Walter K. *Wild Shores: Exploring the Wilderness Areas of Eastern North Carolina*. Asheboro, N.C.: Down Home, 1993.

Temple, Robert D. "Troublesome Boundaries: Royal Proclamations, Indian Treaties, Lawsuits, Political Deals, and Other Errors Defining our Strange State Lines." *Carologue*, Summer 2011, 12–19.

Thompson, Hope. "Civil Rights in Carolina: A Native American's Story." http://www.candidslice.com/civil-rights-in-carolina-a-native-americans-story/. Accessed 2018.

Thoreau, Henry David. *Walden, Walking*, and *A Week on the Concord and Merrimack Rivers*. In *The Portable Thoreau*, edited by Carl Bode. New York: Viking Penguin, 1982.

Thorndike, Joseph J. *The Coast: A Journey down the Atlantic Shore.* New York: St. Martin's, 1993.

Thornton, Russell. "Native American Demographic and Tribal Survival into the Twenty-First Century." *American Studies* 46, no. 2 (April 1982).

Todd, Vincent H. *Von Graffenried's Account of the Founding of New Bern.* Raleigh, N.C.: Edwards & Broughton, 1920.

"Trading Ford: Ten Thousand Years of American History in Piedmont North Carolina." http://www.trading-ford.org/Trading_Ford_on_the_Yadkin_rev _12-09.pdf. Accessed 2018.

Traunter, Richard. *The Travels of Richard Traunter on the Main Continent of America, from Appomattox River in Virginia to Charles Town in Carolina, in Two Journals; performed in the Years 1698 and 1699.* Unpublished manuscript, held in the library of the Virginia Museum of History and Culture, Richmond.

Truett, Randle Bond. *Trade and Travel around the Southern Appalachians before 1830.* Chapel Hill: University of North Carolina Press, 1935.

Tyler, Moses Coit. *History of American Literature of the Colonial Time.* New York: Putnam, 1897.

Tylor, Sir Edward Burnett. *Researches into the Early History of Mankind and the Development of Civilization.* London: John Murray, 1878.

"A Visit to 'Indian Hill,' or The Winter Residence of the One-Eyed King of Sapona." *Carolina Watchman* (Salisbury), December 4, 1879.

Walser, Richard. "Damn Long Time between Drinks." *North Carolina Historical Review* 59, no. 2 (April 1982): 160–71.

Ward, H. Trawick, and R. P. Stephen Davis Jr. *Time before History: The Archaeology of North Carolina.* Chapel Hill: University of North Carolina Press, 1999.

Warren, Jule B. *North Carolina Yesterday and Today.* Raleigh: State Department of Public Instruction, 1942.

Watson, Alan D., ed. *African Americans in Early North Carolina: A Documentary History.* Raleigh: Office of Archives and History, North Carolina Department of Cultural Resources, 2005.

———, ed. *Society in Early North Carolina: A Documentary History.* Raleigh: Office of Archives and History, North Carolina Department of Cultural Resources, 2010.

Watts, May Theilgaard. *Tree Finder: A Manual for the Identification of Trees by Their Leaves.* Rochester, N.Y.: Nature Study Guild Publishers, 1998.

Weeks, Stephen B. *Libraries and Literature in North Carolina in the Eighteenth Century.* Washington, D.C.: Government Printing Office, 1896.

Weisberger, Bernard A., ed. *The WPA Guide to America: The Best of 1930s America as Seen by the Federal Writers' Project.* New York: Pantheon, 1985.

Wells, Bertram Whittier. *The Natural Gardens of North Carolina.* Chapel Hill: University of North Carolina Press, 1932; reprint 2002.

Wetmore, Ruth Y. *First on the Land: The North Carolina Indians.* Winston-Salem, N.C.: John F. Blair, 1975.

Whedon, Parker. Private correspondence with Jack Horan regarding attempt to retrace Lawson's journey in 1961, dated July 28, 2001.

Whitehill, Walter Muir. *Boston: A Topographical History.* 2nd ed. Cambridge, Mass.: Harvard University Press, 1968.

Wiley, Martin. *Estuarine Processes: Uses, Stresses, and Adaptation to the Estuary.* New York: Academic Press, 1976.

Wilson, Charles Reagan, and William Ferris, eds. *Encyclopedia of Southern Culture.* Chapel Hill: University of North Carolina Press, 1989.

Wilson, David Scofield. *In the Presence of Nature.* Amherst: University of Massachusetts Press, 1978.

Winston, Sanford. "Indian Slavery in the Carolina Region." *Journal of Negro History* 19, no. 4 (October 1934): 431–40.

Works Progress Administration. *North Carolina: The WPA Guide to the Old North State.* Chapel Hill: University of North Carolina Press, 1939; reprint, Columbia: University of South Carolina Press, 1989.

Wulf, Andrea. *The Invention of Nature: Alexander von Humboldt's New World.* New York: Knopf, 2015.

INDEX

Italic page numbers refer to illustrations.

relationship with Native Americans, 23, 26–27, 50–51, 54, 55, 61, 102, 103, 117, 155–56, 158, 162, 201–4, 212, 213, 214, 215; narratives of, 26–27; and deforestation of longleaf pines, 38; and fugitive indentured migrants, 54; and dams on creeks, 123; town design of, 184

Falls Lake, North Carolina, 165, 167
farms: of Native Americans, 35; tree farms, 45, 49, 67, 70, 71, 73, 145; corporate farms, 76, 81, 145; hobby farms, 86; companion farms, 97; and European settlers, 103, 123; as event venues, 107; and pollution, 124; keep-busy farms, 130; dairy farms, 145; solar farms, 151–52; goat farms, 155
Ferber, Edna, 193
Ferguson, South Carolina, 64
Fernandez, Juan, 89
filter feeders, 14
Flat Rock Road, 86, 87, 88, 90, 97
Flat Swamp Road, 140
Flowers, Joshua Percy, 169
Flowers Crossroads, North Carolina, 169, 170
Flowers Plantation, North Carolina, 169–70
Forbes, Esther, 41
forest conservation, 37–39, 45
Fort Watson, South Carolina, 54
Forty Acre Rock Heritage Preserve, South Carolina, 88–89
Francis Marion National Forest: swamps of, 30, 32, 35, 39, 65, 96, 143; longleaf pine of, 38–39; moonshine stills of, 40; walking in, 45; lakes of, 61, 62; plants of, 94

French and Indian War, 4
French traders, and John Lawson's journey, 179–81
frogs, 91, 154, 155
Fundamental Constitutions of Carolina, 41

Gaillard, Barthelemy, 43
Gale, Christopher, 8–9, 202–4
Gallay, Alan, 51
Gallian (elder Huguenot settler), 33
Gallian (younger Huguenot settler), 33–34
Garner, North Carolina, 167, 168, 216
Garris, Beckee, 109
geographical information systems (GIS), 111, 114
George II (king of England), 82
Georgetown, South Carolina, 42
Georgia Stone Industries quarry, 87, 90
Goat Island, South Carolina, 20
Goat Island Yacht Club, 21
Golden Meadow Road, 145
goldenrod, 15, 155, 176, 209
Goldsboro, North Carolina, 178
Google Maps, 40, 177, 185, 217
Goose Creek, South Carolina, 179–80
Goose Creek Men, 179–80
Gourdin, South Carolina, 66
grasshoppers, 154–55, 184
Gray, Freddie, 131
Great Trading Path, 86
Great Wagon Road, 114, 137
Green, Val: and John Lawson's journey, 47, 50, 58–61, 83, 122, 137, 138, 147, 161, 162, 167, 170, 177, 178, 179–82, 183, 191; photograph of, 48; on Santee Indians, 57; and Old River Road, 69–70; and Poinsett State

scription of cultures, 1–2, 4, 5, 8–9, 26–27, 34–35, 50, 52–53, 55–57, 61, 84, 93, 94, 101–3, 105, 106, 108, 109, 128–29, 132, 136–37, 146, 147, 156–57, 159, 160, 162, 163, 184, 197, 210, 211, 212–15; and John Lawson's guides, 7, 17, 33–34, 50, 59, 60, 69, 71, 93, 128, 132–33, 156–57, 160, 162, 177, 179, 184, 190, 202; and canoe building, 16–17, 217; John Lawson on hunting of, 17, 18, 93, 211; relationship with European settlers, 23, 26–27, 50–51, 54, 55, 61, 102, 103, 117, 155–56, 158, 162, 201–4, 212, 213, 214, 215; and farming, 35; trade of, 35, 42, 50, 60; and tobacco, 35, 101, 120, 158, 160, 162, 175; and alcohol, 50–51, 103, 144, 212, 213, 214; John Lawson on destruction of population, 50–51, 103, 212; and inter-tribal wars, 51, 93; as slaves, 51, 103, 180, 201, 213, 215; recognition of tribes, 54, 55–57, 66, 84, 99, 100, 104, 158, 204, 215; education of, 55; powwows of, 56–57, 104, 158; and U.S. termination policy, 104; communications of, 121; and segregation, 158. *See also specific tribes*

Native American Studies Center, University of South Carolina–Lancaster, 88, 99–101, 104, 106, 109, 119

Natural History Museum, London, 8, 94, 206, 207–9

Natural Resources Conservation Service, 116

naval stores industry, 38, 65, 193

Netherton, Henry, 180–81

Netherton (son), 180–81

Neuse River, 165, 166–67, 169, 170, 177, 186, 192, 200, 202, 217

New Bern, North Carolina: John Lawson's role in founding of, 2, 8, 117, 151, 193, 200–201; and Pamlico Sound, 165; John Lawson living in, 191–92

New England, 29

New Hope Creek, 160

New Jersey, 13

New Orleans, Louisiana, 29

Newsom, Mary, 123–26

Newton, Isaac, 6, 195

Nisbet, James, 107

North Carolina: industries of, 10; and Carolina bays, 58; view of countryside, *112*; borderline of, 113–14, 197; Piedmont region, 118, 123, 124, 125, 133, 145, 152–53, 154, 159, 164, 165, 168; and riparian buffers, 124–25; wetlands of, 124; barbecue of, 126; coastal plain, 168, 171, 172, 177, 183; Outer Banks barrier islands, 186, 193. *See also specific towns and cities*

North Carolina Estuarium, 186–87

North Carolina Office of Archives and History, 193

oaks, 23, 37, 39, 58

Occaneechi Indians, 7–8, 155, 156, 157–60

Ocracoke Inlet, 193

Old Brick Church (Wambaw Church), 43

Old Hillsborough Road, 155

Old River Road, 69–71

Old Salisbury-Concord Road, 132, 134–35

Oneiscau, 23. *See also* Bulls Island, South Carolina

ospreys, 14, 28, 49

Ossabaw, 127

Route 261, South Carolina, 71
Royal Society of London for Improving Natural Knowledge, 6, 31, 33, 195
Rutledge, Archibald, 43

Salisbury, North Carolina, 136–37, 139–40
salt cedar, 15
salt marsh: and John Lawson's journey, 11, 13, 14, 16; plants of, 11–12, *12*, 13, 15, *15*; bird life of, 12, 14; fish of, 12, 14, 15; changes in, 13, 16; runoff threatening, 29
sand dollars, 23
sanderlings, 14
sandpipers, 14
San Francisco, California, 29
Santee, South Carolina, 66, 67
Santee Coastal Wildlife Management Area, South Carolina, 13
Santee Dam, 47, 49
Santee Indian Mound, South Carolina, 53–54, 61, 70, 78, 84
Santee Indians: and John Lawson's journey, 7, 18, 34–35, 50, 52–54, 55, 60–61, 62; king of, 47, 57, 60–61; John Lawson's description of deer hunting, 52; burial mounds of, 52, 53–54, *53*, 61; barbecue of, 52, 54, 126; John Lawson's description of burial customs, 52–53, 184; and Siouan language group, 54; recognition of, 54, 55–57, 66, 99, 104; population of, 54, 61, 109; *hickerau* (black house), 61
Santee Jack, 34, 50, 71, 179
Santee National Wildlife Refuge, South Carolina, 47, 53, 57–58, 60, 63
Santee River: and John Lawson's journey, 7, 16, 17, 18, 25–26, 28, 32, 33–34, 40, 49–50, 59, 61–62; and Intracoastal Waterway, 28; damming of, 28, 43, 46, 47, 49, 62, 69, 123; Huguenots of, 32, 42; and Lawson Trek, 32–33, 40, 42, 44, 47; steamboats on, 44; ecosystem of, 62–63, 65; and swamps, 64, 65, 70–71; tributaries of, 79
Sapona Indians, 136, 137–38, 144, 147, 153, 159
Savage, Henry, Jr., 63–64
Saxapahaw, North Carolina, 153
Schiffert, Vince, 218
Scott, Peggy, 55–57, 66, 104, 122
Scuffleton, North Carolina, 183
Seneca Indians, 121, 136
settlers. *See* English settlers; European settlers; Huguenot settlers
Sewee Indians: and John Lawson's journey, 7, 18, 25–26, 33, 34, 50; and European settlers, 23, 26; and McClellanville, 24; canoes of, 26, 34; trading voyage of, 26, 50; John Lawson's description of, 27; population of, 109
Sewee Shell Ring, South Carolina, 24–25, 26
Shakespeare, William, 209
Shakori Indians, 156
shell rings, 24–25, 26
shells, 22, 23
Sherman, William Tecumseh, 83
short-billed dowagers, 14
shrimp fishery, 24, 27
Sides, Susan, 137
Simons, Joseph, 64
Simpson, Susan, 82
Simpson, Vollis, 173, 178
Singer, Michael, 79, 80, 84, 86, 87